POETRY OF HAITIAN INDEPENDENCE

POETRY OF HAITIAN INDEPENDENCE

Edited by Doris Y. Kadish and Deborah Jenson

Translations by Norman R. Shapiro

Foreword by Edwidge Danticat

Yale UNIVERSITY PRESS / NEW HAVEN AND LONDON

Published with assistance from the foundation established in memory of Calvin Chapin of the Class of 1788, Yale College.

Yale University Press books may be purchased in quantity for educational, business, or promotional use. For information, please e-mail sales.press@yale.edu (U.S. office) or sales@yaleup.co.uk (U.K. office).

Designed by Nancy Ovedovitz. Set in Sabon and Brandon Grotesque type by Integrated Publishing Solutions, Grand Rapids, Michigan. Printed in the United States of America.

Library of Congress Cataloging-in-Publication Data
Poetry of Haitian independence / edited by Doris Y. Kadish, Deborah Jenson ; translated by Norman R. Shapiro ; foreword by Edwidge Danticat.
pages cm
Includes bibliographical references and index.
ISBN 978-0-300-19559-0 (hardback)
1. Haitian poetry—Translations into English. I. Kadish, Doris Y., editor. II. Jenson, Deborah, editor. III. Shapiro, Norman R., translator.
PQ3946.5.E5P64 2015   841.008'097294—dc23   2014041574

A catalogue record for this book is available from the British Library.

This paper meets the requirements of ANSI/NISO Z39.48–1992 (Permanence of Paper).

10 9 8 7 6 5 4 3 2 1

Contents

Foreword

Journalism is often described as the first draft of history. I often think of poetry as an alternate draft. Shameless in their partiality and their unabashed willingness to exult as well as excoriate— especially after extraordinary events—poets have the type of creative license that neither historians nor journalists have. They can subjectively describe personal pleasures and pains, all while trying to speak for an entire nation. This is what many of the poets featured in *Poetry of Haitian Independence* tried to do after 1804, when, following decades of a revolutionary war, Haiti officially became the world's first black republic.

As the Haitian historian Bayyinah Bello has often pointed out, and as the poet Coriolan Ardouin highlights here in his epic poems, the fight for Haitian independence began as soon as Africans were kidnapped from their home continent and sold to slave traders operating in the so-called New World—a world that required new words to describe its horrors and cruelties, and eventually its battles, villains, defeats, heroes, and triumphs.

A notable precursor to Haitian independence poetry is Boukman Dutty's prayer at the Bois Caïman Vodou ceremony which launched the Haitian revolution on August 14, 1791. Both invocation and call to arms, Boukman's plea is poetic at its African and Aristotelian core. It is a call-and-response indictment that pits good men and women against an obvious evil.

Some scholars have suggested that the Bois Caïman ceremony falls in the realm of poetic imagination, that it might not have happened at all. However, its central players—Boukman and the Vodou priestess Cécile Fatiman—lived and breathed in the world, and the words supposedly uttered by Boukman remain. *Bon Dye ki fè la tè. Ki fè solèy ki klere nou enro . . .* They are wonderfully rendered here in the voice of the poet Hérard-Dumesle, as translated by Norman Shapiro:

That God, whose torch—the sun—flames overhead;
Who makes the winds to roar, the seas to swell—
Cloud-hidden—to be sure, he knows full well
The white man's sins against your land, your race.
His worship leads to crime; ours leads to grace
And goodliness. But God's virtue supreme
Demands revenge; he will our strength redeem
And guide our blows. Let us, with trampling feet,
Their idol crush: he who would find it meet
That bitter tears fill our eyes endlessly!
Liberty, come! May you our hearts' voice be!

This would not be the last time that the voice of liberty would be invoked. Haiti's Declaration of Independence, a document drafted in 1804, was itself a poetic text, filled with poignant and elaborate imagery and passionate language. Written as both testimonial and direct address, it is, like most poems, a plea from one heart to the next, in this case a patriotic heart. And the fact that it was supposedly drafted by a young poet, Louis Boisrond-Tonnerre, who is reported to have said that it should be written with the skin of a white man as parchment, his skull as an inkwell, his blood for ink, and a bayonet for a pen, makes it even more formidable.

> Le Général en chef au Peuple d'Haïti
> Citoyens, Ce n'est pas assez d'avoir expulsé de votre pays les barbares qui l'ont ensanglanté depuis deux siècles; ce n'est pas assez d'avoir mis un frein aux factions toujours renaissantes qui se jouaient tour à tour du fantôme de liberté que la France exposait à vos yeux: il faut, par un dernier acte d'autorité nationale, assurer à jamais l'empire de la liberté dans le pays qui nous a vus naître; il faut ravir au gouvernement inhumain qui tient depuis longtemps nos esprits dans la torpeur la plus humiliante, tout espoir de nous réasservir, il faut enfin vivre indépendants ou mourir.

The Commander-in-Chief to the People of Haiti
Citizens: It is not enough to have expelled the barbarians who
have bloodied our land for two centuries; it is not enough to
have restrained those ever-evolving factions that one after an-
other mocked the specter of liberty that France dangled before
you. We must, with one last act of national authority, forever
assure the empire of liberty in the country of our birth; we
must take any hope of re-enslaving us away from the inhuman
government that for so long kept us in the most humiliating
torpor. In the end we must live independent or die. [trans.
Laurent Dubois and John Garrigus]

Since then Haitians have somehow managed to both live inde-
pendent *and* die. Our subsequent struggles have also proven that
this document declared only one type of independence. The rest,
the complete fulfillment of the nation's destiny, would remain to
be won.

"Natives of Haiti! My happy fate was to be one day the sen-
tinel who would watch over the idol to which you sacrifice"; the
voice of the new emperor, Jean-Jacques Dessalines, continues to
echo through the rest of the document. It also reads like a love
letter to one's most cherished beloved. "I have watched, some-
times fighting alone, and if I have been so fortunate as to return
to your hands the sacred trust you confided to me, know that it is
now your task to preserve it."

The passing of batons as part of the birth of a nation is not
all that unusual, especially a nation in which the citizens had
previously been enslaved. Both tough and gentle words must be
spoken to inspire the new republic to rise to the task. Old battles
are revisited to embolden the populace for the new hurdles ahead.
The Declaration of Independence and the national anthem create
a new uplifting national narrative.

It is thus not surprising that the first piece of "poetry" in these
pages should be the "Hymne haytienne," Haiti's first national
anthem. The hymn is credited to an anonymous hand as though

it were, like the country's independence, collectively rather than individually achieved. Many of the poems that follow are in the same vein, showing the urgent and critical need for ordinary men, women, and children to see their own lives reflected in the successes of their predecessors. We hail emperors and kings, but with each laudatory verse we are also elevating ourselves.

Poetry can serve that purpose well, not by producing propaganda but by capturing the heights of emotion, portrayed here by someone identified only as "un enfant d'Haïti" (a child of Haiti) as "Justice, love, pleasure, courage." Praise songs offer endless possibilities for us to declare our ecstasy in our newfound liberties. Tyrants only leer from the past and do not yet loom ahead. We have not yet realized that even under the rule of our own great leaders, we might also suffer.

The anonymous poet who two decades after independence wrote, "Voyez ce vieux colon" (See that old planter) is among the first to remind us of the fragility of these new freedoms. "Fruitless, the revolution," he writes in the old colonist's voice, "That wrought your nation's Constitution! . . . People, take back your chains. / Once more slavery reigns!"

The perception that slavery might return did emerge once forced labor was reinstituted by Dessalines. But the new nation would not totally bend, even as it battled internal strife, even as it was forced, under the rule of Jean-Pierre Boyer, to pay a crippling independence debt to France that was estimated to be worth over 21 billion dollars two hundred years after Independence Day.

Juste Chanlatte, a poet and newspaper editor, brings a few more voices into his choral poem-plays. In "Quels accents tout à coup ont charmé mon oreille?" (What sweet chants, these, that strike, entrance my ear?) he does not ask us to sing only in the "manly" voices of the "Hymne haytienne"; he wants us to sing along with the women and children too. Soldiers and members of the masses attempt to speak of several idealistic goals.

Le Peuple
Puissent de cet état les rameaux divisés,
Se joindre sous l'abri du pouvoir monarchique,
    Et tous les cœurs humanisés
    Former une famille unique!

The People
May all the outspread branches of this tree
Join in the royal shade, together; may
    Each heart—of one humanity—
    Be but one family this day!

If only as a people, we could have managed this type of feat. However, poetry has always been as much about aspirations as realities. And after independence, many of our poets were more euphoric than prophetic. Perhaps this had something to do with the fact that they were among the most privileged members of the new society. Still Count Chanlatte's chorus seems to nudge him in the right direction. "Are we awake? Or are sleep's smiling,/Lying dreams, with fictions beguiling,/Lulling, plying our spirit and our sense?"

Antoine Dupré is more overt in describing his dream for the nascent nation. Framing it as an actual dream, he predates Martin Luther King, Jr., in expressing his desire for a nation in which all (men) are treated equally and are judged only by their deeds and not by their "rank or color." He also looks farther out, toward Washington and Paris, where battles over liberty were still being waged. One senses in his words, and those of many of this book's independence poets, a longing for Haiti to become a beacon of hope to nations where people are still enslaved.

I must confess that I can't help but hope that some of the anonymous poets in this book are women. They certainly might be. Many of the ladies of the new leisure class might have had the time—if they'd had the education—for literary pursuits. Failing that, I will take the women and girl warriors in Juste Chanlatte's choral poems as representatives of the female freedom fighters, such as Sanite Belair and others, who fought valiantly alongside the men on the front lines.

Still the independence poet cannot continue to look back forever. There is the next generation to tend to, the future to think about. The anonymous author of "Mon père, j'aime à voir ces champs et leurs coteaux" (Father dear, how I love to cast my glance over these hills and fields) frames this desire to look ahead in a conversation between an old man and his son. "Know this, my son," the old man declares. "When Revolutions flare, / Searing our beaches with the blood of war—/ Like the one not long past that drenched our shore—/ It is but to assure the happiness / Of those who follow us, nor more nor less."

That happiness was never guaranteed by the revolution, even as, in Haiti's Declaration of Independence, the nation's founders had wished it both for themselves and for their countrymen and women. The "long centuries of grandeur and of peace" they longed for still evade us today.

Haiti commemorated the bicentennial of its independence while it was occupied by a multinational force, which included French soldiers. It was widely believed that they were there in part because then-Haitian president Jean-Bertrand Aristide had deigned to ask that France reimburse Haiti, with interest, the independence debt that Jean-Pierre Boyer had been forced to pay. With French troops on Haiti's soil in 2004, and with United Nations forces there now, what would Haiti's poets of independence think of these armed foreigners who purport to be our saviors?

Some might be turning in their graves. But others might be thinking, *I told you so.* Just as Pierre Faubert warned in "Frères, nous avons tous brisé le joug infâme" (Brothers all, we have now that foul yoke broken): "Forget not, friends. Your brave accomplishments / Made you victors by half! And so, / Now must your virtues and intelligence / Complete your task against the foe."

The foe keeps changing, but the battle remains. Though the battle cries might need to be slightly modified.

One possible dictum might lie in a verse from Faubert's poem.

Oh! par tous ces guerriers qui, pères magnanimes,
    Ont tant souffert pour leurs enfants;
Par tant de sang versé, tant de nobles victimes,
    Haïtiens, serrez vos rangs!

In the name of those fathers, they who bled
    To save their children, gave their all;
Those valiant victims, warriors lying dead...
    O Haitians, close your ranks! Stand tall!

Editorial Note

Because of the confusing similarity in the published titles of many of the poems (e.g., "Hymne," "Couplets," "Cantate"), we have chosen to use the first lines of the poems as titles. The English titles consist of the translation of the French, even when the words do not all appear in the first line. Where applicable, we also include the original title of the poem in parentheses.

We have modernized the orthography of the original for the French-language poems, and we use modern spellings for proper nouns in the translations. Unless otherwise indicated, all translations of quotations in the introduction and notes are our own.

Introduction

The Declaration of Independence in 1804 gave birth to poems
celebrating Haiti's newly gained freedom and its founding prin-
ciples of equality, justice, courage, and national pride. Independ-
ence inaugurated the mission of representing the crucial good
of Haitian autonomy. Passion about this challenge was shared
throughout the African diasporic world. Ideas about freedom that
were developed in Haiti had hemispheric scope and transnational
importance.[1]

Plato memorably proposed that poetry should be banished
from the ideal republic because of its power to influence citizens,
becoming "second nature in body, voice, and mind."[2] The first
republic of former slaves also viewed poetry as a powerfully per-
suasive influence but envisioned it in a positive light as the foun-
dation of all culture, to be embraced in the founding of identities
and practices. The Haitian historian Émile Nau described poetry
in indigenous societies as the voice of the people, "the song of
the multitude, a general outpouring, an epic," which includes
"history, science, beliefs, customs, social institutions, everything,
earth and sky."[3] His words remind us of the sensorial impact of
words and the highly musical nature of poetry, especially the po-
etry of Haitian independence, in which a social mission is served
by the island's oral, rhythmic traditions.[4] Haitian poetry in the
first half of the nineteenth century hailed, praised, and monumen-
talized independence in ways that have both political and literary
significance. The literary critic Amy Reinsel observes that through
poetry, Haitian authors were able to "assert poetic subjectivity
and claim their own modern history." Their writing "constituted
radically unexpected gestures in the global environment hostile
to Haiti's articulations of nationhood." This poetry "constituted
a deliberate practice in the construction, legitimization, and

expression of national identity."[5] The poems included in this volume shed light on Haiti, the Caribbean, the Enlightenment, postcolonialism, poetry, and the history of culture and identity.

The extent to which poetry had a journalistic role at the time and functioned as part of a literature of combat is evident in the motto of the newspaper *L'Abeille haytienne,* published from 1817 to 1820: "Sword and pen in the service of the State."[6] Like other papers, it combined literature with local, international, and commercial news. The journalistic efforts of Haitian poets in the first decades after independence came from the secretarial ranks of the competing leaders of the new nation. Poetry provided the occasion for them to write about historical events, heroic figures, battles, ceremonies, and ideological skirmishes that were central to the creation of a Haitian national identity. The lines between statecraft, military life, and literature were not carefully drawn. Engagement occurred on multiple fronts, in acts and in words. As regimes changed from decade to decade—or even year to year, as in the 1840s—poetic and journalistic allegiances changed too.

The opening article in the first issue of *Le Républicain: recueil scientifique et littéraire* (1836) contains, as the newspaper's subtitle, "Scientific and Literary Collection," suggests, a summation of many of the main features of Haitian journalism in the first half of the nineteenth century. The author, D. Lespinasse, expresses the need to reach out beyond those who read books and address the daily concerns of the public in short, timely articles. He promotes collaborative rather than single-author writing as a reflection of the common spirit that unites the younger generation. He emphasizes the need for all forms of intellectual enrichment—philosophy, law, poetry, history, literature, political economy—to stand side by side within the pages of the newspaper. Most important, he asserts that the paper will serve the good of the country. The days of sorrow and loss are in the past, he states; but that does not mean that in a time of peace the revolutionary past can be forgotten. All must remember the brilliant accomplishments and the memorable days "which imprinted on the brow of the children of Haiti the title of nation."

Who were the poets and where did they publish their works? Juste Chanlatte, Ignace Nau, Coriolan Ardouin, Pierre Faubert: these notable poets played significant literary and public roles in Haitian society. Others—anonymous authors such as "a child of Haiti" and a "grenadier"—produced only occasional works and have left few biographical traces. Still others, such as Jules Solime Milscent and a writer identified only as Delile Laprée, were founders of early newspapers. Although information about their lives is limited, their historical imprint is large. They are responsible for initiating independent Haiti's remarkable journalistic tradition.[7] That tradition includes the papers that we draw from in this anthology: *Gazette politique et commerciale d'Hayti* (1804), *Le Télégraphe* (1813), *L'Abeille haytienne: journal politique et littéraire* (1817), *Le Propagateur haïtien* (1822), *Le Républicain* (1836), and *L'Union: recueil commercial et littéraire* (1837).[8] Haiti's journalistic heritage is all the more impressive when one considers the obstacles faced by the early-nineteenth-century writers and publishers in the new nation: frequent regime changes, the small number of paying subscribers, the restricted readership for French-language publications, the imperfect postal and transportation systems. Freedom of the press was valued greatly, certain noteworthy exceptions notwithstanding.[9] One is the dramatic case of the apparently African-born journalist Félix Darfour, editor of *L'Éclaireur Haytien*), whose opposition to Jean-Pierre Boyer resulted in Darfour's execution in 1822. Boyer denounced Darfour as a "new Christophe," and Boyer's secretary of state Joseph Inginac accused Darfour of stirring up color divisions.[10]

The poems found in early Haitian newspapers present a largely unknown literary corpus for several reasons. The literary history of nineteenth-century Haiti has only recently begun to receive scholarly attention.[11] Moreover, literature from this period has been difficult to access, especially poems, which were rarely published in complete collections. Excerpts or selections of some of the poems have been published in twentieth-century anthologies of Haitian literature.[12] But even they have often been of limited distribution. In addition, they frequently do not contain information about the primary sources of the poems, and in some cases their versions of the poems are faulty or incomplete. The issues of early Haitian newspapers that have survived are found in a sprinkling of research libraries or specialized digital collections. Undoubtedly more poems on the topic of Haitian independence exist than we have uncovered for our collection. It is to be hoped that future research will complete the task of locating them. Other important tasks to pursue are exploring the connections between French-language poetry and whatever remains of Taino oral traditions and establishing connections with the songs, proverbs, stories, and riddles which existed within slave culture in the colonial era or rural and ritual contexts after independence. Haitian poetry of independence represents a transitional moment between the diverse arts and cultures brought from Africa and the poetry later in Haitian history that would represent the black republic in Creole (*Kreyòl*), which was only rarely used to transcribe or preserve cultural productions in the early years of the Haitian nation.

The poems in this anthology pay homage to Haiti's founding fathers: Toussaint Louverture, Jean-Jacques Dessalines, Henry Christophe, Alexandre Pétion, and Jean-Pierre Boyer. They include poetic responses to the indemnity payment through which Haiti negotiated France's belated formal recognition of its independence in 1825, and they expand the symbolism of Haiti's independence heritage. Certain key thematic components recur throughout: rejection of enslavement, denunciation of colonial tyranny, assertion of human rights, commitment to freedom, solidarity in battle, praise for leaders. All these components are in evidence in one of the first poems published in Haiti after the declaration of independence, "La Nature infiniment sage" (Nature, in wisdom infinite), which appeared in the *Gazette politique et commerciale d'Haïti* on August 1, 1804. Its author is listed, significantly, as "un enfant d'Haïti," an appellation which may echo Dessalines's warning in an April 1804 proclamation that the Spanish, on the eastern side of the island, needed to swear fidelity to be recognized as "children of Haïti." This small but telling historical detail is symptomatic of the ways these poems provide affirmations of African diasporic identity.

The poems in this volume demonstrate the socioeconomic and identitarian fluidity of early Haitian politics, a period in which individuals associated with black, white, and mixed-race heritage shared many components of a common historical, cultural, and linguistic background, yet often with different stakes. They also reveal the sharp partisan differences that existed at a time when poets positioned themselves according to the choice of leaders to set the course of the destiny of Haiti. Understandably, then, the question of who most faithfully represented Haiti's independence in the first half of the nineteenth century remained vexed and complicated. Yet all the poets share a fervent belief in and commitment to freedom and the legitimacy of the new nation. As Fischer observes, acknowledgment of Africa was common to black and mixed-race writers: "Indeed, if there was any kind of consensus among the increasingly hostile factions in Haitian political culture in the nineteenth century, it was precisely this— that Haiti was the defender of the 'African race.' That this meant different things for different people is another matter."[13]

The strong association with Africa during the first half of the nineteenth century was closely connected to the founding father of Haitian independence, Dessalines. The poem "C'est toi, grand Empereur" (You, O great Emperor!) was written by one of Dessalines's soldiers, one Gautarel, in 1805 on the occasion of the emperor's feast day, the Feast of Saint James, July 25. The soldier used the power of his "faibles écrits"—his "halting verse"—to celebrate the emperor who had "laid low/French power": "Les vils français en vain te choisissaient des fers . . . Tu triomphes de tout par la force des armes" (you . . . Flout the vile Frenchman's foul and fell design/Ever to shackle you!). This and other poems reveal the close association in the popular imagination of Dessalines and the Vodou tradition, which integrated Catholic and afro-Haitian religious practices even before the Haitian revolution. The fact that July 25, the day celebrated in "You, O great Emperor!," coincided with the Catholic feast day of Saint James raises the possibility that state feasts under Dessalines had mixed Catholic and Vodou elements.[14] Poems by other writers in this volume, including Chanlatte, Hérard-Dumesle, and Ardouin, contain references to Vodou figures and practices. Such works provide historical evidence of the complexity surrounding "Africa," "Vodou," and "Haiti." Fischer observes that the association of Haiti with Africa's Egyptian legacy was especially significant in nineteenth-century Cuba.[15]

The critical reception of the poetry of Haitian independence has from the start identified it as a slavish imitation of the supposedly superior culture of its colonial oppressor, France. As the Haitian ethnographer Jean Price-Mars stated in 1927, "It is this odd approach that in the metaphysics of M. de Gaultier is called collective bovarism, that is, the faculty whereby a society conceives of itself as other than it is."[16] Michael Dash argues that what Price-Mars saw in the Haitian elite was a group who "like tropical Emmas bedazzled by the bright lights of European civilization, were condemned to a blind and sterile imitation of European modernity."[17] Although Price-Mars was advocating a cultural rediscovery of African forms at the heart of Haitian heritage, the notion of a Haitian bovarism signals a long-standing tendency of prescriptive and exoticizing assessments. In reiterating that Haitian poetry had a derivative, imitative relationship to the Western canon, critics have often failed to see that culture evolved in the larger Atlantic world, not in isolation, but in a complex interaction of New and Old World spheres.[18] Such criticism aligns with nineteenth-century French critics such as Alfred Métral and Gustave d'Alaux who urged Haitian poets to include more description of their native land, seek to be more original, and preserve locally rooted traditions. Later nineteenth-century

Haitian critics such as Louis-Joseph Janvier countered that imitation is a complex phenomenon; humans are, following Aristotle's formulation, "imitative," and both individual and cultural development depend on social responses to existing models.[19] Enlightened critics such as Janvier recognized that in the colonial era the slave trade and the Middle Passage had severed slaves' relationships to their home cultures. These critics could see that in the poetry of independence Haiti's first generations of citizens made themselves at home in a heroic political and lyrical tradition with characteristics of a cosmopolitan swath of cultures. Imitation of French models unquestionably exists in the poetry of Haitian independence. Critics have often erred, however, in drawing attention primarily—or, indeed, only—to its imitative nature.[20]

Tensions and paradoxes in Haitians' attitudes toward their former French colonizers culminated in 1825 when France formally recognized Haiti's independence at the price of an astoundingly high indemnity payment—estimated at the equivalent of 21 billion dollars in twenty-first-century terms—to France's displaced colonists. That exorbitant indemnity would undermine the economic viability of Haiti into the 1930s. Yet some Haitian poets clearly viewed it as a second chance not just at national survival—the end of a long series of boycotts, legal challenges, espionage schemes, and threatened attacks—but at international dignity and collaboration as well. Poems from that time which celebrate the union of the two nations and praise the French monarch Charles X were written by poets situated on a wide spectrum of social or racial positions. This ambivalent poetry illustrates the complex economic, political, and cultural relationships that existed between colonizing and (formerly) colonized countries and that have continued to the present time. Such fault lines should not be viewed, however, as obviating the mission of the poetry of Haitian independence to promote national autonomy.[21] Nor should a poem such as Jean-Marie Chopin's "Salut, lointains climats!" (Hail, distant climes!) be dismissed as inauthentic because its writer was presumably white. This and other poems at the time were often written collaboratively with nonwhites and reveal complex and detailed knowledge about or involvement with Haitian politics and culture.

The issue of authenticity based on nationality, ethnicity, or race has special relevance for *L'Haïtiade* (The Haitiade), the only formal epic of the Haitian revolution. The French and Haitian literary collaboration involved in the creation and publication of this poem serves as an illustrative case in point of the challenges involved in establishing the national or racial identities of authors and of the fluidity that surrounded writing in a period in which individuals associated with black, white, and mixed-race heritage shared many components of a common historical, cultural, and linguistic background. *The Haitiade* proclaims itself to be impartial: the French, the Haitians, and those of Creole birth or ancestry all form "un grand peuple de frères" (a race of brethren). In point of fact, however, from a political perspective, the poem favors Toussaint Louverture and contains disparaging remarks about both Jean-Jacques Dessalines and Henry Christophe.

The Haitiade recounts the battle for Haitian independence, with special focus on the period from 1802 to 1804 and on the figure of Louverture. Claims to both French and Haitian authorship of this work have been made. According to Duraciné Vaval, Hérard-Dumesle wrote in 1824, "Juste Chanlatte is at this moment writing a didactic poem entitled the Haiciade." In 1878, Prosper Gragnon-Lacoste stated that Isaac Louverture played a role in writing the notes. In 1922, Louis Morpeau claimed that Isaac Louverture, "in all probability and verisimilitude is the father of *The Haitiade*."[22] The American author, poet, and translator Edna Worthley Underwood seemed to concur, observing that the epic poem had been attributed to Isaac Louverture, whose poetry she included in her translations of Haitian poems published in 1934.[23] In an edition of the epic published in 1945, the author is listed as A. T. Desquiron de Saint Agnan, a Frenchman and magistrate whom Gragnon-Lacoste suspected but was unable to verify was the author. In his introductory remarks to that edition, Michel Desquiron, Desquiron de Saint Agnan's grandson, notes a Haitian connection. The son of Desquiron de Saint Agnan, Michel's father, came to Haiti in 1821; he knew and was esteemed by Boyer, as was his father.[24] Desquiron de Saint Agnan's son married a mulatto, thereby starting the Haitian branch of the Desquiron family. As Jean-Fernand Brierre states in the introduction to the third edition, "It is fitting that a Haitian [Michel Desquiron] is dispelling the mystery surrounding the authorship of the *Haïtiade* and that M. Desquiron de Saint Agnan's name appears for the first time on the front page of a Haitian edition of the poem."[25] Writing in 1986, Vaval claimed that, although Desquiron de Saint Agnan had the initial idea for the poem and was principally responsible for its execution, considering the uncertainty surrounding the poem's authorship, the soundest conclusion to draw was that it was a collaboration between Isaac Louverture and Juste Chalatte.[26] Although Vaval's claim is unlikely to be verified, it is interesting to note that the perspective of the poem fits with the possibility of a collaborative process involving French and Haitian authors. Although the length of the *Haitiade* precludes inclusion of more than the first canto here, the summary of the poem provided in Appendix B reveals that Toussaint's voice, which is heard briefly in Canto 1, assumes narrative control in Cantos 6 and 7. There Toussaint is situated in a French prison, where he recounts the events of the Haitian Revolution beginning in 1790 to the imprisoned General Mallet. Toussaint's voice ultimately occupies roughly one-quarter to one-third of the entire poem, perhaps an indication of Isaac Louverture's influence.

As in the *Haitiade,* neoclassicism was the prevailing artistic and literary style in the decades from the beginning of the poetry of Haitian independence through the 1820s. Its best-known proponent, the French poet Jacques Delille, was immensely popular from roughly 1760 to 1820, although he is hardly read or even recognized today. Neoclassical poetical style, found in poems such as Gautarel's "You, O great Emperor!" and Hérard-Dumesle's "À travers les sillons par la foudre tracés" (About the lightning-flaring furrows), consists of rhymed twelve-syllable alexandrine verses and high-register poetic language. Periphrasis and euphemistic language are common: Hérard-Dumesle refers to the black or mixed-race Haitian as "l'homme au front nuancé" (man, with his brow of many a darksome hue). References to figures of Greek or Roman history and mythology abound. The knowledge about classical antiquity in neoclassicism reflected new values in Haiti, as it did in France during the revolutionary period. In contrast with the baroque, which was the style of palaces and cathedrals, neoclassicism, exemplified in the art of Jacques-Louis David, emphasized simplicity, directness of communication, and art as propaganda "with an unashamedly programmatic emphasis."[27] Neoclassicism's orientation was toward the public. It served to fuel public consciousness. Thus the seemingly incongruous references to mythology and antiquity in early Haitian poetry reflect a tribute to the democratic values of Greek society.[28] Moreover, especially under Christophe's regime, those references evince black Haitians' aspirations to education and knowledge of past cultures. The charge of imitation directed at the poetry of Haitian independence was also leveled at De-lille, whose critics focused, among other things, on the stilted language that recurs so predictably in neoclassical writing. Only later in Delille's poetic career did he, like Haitian writers similarly accused of imitation, gradually move closer to the more varied lexicon characteristic of the Romantic period.[29]

Many of the poems in *Poetry of Haitian Independence* do not systematically conform to neoclassical lexical, rhythmic, or rhetorical patterns. They combine meters and rhythms in informal patterns of various sorts. It was common in the Caribbean to appropriate a variety of themes and materials from the European repertoire in practices originating more in oral recitation and improvisation than in European style manuals. Although not formalistic, self-referential poetry of a modernist strain, the poems are not merely didactic or polemic.[30] Many are songs that possess a performative and musical quality which the rhymed verse translations provided in this volume attempt to capture. These translations are a fitting tribute to a culture in which music played a central role and in which poems presented on ceremonial occasions were often set to music. Juste Chanlatte's "Dans ton variable contour" (Why ply you your fickle ministry?) provides a good example. The orchestral and singing roles within the poem confirm that it was destined for public musical performance. Solos by diverse soldiers and officers, as well as singers ranging from old people and children to an allegorical female warrior-mother, are another sign of the integration of musical poetry into military and state life. The poem echoes the performative structure of Chanlatte's play *L'Entrée du roi en sa capitale, en janvier 1818* (The king's entry into his capital in January 1818), produced at a court celebration for King Henry Christophe. Written in a comedic vein and thus in a lower register than poetry, the play makes use of Creole. But both works intersperse dialogue with music and dance and contain the same central symbol of Haitian freedom, the column to Independence.

Chanlatte provides an especially salient illustration of both the shifting poetics of early Haitian poetry and its mutable partisan politics. Poet, general, and public servant, Chanlatte (1766–1828) served as a secretary to Jean-Jacques Dessalines. After Dessalines's death, Chanlatte became a major figure in the black monarchical regime of Henry Christophe in the North, where he served as editor of the *Gazette royale d'Hayti*. Christophe's politics stood in sharp opposition to those of his republican rival, Alexandre Pétion, who was of mixed ancestry and educated in France. Pétion died in 1818 and Christophe in 1820, at which time Chanlatte was employed by Pétion's successor, Jean-Pierre Boyer. Especially reprehensible in the eyes of Chanlatte's critics was his denunciation of Christophe, whose virtues he had extolled for a decade before switching allegiance to Boyer. Some have derided Chanlatte as anti-progressive and elitist, and yet he was a scribal voice for a range of early Haitian leaders, and an early contributor to the literary tradition in Creole, as well as a key contributor to early French-language poetry in Haiti.

The six poems by Chanlatte included in this volume show his political and poetic evolution across the different regimes in which he served. In "Quels apprêts? Quels moments?" (What hustle-bustle, hurly-burly sound), written under Dessalines's reign, the poet celebrates freedom from slavery, pride in Dessalines's heroic accomplishments as Haiti's founding father, attachment to the island (its cliffs, waves, and tropical climate), and solidarity among its citizens. The poetic language is simple and direct, with no recourse to mythological allusions or neoclassical periphrasis. The key themes that appear throughout our corpus of poems—independence, country, liberty, people, pride, courage—are loudly proclaimed.

"Quels accents tout à coup ont charmé mon oreille?" (What sweet chants, these, that strike, entrance my ear?) shows a different side of Chanlatte's writing. Here is a sample of Christophean poetry, little of which has survived or been printed in accounts of early Haitian literary history. The author is identified as the comte de Rosier, Chanlatte's title under Christophe's reign. The occasion for the presentation of the poem, which was sung by two women in the court, the comtesse de Rosier and Mademoiselle Mells, was the fourth day of the feasts of Christophe's coronation in 1811. Among the notable features of the poem is its heavy usage of mythological references, which may initially strike readers mainly as indications of European influence or attitudes. As noted above, however, the use of such references is a complex matter. For one thing, Chanlatte undoubtedly employed erudite allusions to please the king, who, although he had no formal education, valued high culture greatly. Accordingly, he surrounded himself with educated people who read to him, informed him, taught him history, and advised him.[31] For another thing, classical references are at times overlaid with local references. The words spoken by the "Génie d'Hayti"—"La Discorde sifflait: des lions furieux/La crinière agitée en pointes se hérisse" (Discord hissed. Lions, furious, toss their mane;/As darts of fur prick, spike the air pell-mell)—echo Dessalines's own warning that "the irritated genius of Hayti" would rise up out of the ocean against hostile naval incursions.[32]

The remaining poems, written under Boyer's reign from 1820 to 1843, show a poetic and political evolution in his writing. "Du vieux cercle des ans une face nouvelle" (Scarce does a new face shine forth from the old year's course) begins the pattern of lavish, at times sycophantic, praise for Haiti's new leader. The tendency to use classical references (Phoebus, Apollo, Pallas) as well as neoclassical language displays the poet's will to display erudition. However, the poem also places emphasis on Haitian independence, as its title, "Cantate à l'indépendance" (Ode to Independence), proclaims. Its key themes are the people, freedom from French tyranny, love of the country, and allegiance to the founding fathers. Independence also appears in the title of the poem discussed above, "Why ply you your fickle ministry?," originally titled "Ode à l'indépendance." As already noted, Chanlatte returns in this poem to a dialogic format that he used during the Christophean phase of his career. But here Christophe is denigrated as "inhumain." The column to Independence, a metonymic representation of the nation in the play, is mentioned only once in the poem. Whereas the play features an array of social classes, ages, and professions in both male and female characters who pay tribute to the column from their various perspectives, in the poem the voices merely echo one another in praise of Boyer. With "Quel est ce Roi, dont la bonté?" (What King, this, he whose weal outspread?), written when France recognized Haitian independence in 1825, he joins the chorus of poets situated on a wide spectrum of political, social, and racial positions who found it politically expedient to celebrate the union of the two nations and praise the French monarch Charles X. It is noteworthy, however, that although the two countries are placed side by side in the poem—"Vive Haïti! Vive la France!" (Long live Haiti! And long live France!)—allegiance to Haiti comes first. "Au loin, qui brille à nos yeux étonnés?" (What looms there, shining afar before our startled eyes?), written in the same spirit of praise for Boyer, contains even stronger affirmations of Chanlatte's enduring allegiance to his country. Past battles for freedom are recalled by the phrase "vivre libre ou mourir" (live free or die) repeated twice. But the poem also looks to the future. The key concepts now, Chanlatte states, are "liberté, commerce, indépendance" (liberty, trade, independence). The future of Haiti requires remembering the past, but placing a new emphasis on peace, justice, security, and prosperity.

If little changed under Boyer's regime during the period of the 1830s, a major literary shift did occur in literature, both in Haiti and in France: the rise of Romanticism. Unquestionably, French poets—especially Alphonse de Lamartine and Victor Hugo—played influential roles. Essays on their influence found in journals such as *Le Républicain* and *L'Union* reveal that French Romantic poets' assertions of individuality and universality were viewed by Haitian writers as "a cornerstone of . . . arguments against racism and [the] continued practice of slavery."[33] The French Romantics' messianic vision of the poet and their emphasis on France's national past similarly resonated with their Haitian counterparts. The early citizens of Haiti aspired to create a national literature with special focus on heroic figures of the Haitian Revolution such as Toussaint Louverture and Dessalines: "Nothing ties us more firmly and provokes our interest more strongly than the stories of the revolutionary era of our country. The actors of these inspiring and bloody struggles for our deliverance are still here: they are our fathers. . . . Young people of the new generation, bow your heads when you pass before the venerable authors of our freedom."[34] Haitians were repeatedly admonished to maintain locally rooted traditions: "love and cherish your nationality: you owe it to yourselves, you owe it to the memory of your fathers, you owe it to humanity. Derive inspiration from your history, religiously conserve your country's traditions: without traditions, there is no country. Refrain from servile and partisan copying of other nations. . . . Resemble only yourself, be and remain Haitian."[35]

Much can be learned from juxtaposing Haiti's return to its national past in the 1830s with the similar move that took place in France at the time, as shown, for example, in Lamartine's "Les Révolutions" and Hugo's "À la Colonne." Edward Said has written of a contrapuntal method of analysis, "a simultaneous awareness both of the metropolitan history that is narrated and of those other histories against which (and together with which) the dominating discourse acts."[36] Placing writings by French Romantic poets in the broader context of writings by Haitian writers that share the same themes and concerns invites comparisons and contrasts with respect to nationality, race, and literary style. It prevents the narrow Eurocentric reading that nineteenth-century literature has too often received. Additionally, since Lamartine played a significant role in the history of French abolition and since both Hugo and Lamartine were themselves authors of works about Haiti—Hugo's novel *Bug Jargal* and Lamartine's play *Toussaint Louverture*—significant interconnections exist between Haiti and France.

Poems by the two leading figures of Haitian romanticism, Ignace Nau (1808–39) and Coriolan Ardouin (1812–35), are included in this volume. Nau and his brothers Émile and Eugène, along with Ardouin and his brothers Beaubrun and Céligni, formed a literary group, or *cénacle,* in 1836. They founded *Le Républicain,* which remained in existence for a year until it published an article considered to be offensive to the government. *Le Républicain* was followed by *L'Union,* founded by Nau, which ceased publication in 1839.[37] Nau's poems appeared in *Le Républicain* and *L'Union* as well as in *La Revue des colonies,* published in France. Ardouin's poems were also included in the French publications *La Revue contemporaine* and *La Revue des deux mondes.* Ardouin's poems were published after his death by Nau and then reissued in

1881 by Coriolan's brother Beaubrun Ardouin. It was not until 2000 that Nau's poetry was published in a collected edition.

Ignace Nau stands out among the poets included in this volume for his interest in indigenous writing. Although that interest is not directly apparent in his poems, it can be seen in three creole stories he contributed to *L'Union,* including "Le Lambi," situated in 1791 during the revolution in Saint-Domingue. The combination of French and local creole-language expressions in these stories is noteworthy. Nau was undoubtedly influenced by his brother Émile, who published *Histoire des Caciques* in 1843. This work, which emblematizes Haitian Romanticism's return to its past, foregrounds the loss of freedom over a period of roughly twenty-five years of more than a million indigenous inhabitants of Haiti, whose betrayal and enslavement by Europeans is analogous to that which Africans were subjected to under slavery. The term *cacique* is used to refer to the original inhabitants of the island of Hispaniola, the Taino Indians. Émile Nau addresses the issue of cacique literature, concluding that "without a doubt Haiti had a literature. It was popular poetry. This sort of poetry is found among all people who have a national existence, a language, and traditions."[38] They sang poems, called *areyetos,* as expressions of their daily lives and on special occasions such as funerals, feasts, and games. Émile deplores the failure of the Spanish to write down any of the cacique literature. Although there is no way of knowing what the poems were like, he assumes that, as songs, they had cadence and rhythm; and he calls attention to the interest that Henry Christophe showed in the Caciques, especially concerning his namesake Henry the last heroic defender of Indian freedom.

The poetry of Ignace Nau does not typically address social or political issues. However, the poem ("Dessalines!... À ce nom, amis, découvrons nous!" [Dessalines!... At that name, doff hats, my friends!]) provides a notable exception that, like his brother's work on the Caciques, reveals a preoccupation with Haitian history. In this poem, Nau chose to pay homage to the founder of the Haitian nation and to condemn the plot that led to his death. Like others of the Romantic generation, he pleads for unity and peace in the march toward progress. And he worships heroes who spilled their blood for their country. The people are admonished to remember their heroes: especially the "aigle africain" (African eagle), in whose guise Nau chooses to recall the former slave Dessalines. A new generation of Haitians may fail to remember or appreciate the revolts that slaves initiated, the battles in which they fought, and the freedom they gained. But this collective past constitutes a patrimony which serves as the bedrock of Haitian identity. Nau foregrounds this heroic past, rather than the partisan allegiance to specific leaders found in poems written in the early decades of Haitian independence. Boyer, the president at the time of the poem's composition, is not even mentioned. Also, in keeping with the Romantic phase of Haitian poetry to which Nau belongs, nature plays a key role in "Dessalines!... At that name doff hats, my friends!" Nature, not politics, forms the basis of the national consciousness that the poem evokes. Haiti's brilliant climate is a source of joy and pride: "demain le soleil se lèvera plus pur/Et plus majestueux dans sa courbe d'azur!" (tomorrow's sun shall rise/In its majestic sweep through azure skies!). Promise for the future is expressed through natural rebirth and regeneration: "Et nos fleuves taris jailliront en torrents,/Et nos lacs rouleront des flots plus transparents" (Our arid riverbeds shall gush and pour;/Our lakes shall, crystalline, shine shore to shore).

Nau's "Au Génie de la patrie" ("Qu'ils sont délicieux tes jours de liberté!" [Oh, the delight of your days freedom-spent!]) reveals a similar preoccupation with Haitian history. In this case, sorrows afflict both the nation and the individual, who loses the woman he loves. The enduring male "Génie de la patrie," the hope for the future, is contrasted with the transient feminine presence whose absence the poet mourns. The poem pays homage to another founder of the Haitian nation, Pétion. The message in "Au Génie de la patrie" complements that found in "Dessalines!... At that name doff hats, my friends!": movement forward requires harmony, peace, and commitment on the part of the young generation to sustain the virtues of the nation's heroes. Although Pétion was viewed as a partisan figure for mulatto interests in the past, Nau evokes him as a unifying figure committed to the sacrifices made for freedom by all the founding fathers of Haitian independence.

Coriolan Ardouin's poetry focuses on subjects related to slavery and Haitian independence more consistently than Nau's.[39] *Les Betjouanes* (The Bechouans) consists of five poems which trace the narrative trajectory from a peaceful existence in Africa to the tragic chapters of capture, enslavement, and the dreaded Atlantic Passage. This trajectory is the foundation of Haiti's history before independence. The poems do not refer to Haiti; instead, various locations in south-central and eastern Africa evoke the prehistory of slavery. The specificity of place names, flora, fauna, and cultural practices conforms to the Romantic notion of "local color" while at the same time marking these poems as distinctively non-European. The first three poems evoke the daily lives and joys of Africans, who dance, frolic in the water, and revel in the rhythmic sounds of the jungle and the music produced on indigenous musical instruments. The feelings of the African girl Minora are expressed in relation to her setting: her feelings at the loss of her lover are compared to those of a lioness yearning for her mate, and her sorrow is likened to the closed petals of a mimosa flower. Reference is made to the Amirantes, outer islands of the Seychelles, and the Kuruman, an African river, as well as to such local flora as date trees, coco-palms, boxwood, and lotuses. The beauty and sensuality of African women, a key motif, is illustrated in the persona of Minora, who enjoys the warm embrace of the river's waters. Her separation from her lover, whose sudden disappearance puzzles and then alarms her, introduces the theme of the slave trade and its horrific effects, which her story dramatizes. The fourth poem presents a chilling description of the process of enslavement, in which Africans play a key role. The inhuman treatment of unsus-

pecting victims like Minora is initiated by the Bushmen (Boschis-
mens), who were feared for their bloodthirsty ways. Like animals
(hyenas, apes, vultures), they capture their unsuspecting prey. The
fifth poem suggests the point of view of Minora on board the slave
ship and deplores the cruel fate of the victims.

The remaining poems by Ardouin included in this volume
have direct relevance to Haitian history. "Pétion" ("Quand le ciel
se dorait d'un beau soleil couchant" [When the sky donned the
setting sun's fine golds]) reflects upon the internal political threats
the country faces. It depicts a pensive, compassionate, melan-
choly Pétion, situated in a natural setting. He recalls the glory
of past military victories and fears for the future of the republic,
which Ardouin compares to a ship whose helmsman sees an ap-
proaching storm and suspects that survival is unlikely. The poem
compares the storm to the civil wars that have afflicted Haiti. It
ends with the uncertainty for the future that surrounds Pétion's
legacy. The six parts of "Mila" ("Hélas! je me souviens de ce
jour" [Oh! I recall that day]) tell the tragic story of a young girl
under slavery. The events occur in a New World setting although
the star-crossed lovers, Mila and Osala, are African born. The
story is a familiar one from the body of nineteenth-century slave
stories: a wicked master named Elbreuil desires Mila, who rejects
him; Elbreuil sends Osala away in chains in a fit of jealous rage;
Mila dies of grief. Romantic features of the Mila poems are simi-
lar to those found in *The Bechouans*. The elements in nature that
are evoked, such as sugarcane, frangipane, and thatched huts,
are representative of the Haitian landscape. "Le Pont rouge"
(The Pont-Rouge), which is set in the place where Dessalines was
assassinated by political and military rivals in 1806, suggests
similarities and differences between Dessalines as emperor and
Napoleon's corresponding role in France—even though Dessa-
lines's adoption of the structure of empire was arguably a gesture
of resistance to French hegemony, rather than an imitation of it.[40]
The poem begins by acknowledging Dessalines's bloody acts but
goes on to glorify and justify him: "Dessalines apparut superbe,

grand, immense!" (Then Dessalines, superb, appeared, stood tall!).

The poetry of Pierre Faubert (1806–68) illuminates the efforts by Haitian writers in the 1840s to bolster and maintain a strong sense of national consciousness. Faubert, an educator who directed the Lycée Pétion at Port-au-Prince from 1837 to 1842, served administrative roles under both Pétion and Boyer. The 1840s were a time of growing political and economic instability. Opposition to Boyer's regime, led by Hérard-Dumesle, increased steadily. In 1843, Boyer resigned and fled to Jamaica. After years of growing resentment, the Dominican Republic declared its independence from rule by Haiti, which Boyer had instituted in 1822.[41] Under Faubert's direction, the Lycée Pétion revived interest in the history of Haitian independence and addressed the pressing issue of the color prejudices that lingered and were undermining Haitians under the Boyer regime. "The pupils of the national lycée were told that the country must develop, not only because this would lead to material benefits, but in order to destroy completely the prejudice which existed against their race."[42] His leadership bore fruit, creating a cadre of educated young men who demanded more inclusive racial attitudes as well as political and economic reforms.

Two of Faubert's poems—"Persécutés sur ce rivage" (Harried, we stand upon this shore) and "Du Dieu des opprimés célébrons la puissance!" (All praise his power, the God of the oppressed!)—are drawn from the play *Ogé ou le préjugé de couleur* (Ogé; or, The Prejudice of Color), which Faubert's students performed at the Lycée Pétion in 1841. The play raises the controversial subject of color prejudice. In the introduction to the play, Faubert defends himself against charges made in 1843 by the abolitionist Victor Schoelcher, who attended the play. Faubert justifies the play by arguing that color prejudice extends to all races, white and mulatto as well as black. Faubert also defends the subject of the play, the mulatto martyr Vincent Ogé (1755–91), who lived at a time when achieving equality for free persons of color was a primary abolitionist goal. Ogé was not alone in the eighteenth century in being unable or unwilling to envision the possibility of the emancipation of slaves. Faubert observes that as late as 1830 Schoelcher himself did not speak out for emancipation and adds that such respected abolitionists as the Amis des noirs, the marquis de Condorcet, Henri Grégoire, and Lamartine shared his admiration for Ogé. "Harried, we stand upon this shore" is a song that is sung in the first act of the play, which takes place in the home of members of the prejudiced white planter class. Their unwillingness to acknowledge the existence of oppressed people living among them or the validity of the people's cause is suddenly disrupted, however, when a group of rebel insurgents arrives. The song is the insurgents' rallying cry and call for action. "All praise his power, the God of the oppressed!" is the marching song that opens act 2. It celebrates Ogé's fight for freedom and asserts solidarity between persons of color and slaves.

Two other poems—"Je suis fier de le dire, ô négresse, je t'aime" (Proudly I say, "I love you," negress mine) and "Frères, nous avons tous brisé le joug infâme" (Brothers all, we have now that foul yoke broken)—are included in a collection of poems titled "Poésies fugitives" (Fleeting Poems) published in the same volume as Ogé. The first adopts the point of view of a white man who desires a black woman. Faubert highlights the woman's subjective experiences. He deplores the sufferings she has had to endure and the arrogance of whites who assume they are superior. He affirms equality of the races and calls for justice and freedom. Many of the same themes found here are central to the meaning of "Brothers all," written eight years later, in 1850. It too calls for justice, freedom, and equality, and for the recognition of past sufferings. Faubert goes farther in this poem, however. While celebrating British and French abolitionists from the past, he emphasizes that the future will rely on the physical and intellectual strength of Haitians. Most important, he stresses the need for unity. Broadening the scope of the poem to the international stage, he contrasts Haiti with the United States and

Hungary, countries where prejudice and dissension prevailed.[43] Haiti must be a country that achieves "union," a divine word that depends on setting aside color prejudices: "Mais voulez-vous compléter votre gloire?/Noirs et Jaunes, soyez unis" (But to complete your glory's course,/Blacks and Mulattos, stand united!); and he concludes that God "estime/L'âme seule et non la couleur" (judges Man's soul and not his skin). Like Ardouin and Nau, Faubert evokes the blood shed by warriors and heroes of the past. But in addition, he adopts a political stand, calling for adherence to the notion of union among diverse factions and races. Assimilationist positions similar to Faubert's provoked controversy in Martinique following emancipation in 1848, setting the politician and antislavery activist Cyrille Bissette at odds with his abolitionist adversary Schoelcher.[44] By thus shedding light on the complex history of abolitionism and race relations at the end of the first half of the nineteenth century, "Brothers all" enriches critical inquiry into a crucial period of Atlantic world history.

The end of the Boyer regime in 1843 and the independence of Santo Domingo (now the Dominican Republic) in 1844, major historical events in Haitian history, mark fitting chronological endpoints for the story of Haitian independence recounted by poets of the first half of the nineteenth century. However, the story does not end there, as is evident in the 1887 poem "Chant national" ("Quand nos aïeux" [When our ancestors]; see Appendix D) by Oswald Durand, hailed by many as Haiti's national bard. The version of the poem that we provide from the original publication *Rires et pleurs* provides an instructive reminder of how important it is to pay close attention to the primary texts of the poetry of Haitian independence, as we have attempted to do in this volume. Most printed versions of the poem omit the second stanza, which highlights Haitians' African origins and the long-standing color prejudice in the country.[45] How, why, and when decisions were made to truncate the original poem, and whether those decisions were aesthetic, practical, or political:

these are among the intriguing questions that future scholars will need to address for this and other poems included here. Finding answers to questions like these will require that Haitian literature of the first half of the nineteenth century continue to attract the attention it deserves and that Haiti continue to occupy a key position in transatlantic studies—a stirring tradition of poems meant to be recited and shared.

Chronology

Dates in nineteenth-century Haitian history are fluid; sparse documentation, or plural but contradictory documentation, of individual events is characteristic. In-depth work on any specific historical entity—event, person, or publication—demands careful assessment of the dynamics and stakes involved. What follows here is a tentative list of historically notable dates, along with dates of the inaugural issues of major Haitian newspapers from the first half of the century.

1803

April 7   Death of Toussaint Louverture in the Fort de Joux in France

November 18   Dessalines leads the Haitian soldiers to victory against the French in the battle of Vertières.

November 29   Proclamation of Independence (Proclamation d'indépendance) by Generals Dessalines, Christophe, and Philippe Clerveaux

1804

Following the general retreat of the French army, General Ferrand establishes command of a French outpost on the eastern side of the island and begins working on legal challenges and interventions of French privateers against trade in Haitian ports, with the first documented seizure of a ship, the American vessel *Mars,* dated February 3, 1804.

January 1   Haitian Declaration of Independence (Acte d'indépendance)

April 28   Following violent reprisals against the remaining white French in Haiti, Dessalines issues a proclamation stating, "I have avenged America."

September 22   Proclamation of the Empire of Haiti

October 6	Coronation of Emperor Jean-Jacques and Empress Marie-Claire Heureuse Dessalines at Cap-Haytien
November 15	Inaugural issue of the *Gazette politique et commerciale d'Hayti*

1805

May 20	Dessalines issues the Imperial Constitution of Haiti.
July 25	Feast Day of Emperor Jean-Jacques (coinciding with the Catholic feast day of Saint James)
August 12	Feast Day of Empress Marie-Claire (coinciding with the Catholic feast day of Saint Claire of Assisi)

1806

October 17	Assassination of Dessalines at the Pont-Rouge on the outskirts of Port-au-Prince
October 18	The "Official Relation" of how Dessalines and General Germain fell into the trap of the "Haytian campaign against Dessalines" is issued by Étienne Gérin, minister of war and the navy; Alexandre Sabès Pétion, commanding general of the Second Division; Yayou, commander general of Léogâne; and Vaval, general of Brigade of the District of Nippes.
October 21	Minister of War Gérin, Commanding General Pétion, Generals of Brigade Sayore and Vaval, and Adjutant General Bonnet write to General Henry Christophe: "Resembling the custom of old warriors, we have publicly acknowledged you to be the chief of the government."

1807

January 10	The city of Jacmel celebrates the victory of Pétion over Christophe after weeks of skirmishes and battles. This date as well as any other inaugurates the establishment of a continuously dynamic North-South or North-Southwest political divide

in Haiti, aligned with "black"-"colored" community identities.

February 17   Henry Christophe issues an address as "president and generalissimo of the land and sea forces of the state of Haiti."

March 9   Alexandre Pétion is elected president of the Republic of Haiti in the South.

Inaugural issue of *La Sentinelle*

1808
November   Following political tensions arising from Napoleon's invasion of Spain, the French are defeated in Santo Domingo. General Ferrand takes his own life.

1809
June 18   Inaugural issue of the *Bulletin Officiel: Gazette du Port-au-Prince*

1810
October 8   Henry Christophe announces the conquest of Saint Nicholas Mole.

1812
June 2   Coronation of King Henry Christophe and Queen Marie Louise at Cap-Henry

February 24 Publication of the Code Henry, a vast legislative compendium for Haiti under the Christophe monarchy

1813
July 22   Inaugural issue of *Gazette royale d'Hayti* (Cap-Henry)

Inaugural issue of *Le Télégraphe*

1814
With the restoration of the monarchy in France in 1814, an initiative to reinforce socioeconomic hierarchies in Haiti and therefore to shore up French interests is launched by the motley crew of

"commissioners": Agoustine Franco de Medina (a French-identified native of the Spanish part of the island of Hispaniola); an author of travel narratives, Dauxion Lavaysse; and a businessman of Gascon, Creole, and German heritage, Herman Draverman.

September 24   Pétion invites Lavaysse to discuss indemnity payments and resumption of commerce.
November   Christophe and his court expose the French plot to reinforce socioracial hierarchies.
December 3   Pétion publicly rejects the French initiative and warns the public to prepare for possible hostilities.

1816
June 2   Republican Constitution of Pétion
October 8   Pétion and Christophe reject the delegation sent by Louis XVIII of France to negotiate terms of an eventual French recognition of Haitian independence.
October 10   Installation of Pétion as president for life

1817
July 7   Inaugural issue of the *Abeille haytienne: journal politique et littéraire*

1818
March 29   Death of Pétion. His body is reportedly buried under the tree of liberty "opposite the Capitol"; his viscera are buried in Fort National; and his heart is bequeathed to his daughter.
March 30   Jean-Pierre Boyer is named president of Haiti.
September 27   Inaugural issue of *Gazette royale d'Hayti* (Sans Souci)
August 17   Inaugural issue of *L'Éclaireur haytien, ou le parfait patriote*

1819
President Boyer begins outreach for asylum to blacks in the United States; he also reportedly reopens negotiations concern-

ing sending a tribute to France, with commercial advantages, in exchange for recognition of Haiti's independence.

1820

April 23	Inaugural issue of the *Hermite d'Hayti: journal historique et littéraire*
October 8	Death of King Henry Christophe
October 18	Massacre of Prince Jacques-Victor Henry and other important political figures under Christophe, including the baron de Vastey and General Jean-Philippe Daut
October 21	Boyer and the Haitian military leadership proclaim that there is now throughout the north and south of Haiti "only one government, and one constitution."

1821

Military ventures by Boyer into what is now the Dominican Republic are documented in journalism from January of 1821. The unification of the eastern and western parts of the island of Hispaniola is conventionally dated 1822–44; however, this represents a complex period of military, political, legislative, and cultural interrelationships of the two regions with heterogeneous dates. "Unification" rarely appears as a motif in documents from this era.

1822

February 9	Boyer enters Santo Domingo and unifies the island of Hispaniola as Haiti.
June 1	Inaugural issue of *Le Propagateur haïtien*
September 9	Boyer denounces the insurgents' proposal to revolutionize Haiti by the afro-European migrant Darfour; Darfour was executed on September 2.

1825

April 17	King Charles X of France conditionally recognizes

the independence of Haiti, imposing an indemnity of 150 million francs.

1827
January 21   Inaugural issue of *La Feuille du commerce: petites affiches et annonces du Port-au-Prince*

1828
January 2   Haiti pays a first installment of 30 million francs to the French.

1830
September 2   Inaugural issue of *Le Phare: journal commercial, politique et littéraire*

1836
August 15   Inaugural issue of *Le Républicain: recueil scientifique et littéraire*

1837
April 20   Inaugural issue of *L'Union: recueil commercial et littéraire*

1838
Haiti's remaining debt to France is reduced to 60 million francs.

1841
July 7   Inaugural issue of *Le Cancanier*

1842
May 7   An earthquake devastates northern Haiti and the city of Cap-Haïtien.

1843
February 13   Boyer's presidency ends.
April 4   Charles Rivière-Hérard is elected president.
December 31   Constitution of 1843

1844

February 27	The Trinitarios declare the independence of the eastern part of Hispaniola from Haiti.
April 4	Jean-Jacques Acaau leads the revolt of the southern Haitian farmers known as the Piquets.
May 3	A coup d'état topples Rivière-Hérard.
May 3	Philippe Guerrier takes over the presidency.
December 12	Inaugural issue of *Le Figaro, barbier-perruquier: journal universel*

1845

February 8	Inaugural issue of *Le Moniteur haïtien*
April 15	Death of President Guerrier
April 16	Jean-Louis Pierrot is installed as president.

1846

March 1	Jean-Baptiste Riché is installed as president.
March 24	President Pierrot is officially deposed.

1847

February 27	Death of President Riché
March 2	Faustin-Élie Soulouque becomes president.

1849

August 26	Coronation of Soulouque as Emperor Faustin I and of Empress Adelina (other dates for his coronation are also reported)

1850

July 9	Death of Jean-Pierre Boyer in France

Translator's Note

I have tried to provide translations of these poems that are faithful not only to their meaning and their tone but also—since they are in formal verse—to their form. This has demanded, for me, the unquestioned use of rhyme and meter, without either of which they would bear only the shadow of a resemblance to the originals.

These ground rules have imposed several challenges: in lexicon and syntax, the use of credible English and the avoidance of jarring anachronism; in prosody, the avoidance of the alexandrine, backbone of traditional French verse but ponderous as a twelve-syllable English line, and its replacement with its canonical equivalent, the ten-syllable iambic pentameter; in spelling, the modernizing of archaic spellings. I have also respected the frequently varying line lengths within some originals, indicated by conventional indents (even where the French neglects to use them), as well as the rendering of odd-syllable (*impair*) French lines by equivalent strategies in English.

Many of these poems also presented a more abstract, more strictly aesthetic challenge. Some of the poems rise to the level of impressive poetry. Others, while observing the technical elements of formal French verse, were written by well-meaning versifiers and untrained amateurs. Translating the latter, I have resisted the temptation to rewrite them and try to make their authors better poets than they were. The aim of this collection, it should be remembered, is not to present deathless literary masterpieces but rather to offer significant historico-social documents from a seminal moment in Haitian history, of interest to enlightened readers and students of French and francophone literature, and of the burgeoning field of Atlantic Studies as well.

POETRY OF HAITIAN INDEPENDENCE

ANONYMOUS

Quoi? tu te tais Peuple Indigène!
(Hymne haytienne)

Quoi? tu te tais Peuple Indigène!
Quand un Héros, par ses exploits,
Vengeant ton nom, brisant ta chaîne,
À jamais assure tes droits,
À jamais assure tes droits?
Honneur à sa valeur guerrière!
Gloire à ses efforts triomphants!
Offrons-lui nos cœurs, notre encens;
Chantons d'une voix mâle et fière,
      Sous ce bon Père unis,
      À jamais réunis,
Vivons, mourons, ses vrais Enfants,
Vivons, mourons, ses vrais Enfants,
      Libres, indépendants.

De nos droits ennemis perfides,
Du Nouveau-Monde les tyrans,
Déjà les Français homicides,
Du Soleil frappaient les Enfants;
Du Soleil frappaient les Enfants;
Ô! du Ciel éclatants prodiges!
Pour lever nos fronts abattus,
Jacque paraît, ils ne sont plus,
Et l'on en cherche les vestiges,
      Sous ce bon Père, unis,
      À jamais réunis,
Vivons, mourons, ses vrais Enfants,
Vivons, mourons, ses vrais Enfants,
      Libres, indépendants.

ANONYMOUS

What? Native race! Would you remain silent? (Haitian Hymn)[1]

What? Native race! Would you remain
Silent, unmoved, when Hero's hand[2]
Avenges you,[3] breaks slavery's chain,
Returns rights stolen from your land,
Returns rights stolen from your land?
Honor this soldier's feats! Rejoice!
His be our hearts, widespread his fame.
Let incense rise to praise his name;
Let us sing with one manly voice:
       "Good Father, he, who thus
       Reigns wisely over us!
Live, die: ever his children, we,
Live, die: ever his children, we,
       United, proud, and free!"

The murderous Frenchman's treacheries
By New World perfidies outdone...
Our rights' villainous enemies
Cast down the Children of the Sun,
Cast down the Children of the Sun.[4]
Lo! Wondrous omens fire the Sky,
And Jacques appears; great warrior,
Lifting our heads! The hounds of war
Leave not a trace to shock the eye!
       Good Father, he, who thus
       Reigns wisely over us!
Live, die: ever his children, we,
Live, die: ever his children, we,
       United, proud, and free!

En mer, en plaine, et sur nos cimes
Écoutez ce bruit, ces éclats;
Amis, c'est le cri des victimes
Dénonçant leurs noirs attentats,
Dénonçant leurs noirs attentats,
Du sang d'une horde cruelle,
Oui, quand vous arrosez leurs os,
Elles font entendre ces mots
Du sein de la nuit éternelle,
  Sous ce bon Père, unis,
   À jamais réunis,
Vivez, mourez, ses vrais Enfants,
Vivez, mourez, ses vrais Enfants,
   Libres, indépendants.

Quel est cet indigne Insulaire,
Ce lâche cœur, ce vil soldat
Qui, désormais sous sa bannière
N'affronterait point le trépas,
N'affronterait point le trépas?
Qu'il parle; au défaut du Tonnerre,
Pour expier cet attentat,
Nos bras levés contre l'ingrat,
Sauront le réduire en poussière,
  Sous ce bon Père unis,
   À jamais réunis,
Vivons, mourons, ses vrais Enfants,
Vivons, mourons, ses vrais Enfants,
   Libres, indépendants.

Amis, que la reconnaissance
Consacre ses faits, sa valeur;
Nous servirons, sous sa puissance,
Le ciel, la justice et l'honneur,
Le ciel, la justice et l'honneur:

Pray hear—over the sea, the plain,
The mountaintops—the anguished cries,
In the black throes of bale and bane,
Of those who, dying, agonize,
Of those who, dying, agonize.
For when you wash their bones, stripped white,
In the blood of the heartless horde,[5]
The victims of their crimes untoward
Cry from the dark eternal night:
        "Good Father, he, who thus
        Reigns wisely over us!
Live, die:[6] ever his children, we,
Live, die: ever his children, we,
        United, proud, and free!"

What island denizen is there;
What coward soldier-wretch draws breath,
Who, warrior vile, is loath to bear
Our flag aloft, and shrinks from death,
Our flag aloft, and shrinks from death?
Let him speak! We need not the flame
Of Thunderbolt[7] to cleanse his sin!
Our arms will smite him, do him in,
And crush to dust his thankless shame!
        Good Father, he, who thus
        Reigns wisely over us!
Live, die: ever his children, we,
Live, die: ever his children, we,
        United, proud, and free!

Friends, let our thanks now sanctify
His valorous deeds—boons freely given;
With justice, honor, serving heaven,
Let us confirm his power thereby,
Let us confirm his power thereby.

Que nos enfants, dès le bas âge,
Aiment à bégayer son nom;
Désormais Jacque est le Patron
De qui repousse l'esclavage,
    Sous ce bon Père unis,
    À jamais réunis,
Vivons, mourons, ses vrais Enfants,
Vivons, mourons, ses vrais Enfants,
    Libres, indépendants.

1804

Cradle-borne, may our children all
Stammer his name in babblings dim:
Blessèd Saint James, Patron[8] of him
Who breaks the bonds of slavery's thrall!
       Good Father, he, who thus
       Reigns wisely over us!
Live, die: ever his children, we,
Live, die: ever his children, we,
       United, proud, and free![9]

1804

C. CÉSAR TÉLÉMAQUE

Chantons, célébrons notre gloire

Chantons, célébrons notre gloire,
Amis de l'île d'Haïti;
Marchons, soutenons la victoire,
Le bonheur de notre pays;
    Chérissons sans cesse,
    Avec allégresse,
Celui qui fait notre bonheur;
    Vive l'Empereur.
    Vive l'Empereur.

C'est lui qui punit l'arrogance
Des Français, nos vrais ennemis;
Et qui par sa douce clémence,
Fait de ses sujets des amis;
    Chérissons sans cesse,
    Avec allégresse,
Celui qui fait notre bonheur;
    Vive l'Empereur.
    Vive l'Empereur.

Son nom, sa valeur, son courage,
Font trembler tous les intrigants;
Ennemi du vil esclavage;
Il voit en nous que ses enfants;
    Chérissons sans cesse,
    Avec allégresse,
Celui qui fait notre bonheur;
    Vive l'Empereur.
    Vive l'Empereur.

C. CÉSAR TÉLÉMAQUE

Let us now sing our glory![1]

Friends of our Haitian island,[2] all,
Let us now sing our glory! Yes,
Let us march onward, standing tall,
Staunch in our well-won happiness;
       Thus, eternally
       Thankful let us be
To him, our joy's great guarantor:
       Hail the Emperor!
       Hail the Emperor!

He it is who flouted the proud
Arrogant French, in battle royal;
Now of his subjects, heads unbowed,
His mercy makes friends, true and loyal.
       Thus, eternally
       Thankful let us be
To him, our joy's great guarantor:
       Hail the Emperor!
       Hail the Emperor!

His name, his valor glorious,
Make scheming traitors quake with fear.
Vile slavery's foe, he thinks of us
All as his children, near and dear.[3]
       Thus, eternally
       Thankful let us be
To him, our joy's great guarantor:
       Hail the Emperor!
       Hail the Emperor!

Reçois de moi les doux hommages,
Mon respectable Souverain;
Que Dieu t'inspire des lois sages,
Et te protège de sa main;
  Je chéris sans cesse,
  Avec allégresse,
Celui qui fait mon vrai bonheur;
  Vive l'Empereur.
  Vive l'Empereur.

1804

Accept, O worthy Sovereign, these,
My simple words of homage; and
May God inspire your wise decrees,
And hold you ever in his hand.
                And eternally
                Thankful shall I be
To him, my joy's great guarantor.
                Hail the Emperor!
                Hail the Emperor!

1804

La nature infiniment sage

La nature infiniment sage
Nous enflamma des mêmes feux;
Justice, plaisir, amour et courage,
Un jour devaient tout rendre heureux;
Mais les tyrans, pour enchaîner nos frères,
Nous ont soumis à de perfides lois;
Au nom de Dieu, ils ont trompé nos pères,
Aux pieds, ils ont foulé nos droits.
Ô jour heureux! Ô siècle de mémoire!
Le peuple a reconquis ses droits.
Chantons, chantons avec courage,
Vive, vive l'égalité!
Chassons, chassons partout l'esclavage,
Vive, vive l'égalité!

C'est en vain qu'on nous fait la guerre,
Nos cœurs sont pris des mêmes feux;
Apprenez tyrans de la terre,
Qu'un peuple est libre quand il veut.
Lancez, lancez vos bombes meurtrières,
Contre nous ralliez vos voisins;
Faites marcher vos hordes sanguinaires,
Tyrans, tigres, rois inhumains!
Venez, venez apprendre aux téméraires,
Que votre sort est dans leur mains.
Chantons, chantons avec courage,
Vive, vive l'égalité!
Chassons, chassons partout l'esclavage,
Vive, vive l'égalité!

Nature, in wisdom infinite[1]

Nature, in wisdom infinite,[2]
Had made us burn with one desire:
Justice, love, pleasure, courage... Each had lit
The joyous flame of freedom's fire.
But shameless tyrants, one day, came to chain
Our fathers, brothers; shackling, trampling us
Straightway beneath their laws' perfidious reign—
And in God's very name! But glorious,
This day, this century! For once again[3]
Freedom is ours, re-conquered! Thus
Sing we, sing we stoutheartedly:
Equality forevermore!
Banished, banished be cruel slavery:
Equality forevermore!

In vain they flout, attack us; for
Our hearts burn with that freedom fire!
Learn, tyrants of the earth, once more:
Free, they who freedom's boons desire!
Hurl, hurl about your deadly bombs of war;
Rally against us your allies;
Let your bloodthirsty hordes play conqueror,
You, tiger-kings, who tyrannize!
Come! Let our evil foes in vain implore
Our doughty race that fate defies!
Sing we, sing we stoutheartedly:
Equality forevermore!
Banished, banished be cruel slavery:
Equality forevermore!

Marche avec nous, chère espérance,
Abandonne nos ennemis,
Jette un regard sur l'indépendance,
Soutiens nos soldats aguerris!
Dieu des combats, maintiens notre vaillance
Livre à nos mains jusqu'au dernier tyran;
Notre Empereur guide notre vengeance,
Haïtiens en voici le moment,
Vaincre ou mourir, et notre indépendance,
Tel est notre dernier serment.
Chantons, chantons avec courage,
Vive, vive l'égalité!
Chassons, chassons partout l'esclavage,
Vive, vive l'égalité!

1804

Fair hope, pray join our hero band;
Forsake our foes, reviled, abjured.
Gaze on the independence of our land.[4]
Sustain our heroes, war-inured!
O Battle God, let us all stalwart stand;
Let earth's last tyrant feel our wrath, as we,
Guided by our great Emperor's mighty hand,
Avenge our wrongs! Haitians, our destiny:
Conquer or die! This, our last promise... And
Ever be independent, free!
Sing we, sing we stoutheartedly:
Equality forevermore!
Banished, banished be cruel slavery:
Equality forevermore!

1804

C'est toi, grand Empereur

C'est toi, grand Empereur, qui maîtrisant la France,
Ramènes dans nos champs, la paix et l'abondance;
Qui sus par ta valeur, ta douceur, ta bonté,
Prendre un si noble essor vers l'immortalité.
En mes faibles écrits, je célèbre ta gloire;
Mais tu t'élevas seul au temple de mémoire.
Les vils français en vain te choisissaient des fers;
Favori du dieu Mars, au milieu des alarmes,
Tu triomphes de tout par la force des armes.
Tel on voit un rocher battu par la tempête,
Méprisant tous les coups qui fondent sur sa tête,
Braver tous leurs efforts en insultant les cieux,
Et repousser au loin les flots audacieux;
Tel on vit la valeur, constante et généreuse,
Du milieu des combats sortir victorieuse.
Ton intrépide cœur garda sa pureté;
Partout tu conservas la noble fermeté.
Et le sort qui toujours règle nos destinées,
S'il eût tissé le fil de tes belles années,
Rome pour couronner tes bienfaits immortels,
Comme à ses demi-Dieux, t'eût dressé des autels.

1805

GRENADIER GAUTAREL

You, O great Emperor![1]

You, O great Emperor![2] You who laid low
French power, restored abundance, let us know
Peace's delights once more; you whose fair grace
Floats you to noble heights to take your place
With the immortals! Here my halting verse
Would sing your praise; you who cast off the curse
Of France; you who alone in memory's shrine
Flout the vile Frenchman's foul and fell design
Ever to shackle you! Ah, but in vain
His base desire! For midst the baleful bane,
Mars, god of war, chose you his favorite son.
Now have you won by force of arms, undone
The scurvy foe! Like a vast cliff—wracked, rattled,
Tempest-scourged, yet staunch—scornful have you battled,
Parried the heavens' every blow; stood strong,
Held fast against tide's surge, righting each wrong,
Till—fruit of constant valor glorious,
Unbowed—you end the fray, victorious!
Your heart remains proud, pure, in honor bred:
In Roman day, had Fate woven your thread,
Like demigod undying would you be
Haloed, enshrined in immortality!

1805

JUSTE CHANLATTE

Quels apprêts? Quels moments?

Quels apprêts? Quels moments? ô jour plein d'allégresse!
Tout un peuple enivré près du trône s'empresse,
Où se forgeaient ses fers, il marche avec fierté,
        Dans sa force et sa liberté,
        Dans sa force et sa liberté.
Il bénit le héros de son indépendance;
Il chante, transporté d'une mâle assurance:
Qui de JACQUES Premier a reconnu la loi,
Célèbre aussi sa fête en celle de son roi.

Que pourrait des tyrans la fureur despotique,
Contre les fiers enfants de ce brûlant tropique,
C'est le flot qui s'irrite et qui court se briser,
        Contre l'immobile rocher,
        Contre l'immobile rocher!
Sous l'abri protecteur d'un invincible égide,
Nous chantons en dépit d'une race perfide,
Qui de JACQUES Premier a reconnu la loi,
Célèbre aussi sa fête en celle de son roi.

Vous qu'il vient d'affranchir de l'antique esclavage.
Pour prix de ses travaux offrez-lui notre hommage;
Qu'un serment solennel soit par vous répété,
        De respect et fidelité,
        De respect et fidelité;
Autour de ces drapeaux, même sort vous rassemble,
Nous vivons à ses pieds, ou nous mourrons ensemble.
Car de JACQUES Premier, qui reconnaît la loi,
N'a qu'un esprit, qu'un cœur, pour l'état et son roi.

1805

JUSTE CHANLATTE

What hustle-bustle, hurly-burly sound[1]

What hustle-bustle, hurly-burly sound,
Day of joy! As the throngs the throne surround
In ecstasy! Where chains were forged, now we
> Abound in newfound liberty,
> Abound in newfound liberty!
We bless our hero[2] for our freedom's prize,
And sing with passion's voice, in manly wise:
"We who accept the rule of JACQUES Premier,
Fete our own feast on our king's[3] holy day!"

The tyrant-despot's fury ill withstands
This tropic isle's brave people's mighty hands!
And as wave upon wave smites angrily
> The cliffs' unmoved serenity,
> The cliffs' unmoved serenity,
So we, beneath a shield unfaltering,
Resist a ruthless enemy and sing:
"We who accept the rule of JACQUES Premier,
Fete our own feast on our king's holy day!"

To him give thanks, who boldly took the pains
To free you from the past's enslaving chains,[4]
And let your solemn oath repeated be,
> To swear respect, fidelity,
> To swear respect, fidelity;
Let us all flock about his flags, proud flying,
Together living at his feet, or dying!
"We who accept the rule of JACQUES Premier
Have one heart, soul, country, and king this day!"

1805

ANONYMOUS

Ce qu'Henry désirait faire

Ce qu'Henry désirait faire
Le nôtre l'accomplira,
Chaque pauvre mercenaire
Dans un pot la poule aura.
Chacun sera philanthrope,
Ami de l'humanité;
On verra toute l'Europe
Rechercher notre amitié.
On verra toute l'Europe
Rechercher notre amitié.

Loin de Hayti les larmes,
Nos malheurs sont à leur fin,
Sous un tel roi plus d'alarmes,
Notre bonheur est certain,
Que notre ange tutélaire,
MARIE, idole des cœurs,
Recueille enfin le salaire
De ses touchantes faveurs.
Recueille enfin le salaire
De ses touchantes faveurs.

1814

ANONYMOUS

As his namesake sought to do[1]

As his namesake sought to do,
Henry[2] shall enhance the lot
Of poor warriors, tried and true,
With a hen in every pot!
Haitians we, with generous hand,
Shall befriend humanity,
As each European land
Seeks our friendship eagerly.
As each European land
Seeks our friendship eagerly!

Haiti, dry your tears! Avast,
Misery and woe! No more!
Under our great king, at last,
Naught but fair days lie in store!
May MARIE[3]—sweet queen of heaven,
And our own!—bestow her grace,
And for all her favors given,
Ever praised be by our race.
And for all her favors given,
Ever praised be by our race!

1814

JUSTE CHANLATTE

Quels accents tout à coup ont charmé mon oreille?
(Cantate: La Ville du Cap-Henry)

Quels accents tout à coup ont charmé mon oreille?
Quels concerts! quels transports! et de quelle merveille
      Se sont embellis ces climats?
Quoi! de l'airain tonnant les échos moins barbares,
Aux trompettes, aux cors, aux clairons, aux fanfares,
      Mêlent leur imposant fracas!

Chœur général
      Veillons-nous? ou l'erreur d'un songe
      Des prestiges d'un doux mensonge
A-t-il flatté nos sens et bercé nos esprits?
   Non: du dieu *Mars* c'est l'immortelle fille
Qui fixant pour jamais le trône en sa famille
      Brille à nos regards attendris!

Le Génie d'Hayti
      Hayti! tressaille d'ivresse;
      Un héros, l'exemple des rois,
      À ton nom son lustre intéresse,
      Et pour consolider tes droits
      Son bras a passé sa promesse.
      À chanter ses fameux exploits,
      Si la messagère aux cent voix,
      Consacre et son temps et sa gloire,
      De *Clio* le sublime emploi
      Les grave au temple de mémoire.

Chœur général
      De l'orgueil l'outrage sanglant
      Flétrit notre vertu première;

JUSTE CHANLATTE

What sweet chants, these, that strike, entrance my ear?
(Cantata: The City of Cap-Henry)[1]

What sweet chants, these, that strike, entrance my ear?
What sheer delights have filled the atmosphere
      Here below, with beauties abounding?
Lo! Hear the blaring brasses joyously
Temper and blend their brash cacophony
      With fanfares' trumpets, horns, resounding!

Chorus[2]
      Are we awake? Or are sleep's smiling,
      Lying dreams, with fictions beguiling,
Lulling, plying our spirit and our sense?
No! It is Mars'[3] immortal daughter, who,
Setting her throne forever hereunto,
      Gleams in resplendent reverence.

The Spirit of Haiti
      Haiti! A-quake with ecstasy,
      Your name shines bright, your rights stand fast;
      A hero[4]—king's exemplar, he,
      Mighty—his promise has surpassed.
      Clio, fair Muse of History,
      Shall sing his exploits, first to last,
      And, hundred-voiced, cause them to shine,
      In glory's light forever cast,
      Engraved in memory's hallowed shrine.[5]

Chorus
      Vile, vicious outrage bloodied us,
      Blemished our pride dispirited.

De l'hydre, Henry triomphant,
Nous ouvre une noble carrière.

Le Génie des Arts
De Thémis le sceptre abattu,
D'une main vigoureuse implorait l'assistance;
Soudain par HENRY combattu,
Des lois le vice a connu la puissance.
Il dit, au même instant d'audacieux vaisseaux,
Défiant la fortune et les vents et les flots,
En longs sillons d'écume ont dessiné leur route;
Il veut, et d'un sommet voisin du firmament,
S'élève par enchantement
L'arsenal du dieu *Mars* vers la céleste voûte.

Le Génie d'Hayti
La Discorde sifflait: des lions furieux
La crinière agitée en pointes se hérisse,
Aussitôt le monstre odieux
Rentre en l'infernal précipice.

Chœur général
Ainsi brille au travers des ombres de la nuit
D'un météore vain l'amorce passagère;
Mais du jour le rayon qui luit
Chasse la vapeur mensongère.

La Marine
Au reflet de nos pavillons,
Du fond de nos grottes humides
Sortez aimables *Néréides;*
Admirez nos hardis sillons.

But Henry slew the Hydra, thus
Yielding a path for us to tread.[6]

The Spirit of the Arts
When god Themis's scepter was
Undone, and when it sought a firmer hand,[7]
HENRY it was whose stern command
Taught vice once more the righteous reign of laws.
He speaks, and suddenly courageous craft,
Coursing the deep—defying, fore and aft,
Fate, wind, and wave—trace wakes of furrowed foam.[8]
He decrees, and there rises to the stars,
Magic-wise, to the heavens' dome,
"La Citadelle," vast arsenal of Mars![9]

The Spirit of Haiti
Discord hissed. Lions, furious, toss their mane;
As darts of fur prick, spike the air pell-mell,
The odious monster, once again,
Retreats unto the cliffs of hell.

Chorus
Whence flashes—vain—amid the shades of night,
A meteor's bright, evanescent trail;
But day sweeps off, in shining light,
Its vaporous, enticing tail.

The Navy[10]
And you, fair Nereids![11] May you
Rise from the ocean's grotto lair,
Among majestic furrows, where
You sport the sea-borne banners' hue.

Les Néréides

Jamais des princes grecs l'impétueuse élite,
Voguant vers la Colchide, où entraînait Jason,
En bravoure, en mérite
N'eût souffert la comparaison;
Tel ne parut le fils d'Anchise,
Alors qu'aux champs rutuliens
Abordant pour former de superbes liens,
Des siens il sut fonder la gloire tant promise.
Henry parle, et soudain les eaux
Se courbent, à sa voix, sous des maîtres nouveaux;
Frappés de tant d'éclat, les sujets de Neptune
Du vaste sein des mers désertent le séjour,
Et du gouffre profond l'inconstante fortune
Par un charme vainqueur voit enchaîner son cours.

Chœur général

Sylvain! dis-nous par quel hasard
De nos Driades éplorées
Les demeures si révérées
Font place aux prodiges de l'art?

Le Dieu Sylvain

Orphée a reparu pour vaincre les obstacles,
Tout s'écroule ou s'élève à ses divins accords;
En faisant des miracles
Son génie a sauvé ces bords.

Chœur général

Ah! si le burin de l'histoire
Destine à l'immortalité
Tant d'éclat, de prospérité,
L'amant des filles de mémoire
S'enivrera de notre gloire!

The Nereids
Never Greek princes rash could one compare,
Colchis-bound—they, the happy, chosen few,
      Jason's companions—with this rare,
      Valiant seafaring retinue;[12]
      Nor even with Anchises' son,
      Approaching fate's Rutulian strand
In hope of a fine conquest to be won,
Founding his line in glory's promised land.[13]
      Henry speaks. All at once, the waters
Bow to new masters; Neptune's sons and daughters,
Awed by his brilliance, surge up from the sea's
Bottomless chasm, and with spell-borne force
See its capricious, untamed destinies
Calmed and transformed into a tranquil course.

Chorus
      Sylvan god! Tell us, by what chance
      Our weeping dryads' habitat—
      So long revered!—became thereat
      The home of art's exuberance?[14]

The Sylvan God
Orpheus rose anew;[15] miracle-wise—
With chords divine that make all rise or fall—
      His soul cast down obstacles all,
      And saved these shores from art's demise.

Chorus
      If graven on the tablature
      Of Man's immortal history
      Is our boundless prosperity,
      Ecstatic will he be for sure;
      Memory's daughters' paramour!

Les Femmes

      À l'état nos flancs généreux
      Toujours se montreront propices.

Les Hommes

      Avec quelle ardeur nos neveux
      Jalouseront nos cicatrices!

Les Enfants

Aux coups que porteront nos bras plus aguerris,
Nos glorieux aïeux reconnaîtront leurs fils.

Les Vieillards

Quant à ce haut degré de gloire et de puissance,
On a vu s'élever le lieu de son berceau,
Avec moins d'amertume on descend au tombeau;
Des traces ont resté de sa noble existence.

Les Soldats

Qu'il est beau de verser son sang au champ d'honneur!
À nos dignes neveux laissons pour héritage
La haine des tyrans; pour titre la valeur;
      La liberté pour apanage.

Le Peuple

Puissent de cet état les rameaux divisés,
Se joindre sous l'abri du pouvoir monarchique,
      Et tous les cœurs humanisés
      Former une famille unique!

Les Femmes

Ô jour, cher à nos cœurs!

Les Hommes

      Ô douce émotion!

The Women

      To the state, ever generous,
      Our wombs will prove what wombs are for!

The Men

      Ardent, the sons who follow us
      Will envy us our scars of war!

The Children

By our arms, long inured against the foe,
Our valorous forebears shall their offspring know.

The Old Men

We beheld glorydom's most mighty reign,
Stood by the cradle of her birth; and we
Descend now to the tomb, less bitterly,
For traces of her noble past remain.

The Soldiers

How fair to shed one's blood in battle! Thus,
Unto our worthy progeny we plight
Hatred of tyrants, names illustrious,
      And liberty, their sacred right!

The People

May all the outspread branches of this tree
Join in the royal shade, together; may
      Each heart—of one humanity—
      Be but one family this day!

The Women

O day, dear to our hearts!

The Men

      O passion sweet!

Le Peuple

À trop de droits HENRY mérite la couronne.

À ce vertueux chef, quand notre cœur la donne,

      Des cieux il suit l'impulsion.

Chœur général

      Quelle pompe majestueuse

      S'est déployée au Champ de Mars!

      Quelle ferveur religieuse

      Saisit les cœurs de toutes parts!

      Couple adoré! HENRY! MARIE!

      Reçois la divine onction;

      Le bonheur de la nation

      À son triomphe se marie.

Toi! *Minerve!* preside aux arts, à nos moissons;

Du Dieu qui nous régit tempère le tonnerre,

      Et verse un baume salutaire

      Dans l'âme de tes nourrissons,

Comme on voit que l'*Aurore,* en sa douce clémence,

Humecte les guérets et rafraîchit les fleurs

Pour mitiger en eux la puissante influence

De l'astre qui succède à tes tendres vapeurs.

1814

The People

HENRY! Virtue-crowned head! Yes, thus it is.
When hearts decree the diadem is his,
> The heavens agree it right and meet.
> Festivity, pomp everywhere,
> Over the Champ de Mars outspread!
> Religious fervor, solemn prayer,
> In every heart, in every head!
> King, queen adored! HENRY! MARIE![16]
> May you heaven-anointed stand,
> As, happiness restored, our land
> Joins our joy to your victory!
And you, Minerva,[17] pray our crops, our arts
Abound; may our God quell the thunder, calm
> The storm, and strew with healing balm
> Our babes', our children's souls and hearts;
Just as one sees Dawn's clement providence
Refresh and cool each flower, each field unsown,
Softening thus the sun's great power intense,
After the morning mists have gently flown.

1814

En rêve j'assistais dans un conseil des Dieux
(Le Rêve d'un Haytien)

En rêve j'assistais dans un conseil des Dieux.
Le Puissant Jupiter, ceint d'un bandeau suprême,
Ordonna ce qui suit aux monarques des cieux:
"Immortels qui sous moi portez le diadème,
       Descendez sur la terre,
       Inspirez aux mortels
D'aimer l'Humanité. Des humains je suis père,
Je les fis tous égaux: mes décrets éternels
       N'admettent ni rangs ni couleurs;
       Je juge l'homme par ses mœurs."
Il dit. Neptune et Mars, portés sur un nuage,
De l'illustre Albion abordent le rivage;
Là, le Grand Frédéric, Wilberforce et Canning
D'abord sont embrasés d'un feu pur et divin,
Là, Whitbread, Sidney Smith, Prothérose et cent autres,
Sont de la Liberté les glorieux Apôtres:
Ces hommes vertueux par les Dieux inspirés,
       Pour les peuples d'Afrique,
       Pour ceux de l'Amérique,
Pour l'Univers enfin plaident les droits sacrés.
Minerve descendit aux champs du Continent,
Et du bon Washington fut le guide prudent.
       Je crus voir le fourbe Mercure
       S'envoler vers Paris.
       La chose est-elle sûre?
       Non; mais par les divers écrits
       Que Malouet nous lance
       Je crois en conscience

ANTOINE DUPRÉ

Ascending to the heavens, I dreamt a dream
(The Dream of a Haitian)[1]

Ascending to the heavens, I dreamt a dream,
Seated among the gods to council come.[2]
Almighty Jove, girt with his sash supreme,
Addressed the monarchs in consortium
      Assembled, thus exhorting them:
      "O ye, immortal subjects mine,
      Who bear the royal diadem,
Hear me, pray, and give ear to my design.
Descend to earth. Inspire mankind to love
The human race. For I, father thereof,
Made all men equal; and by my decree
      Grant little place, eternally,
To rank or color! Nay! No worth have they.
      Man's deeds are all I judge him by!"
      At length, when he had said his say,
Neptune and Mars, cloud-borne, traversed the sky,
Reaching the shore of Albion the Fair.
Emblazing many an ardent champion there,
And many a freedom-firebrand in their course,
With flame pure and divine: good Wilberforce,[3]
Frederick,[4] Canning,[5] Smith[6]—souls by the score,
All god-inspired... Whitbread[7] and Protherose...[8]
Virtuous men, who sought the rights of those—
African and American, and more—
      In slavery's thrall, and staunchly fought
In defense of their sacred liberty.[9]
      In New World climes, Minerva brought
      Wisdom to Washington, as she

Que le Dieu des fripons est maintenant en France.

L'auguste Liberté,
La tendre Humanité,
Et la redoutable Bellone,
(Divinités sans sceptre et sans couronne)
Abandonnant du Ciel les célestes palais,
Furent dans Haïti se fixer pour jamais.

Cette belle et riche contrée,
À des fléaux longtemps livrée,
N'avait plus son premier éclat,
Cependant un auguste Sénat
Que présidait un sage,
Tâchait de réparer les maux et le ravage
Que des cruels Européens,
Par leur affreuse tyrannie,
Firent à la triste patrie
Des malheureux Haïtiens.
Pétion en était et le chef et le père,
Les trois Divinités, d'une sainte ferveur,
Pénétrant ce héros, embrasant son grand cœur,
Une main invisible et le guide et l'éclaire.

Ce vertueux mortel,
Inspiré par le ciel
Bannit de sa patrie
L'affreuse tyrannie;
Écarta l'intrigant,
Rendit nul le méchant;
Éloigna l'hypocrite,
Et dans le premier rang fit asseoir le mérite.
Ici le doux sommeil s'enfuit de ma paupière,
Je revis les humains et revis leur misère;
Mais je me trouvais bienheureux,

Guided his steps. Even knave Mercury—
        Or so I thought—was seen to fly
        Paris-bound. True? Who knows? But I
Can say, thanks to the works of Malouet,[10]
        That this god-trickster surely may,
In all his mischievous exuberance,
Straightway, as dreamt, have found his way to France!...
And scepterless, crownless gods too; gods who
Had flown from skies' palatial luxury
To earth below: tender Humanity,
Liberty the august, Bellona[11] too,
Fierce warrior-goddess; all of them, become
Haitians, thus to remain, *ad libitum*...
        Haiti: once rich and beauteous isle,
        Long ravaged by scourges and woes,
        Restored now by the Senate, while
        A leader—father, chief—arose
To succor those whom tyrant's blows demean,
        And parry Europe's infamies!
PÉTION his name! These three divinities
Enflame him, light his path with hand unseen.
        Heaven-sent mortal, he,
        By virtue crowned, sweeps free
        The tyrant from the land—
        The slaver-scoundrel—and,
    The miscreant's hard-heartedness
        Rendered now powerless,
To worth alone he grants preeminence...
Such, my dream. But when, from my somnolence,
I re-awoke, my eyes were quick to find
Torments of a still-suffering humankind.
And yet, happy to realize was I
        That English sages, by and by,

De voir qu'il existait des hommes vertueux,
 Grâce aux sages nés chez le peuple anglais,
 L'Africain désormais,
 En détestant un maître,
 Sur la terre qui le vit naître,
Ne vendant plus ses fils, deviendra plus heureux;
Obligé d'être libre, il sera vertueux.
 Haïtiens, croyez-vous que mon songe
 Soit entièrement un mensonge?
 Réfléchissez
 Et décidez.

1815

Shall, in their wisdom, right our wrongs: the lot
        Of Africa shall not
        Ever enslaved remain,
        But forthwith shall regain
Freedom from hated, loathsome masters. Men
Shall not their children sell; but, free again,
Shall happy be. For freedom must, no less,
To virtue lead, and thence to happiness...
        Haitians! Pray tell, do dreams deceive?
        Falsehood or truth? Do you believe
           My dream has lied?
           Think... You decide.

1815

ANTOINE DUPRÉ

Soleil, dieu de mes ancêtres (Dernier soupir d'un Haïtien)

Soleil, dieu de mes ancêtres,
Ô toi de qui la chaleur
Fait exister tous les êtres!
Ouvrage du créateur!
Près de finir ma carrière
Que ton auguste clarté
Éclaire encore ma paupière
Pour chanter la Liberté.

Liberté, Vierge chérie!
Quand mon œil s'ouvrit au jour
Pour t'aimer j'aimai la vie
Et toi seule eus mon amour:
Le tombeau détruit ta flamme,
Le sentiment, le désir;
Ah! brûle encore mon âme
Après mon dernier soupir.

Par les lois de la nature
Tout naît, tout vit, tout périt,
Le palmier perd sa verdure
Le citronnier perd sont fruit.
L'homme vit pour cesser d'être,
Mais, dans la postérité
Ne devait-il pas renaître,
S'il aimait la Liberté?

Haïti, mère chérie,
Reçois mes derniers adieux,
Que l'amour de la patrie

ANTOINE DUPRÉ

O you, ancestral lord! O Sun (Last Sigh of a Haitian)[1]

O you, ancestral lord! O Sun,[2]
Whose heat gives life to all of us
Here below, each and every one,
Creatures of the Creator! Thus,
As my days reach their end, pray let
My eyes still bright-illumined be
By your pure, august rays, that yet
I may still sing of liberty!

Liberty, cherished virgin![3] When
My eye this life first gazed upon,
I loved life for your love; for then
My love upon no other shone.
Now the tomb, which quells all desire,
Must needs quench dead your flame; but my
Soul shall yet burn with passion-fire
When, dying, I sigh my last sigh.

Nature decrees that all is born
To live and die. The palm's green hue
Must fade; the lemon tree, forlorn,
Must lose its fruit and perish too.
Man lives for naught but death; but then,
Should it not be his destiny
To be reborn and live again,
If he, indeed, loved liberty?

Haiti, dear mother, take my hand
And hear this last farewell of mine;
Let the love of our fatherland

Enflamme tous nos neveux;
Si quelque jour sur tes rives
Reparaissent nos tyrans,
Que leurs hordes fugitives
Servent d'engrais à nos champs.

1815

Emblazon our progeny's line.
If once again upon our shore
The tyrants their foul faces show,
Let their hordes' blood[4] forevermore
Make our fields still more fertile grow![5]

1815

Haytiens, rallions-nous

Haytiens, rallions-nous
Autour du Héros et du Sage
Qui sut abattre sous ses coups,
L'hydre affreuse de l'esclavage.
Noble émule de Washington,
Du monde sa gloire est chérie:
Chantons tous vive PÉTION!
Vive! vive notre PATRIE!

Favori du Dieu des combats,
Et tout guidé par la prudence,
Le Sénat, secondant son bras,
Il conquit notre Indépendance;
Dicta la Constitution
Que conçut son puissant génie:
Chantons tous vive PÉTION!
Vive! vive notre PATRIE!

Chantons du Sénat la splendeur:
De nos Députés la prudence;
De nos Héros le bras vainqueur;
Et d'Haïti l'Indépendance.
Qu'Honneur, Gloire, Paix, Union,
Soit notre devise chérie:
Et chantons vive PÉTION!
Vive! vive notre PATRIE!

Vous, martyrs de la Liberté,
Humain Ogé, bouillant Chavannes,
Vos noms, dans la postérité,

Haitians all, come and rally round[1]

Haitians all, come and rally round
Our Hero-Sage; for it was he
Who pummeled, beat into the ground
Vile, Hydra-headed slavery,
Inspired by the great Washington!
The world holds dear his glorious tale.
"Long live PÉTION,"[2] sings everyone!
"Long live the FATHERLAND![3] All hail!"

Favored son of the god of war,
With prudence ever as his guide—
And Senate by his side therefor—
His genius freed us far and wide.
Soldier and statesman-paragon,
He wrote our laws midst bane and bale.
"Long live PÉTION," sing everyone!
"Long live the FATHERLAND! All hail!"

Sing we the Senate's splendor, and
The wisdom of each Deputy;
Each hero's mighty, conquering hand,
And Haiti, independent, free.
"Honor, Peace, Glory, Union": none
Unsung! Our cry, through our travail!
"Long live PÉTION," sing everyone!
"Long live the FATHERLAND! All hail!"

Never your names shall fade away;
You, Freedom's martyrs! They shall glow—
Firebrand Chavannes, serene Ogé—[4]

Vivront autant que nos savanes,
Avec nous, sans la trahison,
Sans une infâme tyrannie,
Vous diriez vive PÉTION!
Vive! vive notre PATRIE!

Léguons à nos derniers neveux,
Nos vertus et l'Indépendance,
Et de leurs pères valeureux
Ils garderont la souvenance;
Pour cris de Gloire et d'Union,
D'âge en âge avec énergie,
Ils diront vive PÉTION!
Vive! vive notre PATRIE!

Si jamais des peuples jaloux
L'astucieuse politique,
Voulait saper dans son courroux,
Les bases de la République,
Ayons la noble ambition,
De vaincre ou de perdre la vie,
En chantant vive PÉTION!
Vive! vive notre PATRIE!

1817

As long as our fair grasslands grow.
Nor traitor's treachery be done,
Nor infamy your valor veil!
"Long live PÉTION," sing everyone!
"Long live the FATHERLAND! All hail!"

Let us bequeath to our descendants
Virtues untold... Ours, theirs forever,
And their ancestors' Independence,
Heroes bold! Be forgotten never.
"Union, Glory!... " In unison,
From age to age, our strength prevail!
"Long live PÉTION," sing everyone!
"Long live the FATHERLAND! All hail!"

And should some jealous, wrathful nation—
With craft and guile—decide, at length,
To covet the annihilation
Of our Republic, sap her strength,
Let us all, every mother's son,
Conquer or die! Nor flinch, nor fail!
"Long live PÉTION!" cry everyone!
"Long live the FATHERLAND! All hail!"

1817

ANONYMOUS

Réunissons nos voix

Réunissons nos voix et que l'écho répète
    Les accents de nos cœurs joyeux:
Le jour qui nous éclaire est pour nous une fête
    Dès longtemps demandée aux Dieux.
    Loin du berceau de notre enfance
    Nous ne verserons plus de pleurs:
    D'un preux l'auguste bienfaisance
    A mis un terme à nos malheurs.

Chœur
    Sol d'Haïti, terre chérie,
    Sois l'objet d'un amour ardent,
    Salut, gloire à notre Patrie
    Reconnaissance au Président.

D'injustes préjugés ont longtemps sur la terre
    Asservi les faibles mortels:
Accablés sous le poids des fléaux de la guerre,
    Ils cédaient aux tyrans cruels,
    Mais un héros plein de sagesse,
    En tous lieux aimé, révéré,
    À leur sort enfin s'intéresse
    Et rend leur asyle sacré.

Chœur
    Sol d'Haïti, terre chérie,
    Sois l'objet d'un amour ardent,
    Salut, gloire à notre Patrie
    Reconnaissance au Président.

ANONYMOUS

Join now our voices[1]

Join now our voices. Let the echoes ring
        In accents of hearts' joy and love:
Dawn's light arises on our reveling,
        Boon long sought from the gods above.
        Far from the cradle of our birth,
        Here shall we bitter tears forebear.
        A noble sire has proved his worth
        And put an end to dire despair.

Chorus

        O Haitian soil, belovèd strand,
        Object of love's fire eloquent,
        All hail, O glorious Fatherland!
        Sing thanks to you, our President.

Vile prejudices had their slave-yoke laid
        Upon weak, mortal men, who bore
The tyrant's lash, victims too long arrayed,
        Meekly, before the scourge of war.
        But then a hero wise appeared,
        Quick to their fearsome fate condemn—
        Throughout the isle, adored, revered—
        And blessèd refuge offered them.

Chorus

        O Haitian soil, belovèd strand,
        Object of love's fire eloquent,
        All hail, O glorious Fatherland!
        Sing thanks to you, our President.

Puisque par des bienfaits tu prépares la voie
     Qui doit nous conduire au bonheur;
Reçois, ô Président, l'hommage qu'avec joie
     Nous t'offrons en ce jour flatteur!
     Ces enfants, ces femmes, ces pères,
     Dont tu deviens le protecteur,
     Feront pour toi des vœux sincères
     Et te porteront dans leur cœur.

Chœur

     Sol d'Haïti, terre chérie,
     Sois l'objet d'un amour ardent,
     Salut, gloire à notre Patrie
     Reconnaissance au Président.

Plus d'un mortel ici te doit une patrie;
     Pour s'acquitter de ce bienfait
Il serait toujours prêt à lui donner sa vie,
     Si son pays la demandait.
     Héritiers de notre courage,
     De nos vœux, de nos sentiments,
     Nos enfants soutiendront l'ouvrage
     Dont tu posas les fondements.

Chœur

     Sol d'Haïti, terre chérie,
     Sois l'objet d'un amour ardent,
     Salut, gloire à notre Patrie
     Reconnaissance au Président.

1817

Since, with your kindness, you prepare the way
        That shall lead us to happiness,
We pray, monsieur, that you accept this day
        The praise our flattering tongues express.
        Those fathers, mothers, children, too,
        Protected by your clemency,
        Their fervent wishes bear for you,
        In true, heartfelt sincerity.

Chorus
        O Haitian soil, belovèd strand,
        Object of love's fire eloquent,
        All hail, O glorious Fatherland!
        Sing thanks to you, our President.

To many a soul you give a fatherland;
        Grateful, their very life they would
Lay down to satisfy virtue's command,
        Were it to serve their nation's good.
        Sure may you be that all our kin—
        Our children, their descendants—will
        Be as brave as we all have been,
        And your proud destiny fulfill.

Chorus
        O Haitian soil, belovèd strand,
        Object of love's fire eloquent,
        All hail, O glorious Fatherland!
        Sing thanks to you, our President.

1817

Pour briser des tyrans les ignobles entraves

Pour briser des tyrans les ignobles entraves
  Le Nord appelle le Midi;
Amis, il faut céder aux vœux de tant de braves,
  Et leur prêter un sûr appui.

  Comme nous, aux champs de la gloire,
  Ils ont déployé leur valeur:
  Marchons ensemble à la victoire,
  Pour la patrie et pour l'honneur.

Chœur
  La République est notre mère
  Montrons-nous ses dignes enfants;
  Unis sous la même bannière,
  Nous vaincrons les plus fiers tyrans.

Écartons loin de nous la discorde ennemie:
  Que des fils de la Liberté
Sous les drapeaux de Mars la troupe réunie
  Se livre à la fraternité.

  Notre cause est toujours la même,
  Remplissons le même devoir;
  Brisons le joug du diadème,
  Que la loi seule ait du pouvoir.

1817

JULES SOLIME MILSCENT

To smite the tyrant's shackle-curse[1]

To smite the tyrant's shackle-curse, the North
      Calls on the South: comrades, pray hear
The pleas of heroes... Join us, sally forth
      Against each foeman fusileer!

      They trod the battlefield, like us,
      Of glory spawned and valor spanned;
      Let us join ranks, victorious,
      For honor and the fatherland!

Chorus
      Of the Republic born, may we
      Prove worthy offspring of our mother—
      Under one flag, united, free—
      Lay tyrants low, each with our brother.

Discord be banished from each mother's son—
      Liberty's children!—let us stand
Under Mars' battle-banners, all as one,
      In brotherhood, joined hand in hand.

      Be one and all by duty bound!
      For all, one cause, just as before:
      Dash the crown's yoke upon the ground!
      Law alone rule, forevermore!

1817

DELILE LAPRÉE

Sous un joug odieux Haïti déchirée (Hymne)

Sous un joug odieux Haïti déchirée
    Voyait gémir des malheureux enfants.
Dieu fit naître Alexandre! Haïti délivrée
Jusqu'au ciel, en ces mots, fit entendre ses chants.
Dieu! veille sur les jours du Héros magnanime,
        Par qui je goûte le Bonheur;
Son bras brisa mes fers qu'avait forgés le crime.
Dieu! protège les jours de mon Libérateur.

Pour moi, le plus beau jour était un jour d'orage;
    Pour moi, la nuit n'eut jamais de pavots.
Alexandre s'arma, finit mon long servage,
Et jour et nuit au ciel, je m'adresse en ces mots.
Dieu! veille sur les jours du Héros magnanime,
        Par qui je goûte le Bonheur;
Son bras brisa mes fers qu'avait forgés le crime.
Dieu! protège les jours de mon Libérateur.

Mes fils régénérés se sont couverts de gloire;
    Ils ont vu fuir leurs féroces tyrans.
Alexandre était là: de victoire en victoire,
Ils ont osé marcher libres, indépendants.
Dieu! veille sur les jours du Héros magnanime,
        Par qui je goûte le Bonheur;
Son bras brisa mes fers qu'avait forgés le crime.
Dieu! protège les jours de mon Libérateur.

De la sage Thémis ils suivent la carrière,
    Plus d'une muse a couronné leurs chants;
Alexandre y sourit: déjà toute la terre,

DELILE LAPRÉE

Haiti watched as her children, rent asunder (Hymn)[1]

Haiti watched as her children, rent asunder,
Ever groaned their lament most dolorous.
Then God sent Alexandre.[2] Freed from under
Her odious yoke, she sang to heaven thus:[3]
"God! Grace this Hero's days munificent:
      Sweet now my joy, untrammeled, free!
He smote the sin-forged chains that bound us pent:
God save the author of my Liberty!

"My days, however fair, were filled with woe;
My suffering nights no poppy-dreams were given!
But Alexandre laid vile bondage low;
Whence, night and day, I raised my voice to heaven:
'God! Grace this Hero's days munificent:
      Sweet now my joy, untrammeled, free!
He smote the sin-forged chains that bound us pent:
God save the author of my Liberty!'

"My sons reborn, with glory garlanded,
Have seen the vicious tyrant flee our shore.
Triumph to triumph, Alexandre led
Them on, proud and unshackled evermore.
God! Grace this Hero's days munificent:
      Sweet now my joy, untrammeled, free!
He smote the sin-forged chains that bound us pent:
God save the author of my Liberty!

"With Themis,[4] wisdom's mistress, as their guide,
Inspired by many a muse, they march along;
As Alexandre smiles, from far and wide,

Retentit des accords de leurs nobles accents.
Dieu! veille sur les jours du Héros magnanime,
        Par qui je goûte le Bonheur;
Son bras brisa mes fers qu'avait forgés le crime.
Dieu! protège les jours de mon Libérateur.

Mais quels cris douleureux partout se font entendre?
        Cruelle Mort, respecte la vertu.
Fuis loin de ce Palais: Dieu protège Alexandre,
Que peux-tu contre lui? Dans ces lieux que veux-tu?
Dieu! Veille sur les jours du Héros magnanime,
        Par qui je goûte le Bonheur;
Son bras brisa mes fers qu'avait forgés le crime;
Dieu! Prolonge les jours de mon Libérateur.

Tu l'emportes, ô Mort!... A mes chants d'allégresse
        Il faut mêler les cris de la douleur.
Alexandre n'est plus... Talents, bonté, sagesse,
Rien n'a pu du Destin arrêter la rigueur.
Du sein des immortels où ton âme est placée,
        Illustre Époux, protège tes enfants;
Guide ton successeur; nourris dans sa pensée,
Ton amour pour le peuple et ta haine aux tyrans.

Alexandre n'est plus! Mais l'équitable Histoire,
En poignant ses vertus lui donnera des pleurs.
Du sein des immortels où ton âme est placée,
        Illustre Époux, protège tes enfants;
Guide ton successeur; nourris dans sa pensée,
Ton amour pour le peuple et ta haine aux tyrans.

L'éloquent souvenir de sa mâle constance,
        Me soutiendra contre les coups du sort;

Echo the accents of their lofty song:
'God! Grace this Hero's days munificent:
>   Sweet now my joy, untrammeled, free!
He smote the sin-forged chains that bound us pent:
God save the author of my Liberty!'"

But what laments rise now? What dark despond?
Cruel Death, let virtue thwart your mission grim!
God protect Alexandre far beyond
These palace walls! What would you do with him?
God! Grace this Hero's days munificent:
>   Sweet now my joy, untrammeled, free!
He smote the sin-forged chains that bound us pent:
God save the author of my Liberty!

No! Death, you bear him off![5] O grievous lot!
Song turns to dirge... Gone, Alexandre, he
Whose kindness, wisdom, talents all, could not
Spare him the fate wrought by fell Destiny!
From the immortals' bosom where, above,
Rests[6] your soul, O splendid Progenitor,
>   Let your successor,[7] with his love,
Protect your children and loathe tyrants more.

Gone, Alexandre! But his memory
Shall touch the mourning hearts of men withal.
Gone, Alexandre! But eternally
His virtues shall cause endless tears to fall.
From the immortals' bosom where, above,
Rests your soul, O splendid Progenitor,
>   Let your successor, with his love,
Protect your children and loathe tyrants more.

Remembering his stalwart manliness,
I shall gain strength to parry fate's dire blows!

Et chacun de mes fils, pour mon indépendance,
Bravera les périls, la douleur et la mort.
Du sein des immortels où ton âme est placée,
    Illustre Époux, protège tes enfants;
Guide ton successeur; nourris dans sa pensée,
Ton amour pour le peuple et ta haine aux tyrans.

1818

And all my sons, to keep me despotless,
Shall risk pain, perils, and death's mortal woes.

From the immortals' bosom where, above,
Rests your soul, O splendid Progenitor,
        Let your successor, with his love,
Protect your children and loathe tyrants more.

1818

Du vieux cercle des ans une face nouvelle
(Cantate à l'indépendance)

Du vieux cercle des ans une face nouvelle
Aux bords Haïtiens à peine se révèle,
Que du char de Phœbus les coursiers hennissants,
Impatients d'offrir leur pompeux ministère,
Viennent prêter l'éclat de leurs feux renaissants
À la solennité qui luit pour cette terre.
       Jour d'éternel souvenir
      Où se fête l'Indépendance,
       Ah! consacre à l'avenir
      L'idole que ce peuple encense.
Accourez de ces bords, enfants favorisés,
Du haut des cieux descend votre auguste patronne;
Parfumez ses autels, encensez sa couronne,
Accordez à ma voix vos cœurs électrisés.
La tyrannie en pleurs fuyant de cette plage,
Des civiles horreurs les salpêtres éteints,
Les cieux par elle ouverts et rendus plus sereins,
Voilà de son pouvoir l'éloquent témoignage:
Ah! bénissons sa main dont le soin protecteur
Éteignant tous les feux qui l'avaient embrasée,
À cette terre offrit un héros bienfaiteur,
Et sur elle fixa la céleste rosée.
Les voyez-vous, ces traits, cet œil majestueux?
Contemplez tant d'éclat d'un front respectueux.
Un peuple qui connaît sa liberté chérie,
Qui sait qu'elle est en Dieu, dans ses lois, sa patrie,
Dignes des hauts emplois et de leur noble faix
Des descendants qui font de l'état la parure,
En qui brille déjà notre grandeur future,
Ce sont ses heureux dons, ce sont là ses bienfaits.

JUSTE CHANLATTE

Scarce does a new face shine forth from the old year's course (Ode to Independence)[1]

Scarce does a new face shine forth from the old
Year's course than lo! On Haiti's shores, behold
Phoebus's chariot-steeds, breathless to fly
Their haughty ministry of flame, reborn
Midst neighing cries echoing through the sky,
Ablaze above these strands' fresh, solemn morn.
      Day of deathless memory,
    When we fete Independence,[2] and
      Pray her Idol ever be
    Revered, adored throughout the land.
Come you, all fair isle's offspring! By and by,
From on high, she, your august patroness
Descends... Perfume her shrines, let incense bless
Her crown, and this, my voice, electrify,
Inspire your hearts! See the boons she bestows:
Tyranny's dying tears, fleeing your shore;
Saltpeter tortures, dead forevermore;[3]
Untroubled now, the heavens' sweet repose,
Her power's proof! Let us bless her embrace,
Protecting us, quenching the flaming brands,
Granting to us a hero's clement grace.[4]
Fair features! Ah! Proud orb lighting her face!
And skies' celestial dew sparkling the sands...
Gaze on this splendor, heads bowed low in awe.
You, race who know that this dear liberty—
The fatherland, its labor and its law—
God himself planned;[5] who know yourselves to be
Worthy of your descendants' weighty task,
Laid on their shoulders, and who nobly bask
Already in tomorrow's brilliancy:

Pour répondre aux succès dont rayonne sa gloire
       Où puiser d'assez beaux tableaux?
Dans l'ombre destinée aux filles de mémoire
       Qui pourra tremper mes pinceaux?
Patrie! inspire-moi; ressort des grandes âmes,
Toi qui les fais brûler des plus sublimes flammes,
       Ravive mes couleurs:
Dieux! d'Apollon que n'ai-je et la lyre et les ailes!
Quand pourrai-je, en son temple, en traces immortelles
       Graver tant de faveurs?

          Fendant la nue
          Jà de ce Dieu
          Le luth heureux
          Brille à ma vue.

Mais du haut Hélicon quel nuage pompeux
Balance une déesse en son char radieux!

          Sa voix imposante
          Fait parler les dieux;
          L'égide puissante
          Plane sur ces lieux;
          La lance éclatante
          Éblouit les yeux;
          Soudain la nature
          Renaît et fleurit;
          La fraîche verdure
          De fleurs s'embellit,
          Et de sa parure
          Le sol s'enrichit.

En elle resplendit la sagesse éternelle.
L'armure triomphante a soulagé son bras,
Haïti! lève-toi; sur ta tête elle appelle
Les trésors, les bienfaits qui naissent sur ses pas.
       Sujets de son empire,

Happy gifts, those; resplendent destiny!
Where might I find tableaus of grace so rare
        As to depict her glory-bright
Success? Who will my brushes dip, and dare
        Paint with the shades of shadowed night,
Reserved for memory's daughters? Fatherland!
            You, who ignite—with passion-fire
            Sublime—men's souls; who, to my hand,
            Grant hues afresh! Gods! Pray inspire
My verse! Why have I not Apollo's lyre,
His wings? When might I, in his temple, limn
        Immortal lines engraved to him?
                Already I
                See gleam and shine
                His lute divine
                Cleaving the sky...
Look! High above the Helicon, a cloud
Majestic, and a chariot glorious!
Standing, a goddess, jostled but unbowed.
            Her voice, imperious,
            Makes speak the gods; her shield,
            Hovering, covers us;
            Her glittering lance, revealed,
            Glimmers, dazzles our glance,
            As Nature, suddenly,
            In rich exuberance
            Unbound, luxuriantly
            Spreads round her greenery—
            Fresh, cool—midst flower festoon,
            And on the ground lies strewn.
Eternal wisdom lights her goddess-face.
Triumphant she, steel-clad her mighty arms!
Haiti, arise! For straightway would she place
Upon your head her treasures' wealth, her charms.
            Born of her glance, all art;

Enfants de ses regards,
Les sciences, les arts,
Adressent des concerts aux transports qu'elle inspire.
De l'aimable olivier
La guirlande fleurie
Par sa tresse chérie
Ô Boyer! sur ton front relève le laurier!
Président! dit Pallas, dont ici la puissance
Atteste du Très-Haut la sage prévoyance.
Le sort en t'accordant au peuple Haïtien
Entre ce peuple et Dieu consacra le lien.
Tel que, ce ferme appui de la machine ronde,
L'axe immobile et fier sur qui tourne le monde
À son gré, sans péril, le laissant graviter,
Par son attraction l'aide à se supporter.
Tel, céleste instrument du sort de la patrie,
Inébranlable appui de ce riche climat,
À ses lois, ses ressorts, à la sainte harmonie,
Se prête assidûment le secours de ton bras.
Que tes rares vertus par le ciel couronnées
De ce peuple naissant charment les destinées!
Sans cesse, ici, des dieux sois le vivant portrait;
À leur munificence égale tes bienfaits.
De ces lieux magistrat et protecteur et père,
Sur eux répands toujours, en ta marche prospère,
Les principes heureux de la fertilité,
Ainsi que dans son cours un fleuve tutélaire,
Partout insinuant le serment salutaire,
Entretient les trésors de la fécondité,
Et du grand fondateur de son Indépendance
Qu'Haïti croie en toi voir encore la présence!

1821

All knowledge, her domain;
Whence to this suzerain
We raise paeans of praise that fire the heart.
O Boyer! On your brow
Art's laurel wreath gives way
To olive's peaceful bough,
Flower-tressed garland, set in calm array!...
"President," Pallas cries,[6] "whose power now
Proves the Almighty's sage farsightedness!
For Fate, who placed you on the Haitian sod
To rule over this people, did no less
Than consecrate a link 'twixt you and God!"
And as earth turns in heaven, clockwork-wise,
About its axis never-wavering—
At peace, at its own pace—gravity plies
Its staunch support; so too, beneath your wing,
This isle, graced by Fate's ever-blossoming
Fair climate, tunes, in holy harmony,
Its laws, its every living, moving thing,
To the stout arms of your stability.
May your rare virtues, heaven-crowned, now be
Fate's endless boons cast on this folk newborn.
May you the living portrait be of these,
Our gods! May their generous gifts adorn
This people's ever-blessèd destinies.
Our judge and our protector be! And yes,
Father, no less! Sow, midst prosperity's
Propitious onward course, fertility's
Seeds, never stinting in their lush excess.
And as a sacred stream—now here, now there—
Murmuring in its flow a healing prayer,
Lavishes fecund treasure, so may you,
Father of Independence,[7] ever bear
The glory of our Haiti, sprung anew!

1821

Dans ton variable contour (Ode à l'indépendance)

La Sentinelle
Dans ton variable contour,
En ton inégal ministère,
Toi, de l'Aurore et de sa cour,
Trop paresseuse avant-courrière
Hâte, Phœbe! Hâte ton cours!
Ta pâle et douteuse lumière,
Devant l'aube d'un si beau jour,
Doit précipiter sa carrière.
Doux fruit d'une mâle fierté,
Compagne de la Liberté,
Je te salue, Indépendance!
Don précieux des immortels,
De tes favoris la vaillance
Ici, t'élève des autels.

Un Fifre
L'aurore du jour radieux
Où notre valeur immortelle
S'affranchit d'un joug odieux,
Avec éclat se renouvelle:
Chantons, élevons jusqu'aux cieux
Cette conquête solennelle
Qui rend la face de ces lieux
Encore plus riante et plus belle.
Doux fruit d'une mâle fierté,
Compagne de la Liberté,
Je te salue, Indépendance!
Don précieux des immortels,

JUSTE CHANLATTE

Why ply you your fickle ministry? (Ode to Independence)[1]

A Sentinel
Tarry not, changeling Phœbe.[2] Why
Ply you your fickle ministry,
Harbinger—lolling idly by—
Of Dawn and her dear coterie?
Rather ought you course through the sky,
Pallid in moon's serenity,
Heralding this day, praised on high:
Our noble anniversary![3]
All hail, fair fruit of manly pride,
Freedom's mate, marching side by side,
O Independence! Blest be you,
Immortals' precious gift! The fame
Of valiant champions' derring-do
Builds altar-shrines unto your name.

A Piper
The dawn of this day luminous—
Day when our heroes, stout and strong,
Cast off the yoke long laid on us—
Rises anew. Sing we our song
Unto the heavens, recalling thus
Our solemn righting of that wrong;
As our land, yet more glorious,
Smiles, revels in its joy daylong.
All hail, fair fruit of manly pride,
Freedom's mate, marching side by side,
O Independence! Blest be you,
Immortals' precious gift! The fame

De tes favoris la vaillance
Ici, t'élève des autels.

Un Trompette
Déjà, du vaste sein des eaux,
Fuyant la couche nuptiale,
Le soleil, pour ces bords nouveaux,
S'arrache aux faveurs conjugales;
Astre divin! sacré flambeau!
Poursuis ta course libérale,
Et sur le lieu de mon berceau
Étends ta pompe matinale.
Doux fruit d'une mâle fierté,
Compagne de la Liberté,
Je te salue, Indépendance!
Don précieux des immortels,
De tes favoris la vaillance
Ici, t'élève des autels.

Un Tambour
Par toi, du despote hautain,
Se sont dissipés les vertiges;
Par toi, de Christophe inhumain,
S'évanouissent les prestiges:
Si toujours préside ta main
À notre audace; à ses prodiges,
Un jour on voudra, mais en vain,
Des tyrans retrouver vestiges.
Doux fruit d'une mâle fierté,
Compagne de la Liberté,
Je te salue, Indépendance!
Don précieux des immortels,
De tes favoris la vaillance
Ici, t'élève des autels.

Of valiant champions' derring-do
Builds altar-shrines unto your name.

A Trumpeter
Already, from the waters deep,
Spurning joys of the nuptial bed,
Sun—sacred torch—will scorn his sleep,
Seeking our new-graced climes instead!
Come! Trace your broad, majestic sweep,
Here, where my youth was cradle-bred,
As, star divine! your watch you keep
Over day's pomp, joy-spirited.
All hail, fair fruit of manly pride,
Freedom's mate, marching side by side,
O Independence! Blest be you,
Immortals' precious gift! The fame
Of valiant champions' derring-do
Builds altar-shrines unto your name.

A Drummer
Thanks to you, dizzying thunderings
Of despot vain have vanished; and
Thanks to you, gone the cowerings
Of savage feats by Christophe planned![4]
Now are all bold and wondrous things
Governed by your firm, gentle hand,
And tyrants' murderous martyrings
Leave no fell trace throughout the land.
All hail, fair fruit of manly pride,
Freedom's mate, marching side by side,
O Independence! Blest be you,
Immortals' precious gift! The fame
Of valiant champions' derring-do
Builds altar-shrines unto your name.

Un Officier d'Artillerie

Pour le bon droit et l'équité,
Dans ta main terrible et propice,
Le glaive est sans cesse agité,
Noble fléau de l'injustice!
Du faible la félicité
De tes projets fait le délice,
Et ton invincibilité
Sert aux despotes de supplice.
Doux fruit d'une mâle fierté,
Compagne de la Liberté,
Je te salue, Indépendance!
Don précieux des immortels,
De tes favoris la vaillance
Ici, t'élève des autels.

Un Officier de Cavalerie

"Cherchons," dit ton cœur combattu,
"Un peuple nouveau, magnanime,
Dont on admire les vertus,
Et qui des tyrans sont victimes";
Quand tu vis nos fronts abattus
Sortant glorieux de l'abîme,
Soudain tu briguas nos tributs,
Et guidas notre ardeur sublime.
Doux fruit d'une mâle fierté,
Compagne de la Liberté,
Je te salue, Indépendance!
Don précieux des immortels,
De tes favoris la vaillance
Ici, t'élève des autels.

Un Officier d'Infanterie

De Pétion ton fondateur
Raffermis les lois, les murailles,

An Artillery Officer
Defending right and equity
In your staunch grasp, on justice bent,
Flouting dishonor, brandished free:
Your noble blade omnipotent!
Delighted, you, when happy, he—
The weak, the meek, the innocent—
As your invincibility
Wreaks harsh the tyrants' punishment.
All hail, fair fruit of manly pride,
Freedom's mate, marching side by side,
O Independence! Blest be you,
Immortals' precious gift! The fame
Of valiant champions' derring-do
Builds altar-shrines unto your name.

A Cavalry Officer
Your battered heart cried, "Let us find
A race newborn, a genesis
Of virtue, and leave far behind,
Beaten, its despot nemesis!"
You saw us—bowed but unresigned—
Arising from the dark abyss,
And sought to have your name enshrined
In our proud metamorphosis.
All hail, fair fruit of manly pride,
Freedom's mate, marching side by side,
O Independence! Blest be you,
Immortals' precious gift! The fame
Of valiant champions' derring-do
Builds altar-shrines unto your name.

An Infantry Officer
Strengthen our laws, our bulwarks too,
Set firm by Pétion, stout forebear![5]

Et que ton secours protecteur
Nous brille, au grand jour des batailles!
En faveur de son successeur,
Si d'un zèle ardent tu travailles,
Nos bords au tyran destructeur
N'offriront que des funérailles.
Doux fruit d'une mâle fierté,
Compagne de la Liberté,
Je te salue, Indépendance!
Don précieux des immortels,
De tes favoris la vaillance
Ici, t'élève des autels.

Un Sous-Lieutenant de la Garde
Pour tes nourrissons attendris
Que ton feu chaque jour renaisse
Et que de nos autels chéris
Tu sois l'adorable prêtresse!
Échauffe, épure nos esprits,
D'Haïti propice déesse!
Éternise en ces lieux fleuris
De tes trésors la douce ivresse.
Doux fruit d'une mâle fierté,
Compagne de la Liberté,
Je te salue, Indépendance!
Don précieux des immortels,
De tes favoris la vaillance
Ici, t'élève des autels.

Un Lieutenant de la Garde
Pour prix de l'immortel laurier,
Fruit de la lance si chérie,
Vois-tu du généreux Boyer
Voler vers toi l'âme aguerrie,
Fonder sur ton triomphe altier

Long let your succoring light shine through
The glare of war and battle's blare!
And if, with ardent passion, you
Toil to sustain his doughty heir,
Whatever ill foul despots do,
Naught but the grave shall be their share!
All hail, fair fruit of manly pride,
Freedom's mate, marching side by side,
O Independence! Blest be you,
Immortals' precious gift! The fame
Of valiant champions' derring-do
Builds altar-shrines unto your name.

A Sublieutenant of the Guard
With fire, O spirit limitless!
Inspire your progeny to come,
As you—love-worthy priestess!—bless
The altars of our glorydom!
Make pure our souls in flame, and—yes!—
Goddess of Haiti, favorsome,
Preserve in flowering loveliness
Your treasures' sweet delirium.
All hail, fair fruit of manly pride,
Freedom's mate, marching side by side,
O Independence! Blest be you,
Immortals' precious gift! The fame
Of valiant champions' derring-do
Builds altar-shrines unto your name.

A Lieutenant of the Guard
You, who the deathless laurel bore,
Fruit of the lance's victory,
See you proud Boyer's[6] soul—to war
Inured—pledge you fidelity,
And on your triumph evermore

Celui de sa chère patrie?
Vois-tu ce magistrat guerrier
Te vouer son idolâtrie?
Doux fruit d'une mâle fierté,
Compagne de la Liberté,
Je te salue, Indépendance!
Don précieux des immortels,
De tes favoris la vaillance
Ici, t'élève des autels.

Un Capitaine de la Garde
Un honteux et lâche repos
Amollit l'âme et la déprave,
À ta voix; oui, sous nos drapeaux
Nous saurons briser toute entrave:
"Qu'importe où blanchissent nos os?"
C'est la devise du vrai brave.
Tout homme libre est un héros,
Le lâche seul est un esclave.
Doux fruit d'une mâle fierté,
Compagne de la Liberté,
Je te salue, Indépendance!
Don précieux des immortels,
De tes favoris la vaillance
Ici, t'élève des autels.

Un Vieillard
Nous montrerons à nos neveux
Les nobles sentiers de la gloire;
Ils vont apprendre, sous nos yeux,
Comment on fixe la victoire.
Trouver un trépas glorieux,
N'est-ce pas vivre en la mémoire?
Qu'aux coups de nos bras valeureux
S'ouvre une page dans l'histoire.

Found his dear homeland, risen free?
See you this warrior-judge adore—
Worship!—you with idolatry?
All hail, fair fruit of manly pride,
Freedom's mate, marching side by side,
O Independence! Blest be you,
Immortals' precious gift! The fame
Of valiant champions' derring-do
Builds altar-shrines unto your name.

The Captain of the Guard
Calm rest and coward's peace benight
The spirit, and the heart deprave;
Beneath our banners' lofty height,
Your voice our shackled soul will save.
"What matters where our bones bleach white?"
This, the true motto of the brave.
Every free man, a hero, quite;
None but the craven cur a slave!
All hail, fair fruit of manly pride,
Freedom's mate, marching side by side,
O Independence! Blest be you,
Immortals' precious gift! The fame
Of valiant champions' derring-do
Builds altar-shrines unto your name.

An Old Man
We shall unto our children show
The paths of valor spread before
Our eyes; and they forthwith shall know
How victory crowns the warrior!
Does death with glory not bestow
An honored place in memory's store?
May we, with many a gallant blow,
Fill a proud page in history's lore!

Doux fruit d'une mâle fierté,
Compagne de la Liberté,
Je te salue, Indépendance!
Don précieux des immortels,
De tes favoris la vaillance
Ici, t'élève des autels.

Un Guerrier
Dans la défense du pays
Si notre constance succombe,
Que nous soyons ce vil épi
Qui sous la faux fléchit et tombe!
Mânes de nos aïeux chéris!
Vous aimerez nos hécatombes,
Et vos mains à de dignes fils
Ouvriront la paix de vos tombes.
Doux fruit d'une mâle fierté,
Compagne de la Liberté,
Je te salue, Indépendance!
Don précieux des immortels,
De tes favoris la vaillance
Ici, t'élève des autels.

Un Jeune Guerrier
Oui, sur la trace de vos pas,
Contre une horde meurtrière,
Nous produirons dans les combats
Vos coups, votre valeur guerrière.
Plus jaloux d'égaler vos bras
Qu'épris d'une longue carrière,
Trouvons du héros le trépas
Ou les honneurs de la lumière.
Doux fruit d'une mâle fierté,
Compagne de la Liberté,
Je te salue, Indépendance!

All hail, fair fruit of manly pride,
Freedom's mate, marching side by side.
O Independence! Blest be you,
Immortals' precious gift! The fame
Of valiant champions' derring-do
Builds altar-shrines unto your name.

A Warrior
In staunch defense of fatherland,
Should we grow weak and fail withal,
Let us, like withered grain outspanned,
Feel the scythe's blade and straightway fall!
Shades of our forebears! You shall stand
In awe of death's loud-thundering call;
Unto our worthy sons, your hand
Will offer your tombs' peace to all.
All hail, fair fruit of manly pride,
Freedom's mate, marching side by side.
O Independence! Blest be you,
Immortals' precious gift! The fame
Of valiant champions' derring-do
Builds altar-shrines unto your name.

A Young Warrior
Yes, we will tread your glory-ways.
Against a horde on carnage bent,
We will rain blows that awe, amaze,
Striking our foes with one intent:
To rival you! Brief though our days,
We shall nor weaken nor relent,
But welcome death midst heroes' praise,
Honored by your enlightenment.
All hail, fair fruit of manly pride,
Freedom's mate, marching side by side.
O Independence! Blest be you,

Don précieux des immortels,
De tes favoris la vaillance
Ici, t'élève des autels.

Une Jeune Guerrière
Haïtiens! soyez vainqueurs,
Lavez nos antiques blessures;
Pour s'insinuer dans nos cœurs,
Oui, c'est la route la plus sûre.
Ah! qu'un amant est séducteur
Quand son sang devient sa parure.
Eh! comment rejeter l'ardeur
De qui venge, ici, la nature?
Doux fruit d'une mâle fierté,
Compagne de la Liberté,
Je te salue, Indépendance!
Don précieux des immortels,
De tes favoris la vaillance
Ici, t'élève des autels.

*Une Femme guerrière montrant à son jeune enfant la colonne
élevée à l'Indépendance*
Vois cet auguste monument
Qu'ont élevé nos flétrissures;
De son vrai but noble instrument
Promets de venger nos injures.
À ce magnanime serment
Si jamais tu deviens parjure,
Que ton cœur du cruel cayman
Devienne l'affreuse pâture!
Doux fruit d'une mâle fierté,
Compagne de la Liberté,
Je te salue, Indépendance!
Don précieux des immortels,

Immortals' precious gift! The fame
Of valiant champions' derring-do
Builds altar-shrines unto your name.

A Young Female Warrior
Haitian lads! Victors be! Thereby
You cleanse our long-wrought wounds. For lo!
Such is the surest path to ply
If you would reach our hearts. For no
Lover shall fail to satisfy,
When his blood beautifies the beau!
Can we a lover's zeal deny
When he avenges nature's woe?
All hail, fair fruit of manly pride,
Freedom's mate, marching side by side.
O Independence! Blest be you,
Immortals' precious gift! The fame
Of valiant champions' derring-do
Builds altar-shrines unto your name.

*A Woman Warrior pointing out to her young child the column
erected to Independence*[7]
Look! See that monument, proud-wrought,
Erected by our wounds erstwhile.
Its soaring eminence has taught
Us not to yield or reconcile.
Rather, swear vengeance, as you ought.
But should you not, then—traitor, vile
Deceiver!—may your heart be caught
To feed the fearsome crocodile!
All hail, fair fruit of manly pride,
Freedom's mate, marching side by side,
O Independence! Blest be you,
Immortals' precious gift! The fame

De tes favoris la vaillance
Ici, t'élève des autels.

Le Jeune Enfant
Je jure à l'appareil nouveau
Qui brille à ma tendre carrière
Haine éternelle à nos bourreaux,
Fidélité pour nos bannières,
Et si le dard de mon berceau
S'émousse, au secours d'une mère,
J'irai trouver dans le tombeau
Les restes glorieux d'un père.
Doux fruit d'une mâle fierté,
Compagne de la Liberté,
Je te salue, Indépendance!
Don précieux des immortels,
De tes favoris la vaillance
Ici, t'élève des autels.

Un Garde national
Par le sort longtemps condamnés
À subir sa rigueur extrême,
Nos fronts, avilis, consternés,
Pâlissent d'un fatal système;
Aux yeux des tyrans prosternés,
Brillants d'une faveur suprême,
Nos fronts de lauriers couronnés
Plaisent aux immortels eux-mêmes.
Doux fruit d'une mâle fierté,
Compagne de la Liberté,
Je te salue, Indépendance!
Don précieux des immortels,
De tes favoris la vaillance
Ici, t'élève des autels.

Of valiant champions' derring-do
Builds altar-shrines unto your name.

The Young Child
I vow, by weapons gleaming bright
On my tender young years, that I
Will flout fell butchers' murderous might,
True to our banners, waved on high.
And if, to spare a mother's plight,
My cradle-dart—dull—fails to fly,
I shall seek, in the tomb's dark night,
A father's bones that fain not die.
All hail, fair fruit of manly pride,
Freedom's mate, marching side by side,
O Independence! Blest be you,
Immortals' precious gift! The fame
Of valiant champions' derring-do
Builds altar-shrines unto your name.

A Soldier of the National Guard
Long condemned by a hostile fate
To suffer dire iniquities,
Our woe-bent brows, disconsolate,
Grew pale at despots' tyrannies.
But foe, soon spent, laid low—of late
Our master!—gazes, gapes at these
Brows, laureled now, that consecrate
And please the deathless deities.
All hail, fair fruit of manly pride,
Freedom's mate, marching side by side,
O Independence! Blest be you,
Immortals' precious gift! The fame
Of valiant champions' derring-do
Builds altar-shrines unto your name.

Un Magistrat
Grand Dieu dont on voit les desseins
S'accomplir, comme les menaces,
Contre d'infâmes assassins
Daigne protéger notre audace!
Verse les trésors de ton sein
Sur Boyer, sur ses belles traces,
De tes faveurs répand l'essaim
Sur Haïti, sur notre race!
Doux fruit d'une mâle fierté,
Compagne de la Liberté,
Je te salue, Indépendance!
Don précieux des immortels,
De tes favoris la vaillance
Ici, t'élève des autels.

L'Ombre de Pétion
Réunis en un seul faisceau
Sous un Gouvernement unique,
Embarqués à bord du vaisseau
De notre sainte République,
Jurez, par d'immortels travaux
D'illustrer ce brûlant tropique,
Et que d'Haïti le flambeau
Soit le phare de l'Amérique.
Doux fruit d'une mâle fierté,
Compagne de la Liberté,
Je te salue, Indépendance!
Don précieux des immortels,
De tes favoris la vaillance
Ici, t'élève des autels.

Le Génie d'Haïti
Oui, du Ciel les rares bontés,
Planant sur cette île opulente

A Magistrate
Great God, whose plans we watch unfold
Before our eyes: blest, cursed, worst, best!
Pray deign protect our efforts bold
To thwart the base assassin's quest!
Rain on Boyer your wealth untold—
The treasure pent within your breast—
And those who follow, grace-extolled:
Haiti! O bounteous race, boon-blest!
All hail, fair fruit of manly pride,
Freedom's mate, marching side by side,
O Independence! Blest be you,
Immortals' precious gift! The fame
Of valiant champions' derring-do
Builds altar-shrines unto your name.

The Shade of Pétion
United, all, in harmony:
One Government before men's eyes!
May you set sail on tranquil sea—
Ship of state, under azure skies!
Swear that unceasing industry
Shall light this tropic island-prize.
May Haiti's torch the beacon be:[8]
The hemisphere's sheer paradise!
All hail, fair fruit of manly pride,
Freedom's mate, marching side by side,
O Independence! Blest be you,
Immortals' precious gift! The fame
Of valiant champions' derring-do
Builds altar-shrines unto your name.

The Spirit of Haiti[9]
Yes, long shall heaven her opulence—
Her bounty rich and rare—protect

Veilleront aux prospérités
D'Haïti libre, indépendante.
Ces beaux cris seront répétés:
Vive Haïti libre et puissante!
Vive la douce Égalité
Et la Liberté triomphante!
Doux fruit d'une mâle fierté,
Compagne de la Liberté,
Je te salue, Indépendance!
Don précieux des immortels,
De tes favoris la vaillance
Ici, t'élève des autels.

Un Coriphée
Quels sons! quels accents séducteurs!
Est-ce donc l'âge heureux d'Astrée?
Que vois-je? Ô délire enchanteur
Digne du beau siècle de Rhée?
Enchaînés par des nœuds de fleurs
Les enfants de cette contrée
Jurent, sur l'autel de l'honneur,
De paix éternelle durée.
Doux fruit d'une mâle fierté,
Compagne de la Liberté,
Je te salue, Indépendance!
Don précieux des immortels,
De tes favoris la vaillance
Ici, t'élève des autels.

1821

Midst liberty unshackled; whence
Ever shall rise these cries unchecked:
"Long live Haiti's magnificence—
Equality, pride, self-respect!—
And standing tall in confidence:
Freedom triumphant, proud, erect!"
All hail, fair fruit of manly pride,
Freedom's mate, marching side by side,
O Independence! Blest be you,
Immortals' precious gift! The fame
Of valiant champions' derring-do
Builds altar-shrines unto your name.

A Coryphaeus[10]
What sounds! What notes enchant the air!
Astraea's gilded century?[11]
Happiness—here, there, everywhere!—
The age of Rhea's[12] ecstasy?
Garlanded round with flowers fair,
Joyous, this land's youth frolic free
At honor's altar, there to swear
Endless peace and tranquillity!
All hail, fair fruit of manly pride,
Freedom's mate, marching side by side,
O Independence! Blest be you,
Immortals' precious gift! The fame
Of valiant champions' derring-do
Builds altar-shrines unto your name.

1821

ANONYMOUS

Voyez ce vieux colon

Voyez ce vieux colon
Vous traiter de peuple félon;
Usé, rossé, cassé,
Il s'est encore encuirassé.
En sa noble ardeur
Ce grand pourfendeur,
D'un ton arrogant
Nous jette le gant.
À genoux! à genoux!
Jaunes et Noirs, soumettez-vous.

Depuis bientôt vingt ans,
Vous vous croyez indépendants:
Malgré tous vos hauts-faits
Vous êtes toujours nos sujets.
Généraux, soldats,
Et vous Magistrats,
Et vous Sénateurs
Voyez vos seigneurs!
À genoux! à genoux!
Jaunes et Noirs, soumettez-vous.

La Constitution,
Qui vous érige en nation,
Ne peut vous protéger:
Le code noir seul doit juger.
Les quatre-piquets,
Les coupe-jarrets,
Les chiens dévorants:
Voilà vos garants!
À genoux! à genoux!
Jaunes et Noirs, soumettez-vous.

ANONYMOUS

See that old planter[1]

See that old planter,[2] who
Scorns you as felons, through and through;
    Battered and broken... Yes,
But girt for battle nonetheless.
    See him a-swagger there,
    With his proud, noble air.
    Ever quick to despise us,
    Haughty, he still defies us![3]
Bow! Bow beneath the whip, all ye
Blacks and Mulattos, bend the knee![4]

    Two decades soon have passed[5]
Since deeds heroic sought to cast
    Us out. But no! In vain!
Lo! Yet your masters we remain!
    You, worthy Senators,
    Magistrates, Councillors,
    Generals, soldier-hordes...
    Behold us, still your lords!
Bow! Bow beneath the whip, all ye
Blacks and Mulattos, bend the knee!

    Fruitless, the revolution
That wrought your nation's Constitution![6]
    Naught but the old Code Noir[7]
Protects you with laws' repertoire.
    Four pikes stuck in the ground,[8]
    Cruel cut-throats profligate,
    The hungry hunting hound...[9]
    These now your certain fate!
Bow! Bow beneath the whip, all ye
Blacks and Mulattos, bend the knee!

Vos fils, vos petits-fils,
Nous sont par tous les droits acquis.
    Pour vos jolis tendrons,
Nous vous en débarrasserons.
        Le jour au travail,
        La nuit au sérail,
            Comme au bon vieux temps
            Ils tueront le temps.
        À genoux! à genoux!
Jaunes et Noirs, soumettez-vous.

        Vos dons nationaux
Sont nuls: car ils sont illégaux.
    Pétion et Boyer
N'avaient droit de les octroyer.
            Ces biens sont à nous;
            Le comprenez-vous?
            Reprenez vos bâts
            Peuple de forçats.
        À genoux! à genoux!
Jaunes et Noirs, soumettez-vous.

    Trois fois mille colons
Aiguisent leurs estramaçons
        Armés de pied en cap,
Tout d'abord nous prenons le Cap.
            L'Est se remuera,
            L'Ouest tremblera,
            Le Sud tombera,
            Et Boyer mourra.
        À genoux! à genoux!
Jaunes et Noirs, soumettez-vous.

1822

Your sons, your progeny
Are once again our property.
Your daughters, lovely flowers!...
No longer yours are they, but ours!
Days: for their labor bred,
Nights: for the master's bed,
As in sweet bygone day,
Whiling the hours away.
Bow! Bow beneath the whip, all ye
Blacks and Mulattos, bend the knee!

Illegal are the rights
Bestowed by lawless parasites—
Pétion, Boyer![10] For they
Had not the power to grant them. Nay!
Those rights, let it be known,
Are ours and ours alone.
People, take back your chains.
Once more slavery reigns!
Bow! Bow beneath the whip, all ye
Blacks and Mulattos, bend the knee!

Their broadswords sharpening,
Three thousand settlers sallying,
Le Cap will once again
Be ours, armed head to toe. And then
The East will shudder, shake,[11]
The West will quail and quake,
The South in ruins lie...
And your Boyer shall die!
Bow! Bow beneath the whip, all ye
Blacks and Mulattos, bend the knee!

1822

Du Sud et de l'Ouest

Jean-Philippe
Du Sud et de l'Ouest les lâches révoltés
Restes de ceux par vous ou réduits ou domptés,
Pour de nouveaux combats arment leurs mains perfides
De dépouilles, de sang, leurs phalanges avides,
De la rébellion ont proclamé les lois,
Et prêchent hautement le mépris de vos droits.
Dans les murs de Saint-Marc, une troupe infidèle,
Désertant vos drapeaux, épouse leur querelle.
Boyer, de Pétion l'odieux successeur,
Accueille leurs serments, se dit leur protecteur;
À marcher contre vous soyez sûr qu'il s'apprête.
Du généreux Jean-Claude ils ont tranché la tête,
Et, portant dans l'Ouest ce gage de la paix,
Avec nos ennemis sont unis à jamais.
Peindrai-je à vos regards la surprise et la joie
Qu'excita dans le Sud cette sanglante proie?
De cet événement ils crurent que le sort
Avait été réglé par l'Ange de la Mort;
Et que le Tout-Puissant, armé pour leur défense,
Avec eux contre nous était en alliance.

Christophe
Ami, je ne crains point tous ces vils scélérats:
Ils recevront le prix de leurs noirs attentats.
Je vis, et c'est assez pour que leur perfidie
Cesse longtemps encore de se croire impunie.

JEAN-BAPTISTE ROMANE

From South and West[1]

Jean-Philippe
From South and West,[2] the craven rebel band,
Remnants of those crushed by your royal hand,
A tattered, bloody few, would rise again
Against you—loftiest, mightiest of men
Lawgiver of our land—and loud proclaim
Abhorrence of the rights writ in your name.
In Saint-Marc's ramparts,[3] rebel turncoats pledge
Allegiance to the odious sacrilege,
Our flag's deserters all... Hateful Boyer,
Who seized Pétion's reins,[4] affirms that they
Are under his protection, willingly
Welcomes them to his ranks... No doubt does he
Prepare to march against you. Lo! By God,
See how the noble head of our Jean-Claude,
Rent from his body—foul *ex voto*—was
Brought to the West, a tribute to the cause
Of peace betwixt our foes! Need I express
The awed surprise, the utter joyousness
This bloody token wrought! The enemy
Thought now the battle done and won; that he,
Angel of Death, had conferred victory
Upon them; that God, from that moment hence,
Stood stalwart, ever armed in their defense!

Christophe
Friend, I fear not those blackguards base. They shall
Reap the rewards sown by their criminal
Misdeeds! They see that I live yet! Proof quite
Enough that their vile perfidy, their spite—

Mais, dis-moi, depuis quand, par l'honneur animés,
En Brutus, en Catons, mes sujets transformés,
Veulent venger des lois la majesté flétrie,
Parlent de liberté, de gloire, de patrie?
Qui donc leur révéla tous ces mots imposants,
Dont leur faible raison méconnaît le vrai sens?
Je saurai par le fer guérir cette folie,
Et des cerveaux ardents calmer la frénésie.
Si le ciel, de mes maux tempérant la rigueur,
Permet que vers ces champs connus de ma valeur,
Où des vainqueurs du Môle on retrouve la trace,
D'un coursier belliqueux j'aille guider l'audace.
Les timides pigeons, en bataillons épars,
De l'aigle oseraient-ils affronter les regards?
Tels, de mes vœux secrets si j'en crois l'assurance,
Les soldats de Boyer soutiendront ma présence.

Jean-Philippe
Ce fut dans le mystère et la nuit du secret
Que vos sujets, Seigneur, ourdirent ce projet.
Longtemps il demeura couvert par des nuages
Où se formaient sans bruit la foudre et les orages:
Nous échappons enfin à ce sommeil affreux;
La Discorde, il est vrai, partout sème ses feux.
Eh! bien, à ce péril opposons le courage
De vous, de votre sang ordinaire partage.
Puisque ces assassins, foulant aux pieds vos lois,
Abjurent le respect et le pouvoir des rois,
De ce pouvoir sacré sauvez la révérence,
Et que des flots de sang coulent pour sa vengeance.

1823

Their villainy!—shall not for long remain
Unpunished... But pray tell, when did my reign
First spawn those would-be honor-driven men,
Those Catos, Brutuses, [5] risen again,
Spouting words—*freedom, glory, fatherland*—
To scorn the majesty of laws my hand
Designed! Words pompous, grave... Words ill-defined
And meaning naught to their enfeebled mind!
My blade will quell their folly, and shall cure
Their burning brains' frenzied discomfiture!
If heaven, calming my passion, lets me ride
Once more through fields of valor past, astride
My steed—as when La Mole fell to me there—
Could ragged pigeon troops, a-scatter, dare
Confront the eagle? No! Boyer's men, too—
So says my dream!—will bid the fray adieu!

Jean-Philippe
It was in night's dark secret mystery
That these base subjects of Your Majesty
Plotted, conspired... So, silent, in a cloud,
The lightning-storm is born, before its loud
Thundering blast growls forth! But lo! At last,
We waken from our frightening sleep, aghast!
The flames of Discord spread... And now must we
Defend your royal blood's nobility!
Your laws they trample underfoot, and thus
Shame monarchs' name in wise most blasphemous.
You, Sire, must save divine right sovereign,
And with blood's vengeance purge their heinous sin!

1823

À travers les sillons par la foudre tracés

À travers les sillons par la foudre tracés,
Où brille la lueur de cent feux éclipsés,
Des groupes d'opprimés s'assemblent en silence;
Ils prosternent leurs fronts invoquant l'assistance
Du Dieu qui réveilla chez un peuple brillant,
L'illustre Spartacus, cet esclave vaillant,
Victime du destin, mais des siècles l'exemple,
Dont le nom, les vertus méritèrent un temple
Qu'eût sans doute obtenu son sublime dessein,
Si l'aveugle égoïsme, au cœur froid et d'airain
De l'unique intérêt n'eût fait l'apothéose;
Si le monde eût proscrit les tyrans et leur cause.

À leurs accents plaintifs, assemblés sur ces bords,
Les fougueux fils d'Éole aux lugubres accords,
Mêlent leurs sifflements à l'horreur des ténèbres;
Le flexible bambou dans ces concerts funèbres
Ébranlé par leurs chocs se rompt en mugissant,
Et retentit au loin d'un éclat frémissant.

La nature s'émeut... Leurs lamentables voix
S'élèvent vers son trône; elle suspend ces lois
Qui font du mouvement éclore l'harmonie,
Et rendirent fameux le chantre d'Ausonie.
Elle vit le Colon, délirant par accès,
Se livrer aux transports de criminels excès;

About the lightning-flaring furrows[1]

About the lightning-flaring furrows, where
Hundreds of fires, bright-burning, blaze the air—
Now flashing, now grown dim—in silence stand
The poor oppressed, brows low, begging the hand
Of God himself; he who inspired the brave
Spartacus[2]—famous race's scion, slave
Illustrious—to wrest them from their woe.
Victim of fate, sung centuries ago
For his example, his name might have earned
A temple to the flame sublime that burned
Within him, but for Man's blind, selfish pride—
Heart cold as brass!—that ever glorified
Base interest; and had the world, without
A doubt, cast tyrants and their crass deeds out!

Whistling about these shores, the progeny
Of Aeolus,[3] in dread cacophony
Chaotic, blend their deadly accents, stark,
Amid the terrors of the doleful dark.
Frail, the bamboos,[4] laid low, wail, shudder, shake,
Split by the gale winds howling in their wake.

Nature is touched... Their voices' dour laments
Rise to her throne,[5] and she holds in suspense
The rules that raise to life her harmony.
Extolled by the Ausonian poet[6]—he
Who sang her praise and earned great fame... Then, lo!
See? The Colonist revels—fulsome foe!—

Trois siècles l'esclavage, outrageant sa clémence,
Souilla par ses forfaits son auguste présence;
Et, jouet malheureux des plus lâches fureurs,
L'homme au front nuancé gémit sous tant d'horreurs.

La Vengeance s'éveille et fait briller le glaive
Qui jadis délivra les voisins de Genève:
Elle excite des cœurs les rapides élans;
Cette soif inutile, étonnement des sens,
Guide du désespoir et précurseur du crime,
Par la nécessité devenue légitime.

Soudain le calme naît, les fougueux aquilons
Au règne du Zéphir ont livré ces vallons;
Borée a de ces bois fui l'épaisseur profonde;
La nymphe épouvantée à sa fuite le gronde;
Mais qui frappe les yeux! Quelle est cette clarté
Qui jaillit d'un bûcher en ces lieux apprêté!...
L'Attique a-t-il transmis son culte et ses usages
Aux enfants malheureux de ces lointains rivages.
Mais un taureau paraît, et ce noir coloris,
Cet appareil funèbre et ces liens fleuris
Sont pour un sacrifice offerts par l'innocence
À cette déité qu'adore l'Espérance.

Parmi les assistants se lève un orateur:
Il a l'auguste emploi de sacrificateur.
Muni d'un fer sacré, son bras à la victime
Porte le coup fatal, dans l'ardeur qui l'anime
Elle meurt... Aussitôt il consulte son flanc...

In his foul crimes' duress: three centuries
Of pain! Gone, now, clement tranquillity's[7]
Domain, sullied by slavery's excess!
Plaything of most foul vile cowardliness,
Man, with his brow of many a darksome hue,[8]
Groans at the horrors he must bend unto.

Vengeance awakes, brandishes bright the sword
That freed Geneva[9] from the scaling horde
One night; heart pounding, senses thirsting for
Revenge, here, now... Yearning still, ever more
Spurred on by sheer despair, theirs, presently,
A crime—blameless—wrought by necessity!

Suddenly all grows calm: the North Winds deign
Give way to Zephyr, yield him the terrain;
Boreas[10] too has fled the woodland deeps.
Startled, the nymph, appalled at his flight, heaps
Insults upon his head... But wait! What sight
Is this that strikes the eye? What is that light
Flickering from a pyre, here, in this wood?...
Has Attic cult found its way hither? Could
It be? That fire... Here, on this distant shore,
Among this piteous band?... Look! To the fore,
A bull!... And mid this black, this panoply
Of death, flower-bedecked, there is to be
A sacrifice! *Ex voto* rising hence
To their god, worshiped in Hope's innocence!

Then stands an orator amongst the throng,
Who in pose grave, august, clutches a long,
Sacred blade poised above the beast, and who
Will deal the blow—no delay, no ado—
In passion's burning flush... The victim dies!

Délire prophétique!... holocauste de sang!...
"Vous dévoilez le sort de la noble entreprise
Qui forme les héros et les immortalise!..."

Il parle, et ce langage aimé de nos aïeux,
Ce langage ingénu qui semblait fait pour eux,
Dont les accents naïfs, peinture de leur âme,
Prêtant plus d'onction à ce discours de flamme,
Électrisa les cœurs par un transport nouveau:

"Ce Dieu qui du soleil alluma le flambeau,
Qui soulève les mers et fait gronder l'orage,
Ce Dieu, n'en doutez pas, caché dans un nuage,
Contemple ce pays, voit des Blancs les forfaits,
Leur culte engage au crime, et le nôtre aux bienfaits,
Mais la bonté suprême ordonne la vengeance
Et guidera vos bras; forts de son assistance,
Foulons aux pieds l'idole avide de nos pleurs,
Puissante Liberté! Viens... parle à tous les cœurs..."

L'Oracle est prononcé. La flamme dévorante
S'élance en tourbillons vers la voûte éclatante,
D'où mille diamants de leurs feux étoilés,
Dardent sur ces déserts en leurs ombres voilés
De leurs pâles rayons la tremblante lumière,
L'encens fume et, déjà sur une ample litière,
On livre la victime offerte au dieu vengeur,
Et que vient d'accueillir ce dieu libérateur.

The priestly orator stands, casts his eyes
Over its gushing flank, consults each sign
Awash in blood... And, prophet sybilline,
Rants, cries... "Now you the noble purpose see
Whence heroes rise to immortality!"

He speaks. And that tongue[11] that our forebears used,
So simple that it seemed to have suffused
Their very breath; tongue natural, naive,
So much their own that one could well believe
It had been forged for them alone; that tongue—
Anointing his soul-searing words—unstrung
Their minds, electrified their hearts. He said:

"That God, whose torch—the sun—flames overhead;
Who makes the winds to roar, the seas to swell—
Cloud-hidden—to be sure, he knows full well
The white man's sins against your land, your race.
His worship leads to crime; ours leads to grace
And goodliness. But God's virtue supreme
Demands revenge; he will our strength redeem
And guide our blows. Let us, with trampling feet,
Their idol crush: he who would find it meet
That bitter tears fill our eyes endlessly!
Liberty, come! May you our hearts' voice be!"

Thus is the oracle pronounced. The fire
Swirls in an all-devouring hunger, higher...
Higher... A-whirl unto the heavens' height,
Where myriad diamond-stars cast darts of light,[12]
Flickering pale over the dark-veiled, vast,
Barren expanse... Incense-clouds smoke... At last,
Votive gift to that god, vengeance-possessed...
Our freedom's god holds it fast to his breast.

Le bûcher consumé n'est plus qu'un tas de cendre.
Ils consacrent ce bois, leurs chants s'y font entendre.
Ils vont porter leurs pas dans le prochain hameau.
Mais leurs yeux sont frappés d'un prodige nouveau...
Près du bûcher fumant une chouette tombe,
La chute, des pervers annonce l'hécatombe.

L'interprète des dieux explique leurs desseins,
Tout est purifié dans ses pieuses mains.
Chacun des conjurés décoré d'une plume,
Dans ce frêle ornement voit, suivant la coutume,
De ces rites divers que proscrit la raison,
L'amulette sacrée inconnue à Jason,
Que l'Europe adora sous la Loi d'un pontife,
Fanatique rival de l'indigne Calife.

1824

The pyre, consumed, is naught but ashes now.
With prayer-chants and many a sacred vow,
They consecrate this wood; and as, straightway,
They would make for a nearby hamlet, they
Witness an omen, one most strange!... Hard by
The smoking pyre, a screech owl, from on high,
Comes falling earthward: portent dire that one
And all will perish... Doomed to die... Undone...

Whereat, the prophet of the gods explains
That he will purify the owl's remains
And give to each conspirator a feather—
Reasonless rite! And yet who can doubt whether
Talisman plumes were known to Jason![13] Or
If Europe—credulous!—allegiance swore
To amulets blest by the Papal State,
Rival dupe of the lowly caliphate.[14]

1824

JEAN-MARIE CHOPIN

Salut, lointains climats! (Ode sur l'indépendance d'Haïti)

Salut, lointains climats! terre libre et féconde,
Dont la plage à l'Espagne ouvrit un nouveau monde,
Et qui depuis forgea tes glaives et tes fers!
Salut! de tes soldats désarme le courage.
    Partout sur ton rivage
Le signal de la paix vient d'ébranler les mers!

Sur les coteaux riants où les palmiers verdissent,
Nos jeunes oliviers s'élèvent et fleurissent,
Leur ombre tutelaire au loin couvre tes bords!
Salut! le bras vainqueur de tes fils magnanimes
    À tant d'illustres victimes
Présente noblement tes fruits et tes trésors.

Et toi, chef citoyen, Boyer, dont la mémoire
Se présentera pure à l'équitable histoire,
Salut! À tes désirs l'aîné des rois répond,
Ce triomphe est plus grand que la gloire des armes;
    Ni le sang ni les larmes
N'altéreront l'éclat des palmes de ton front!

De ces bords fortunés où règne ton génie
Embrasse d'un regard la France rajeunie,
Vois nos vieux préjugés tombant de toutes parts;
Et, malgré les efforts d'un parti frénétique,
    Vois la jeune Amérique
Jetant l'ancre des lois sur ses débris épars!

Trop longtemps ont duré ces indignes entraves!
L'Européen disait: Les noirs sont nos esclaves;

JEAN-MARIE CHOPIN

Hail, distant climes! (Ode on Haitian Independence)[1]

Hail, distant climes! O land fertile and free,
Whose New World sands fell to Spain's tyranny,
Forging the blades that long held you in thrall.
Hail, your courageous soldiers, armed no more,
      Stirring the sea from shore
To shore, echoing sounds of peace for all!

On the fair, smiling hillsides, where—between,
Betwixt—sprout palms and olive trees of green,[2]
Whose shade protects, in lush magnificence,
Your far-flung strands... Hail, brave sons, who bestow
      On those once steeped in woe,
Your bounty and your fruits' fair succulence.

Hail, Boyer! You, citizen-chief! Your name
Long deserves memory's unblemished flame.
To you, Royalty's eldest son accedes:[3]
Triumph, this, sweeter than war's fame, dear bought!
      Nor blood, nor tears do aught
To dim your laureled brow's bright hero-deeds.

From your wealth-blessèd isle, let clasp your glance
About old France's fresh exuberance.
Watch age-old vice go crumbling, buffeted;
And see even a frenzied land unstrung—
      America: brash, young—
Cast her laws' anchor midst the flotsam spread.

Shackled too long, this race; too long the battle.
The European said: "The blacks are chattel.

Un Dieu les a marqués d'un sceau réprobateur!
Notre luxe a besoin de toute leur misère;
             Non! Dieu n'est point leur père,
Et son indifférence accuse leur malheur!

Mais l'Africain s'élève... et déjà les victimes,
De trois siècles d'horreur ont expié les crimes.
Sur ce tableau fixons notre œil épouvanté;
Oui, ces brusques revers sont des leçons publiques,
             Nos crises politiques
Étonneront les rois et la postérité!

Ô des décrets d'en haut, abîme impénétrable!
Ces bords où l'avarice aveugle, insatiable,
Changeait en vils troupeaux de malheureux mortels;
Ces bords ont vu régner la liberté sacrée,
             Vierge auguste, adorée,
Dont trop souvent l'erreur profana les autels!

Mais il manque un trophée à ta noble couronne;
Vois ces Léonidas que la terre abandonne.
Devant tes pavillons fais pâlir le croissant!
Viens relever la croix sur la cendre d'Homère,
             Et que l'Europe entière
À tes pieux efforts se joigne en rougissant!

Alors, heureuse et grande, achève ta carrière;
Ouvre au commerce actif ta plage hospitalière;
De la France à ta voix les arts vont accourir
Mais garde tes enfants de nos mœurs corruptrices!
             N'achète point nos vices.
On sait tout, quand on sait vivre libre et mourir!

1825

An irate God's reproof has marked them so!
We need their pain to feed our luxury.
        God's children, these? Nay! He
Cares little for their stark and darksome woe!"

Then, lo! The African's avenging hand
Repays three centuries by terror spanned.
Gaze on this piteous land's tableau, with eyes
Aghast in horror; eyes quick to discern
        How swiftly tables turn—
Much to kings' awe and history's surprise!

Vast, dark abyss of lofty laws decreed!
This isle where—blind, unsatisfied—pure greed
Transformed poor mortals into herds run wild;
These skies that now see Freedom's reign restored—
        Virgin august, adored—
Whose altars had lain soiled, profaned, reviled!

One gem your crown yet lacks, noble and proud:
Like brave Leonidas[4]—exiled, unbowed—
Let Turk before your banners quake, grow pale.
Raise the cross over Homer's ashes spread![5]
        May Europe—one, blood-red—
Join in your noble piety's travail.[6]

In grandeur let your course be plied; pray let
Your happy isle rich thriving trade beget;
May our French arts come soon to grace your shore.
But let your children not corrupted be
        By our depravity![7]
How to live and die free... Need Man know more?

1825

JUSTE CHANLATTE

Quel est ce Roi, dont la bonté?

Quel est ce Roi, dont la bonté
Tarit les pleurs de l'Amérique?
Quel est ce Roi, dont l'équité
Reluit sous ce brûlant tropique?
Veut-il sur ces bords, désormais,
Enchantant une république
Par le doux lien des bienfaits,
Tout soumettre à son sceptre unique?
C'est Charles-Dix qui, par sa loi
Est un Dieu pour l'indépendance.
Que l'écho répète avec moi:
Vive Haïti! Vive la France!

Que trop sûr d'un fatal appui,
Un monarque afflige la terre,
Et place entre son peuple et lui
L'attirail affreux du tonnerre;
Cela n'est point rare aujourd'hui;
Des grands, c'est l'usage ordinaire:
Et l'on admire encore celui
Qui sur nous déploya la guerre.
Mais un Roi qui, par ses bienfaits,
Dompte le plus opiniâtre,
Vous ne le trouverez jamais,
Que dans le fils d'un Henri-Quatre.

Triomphant d'un usurpateur,
À peine de l'éclat du trône
Le front d'un Roi, d'un bienfaiteur,
Brille à ceux auxquels il pardonne,

JUSTE CHANLATTE

What King, this, he whose weal outspread?[1]

What King, this, he whose weal outspread
Dries tears America weeps, cries?
What king, this, whose laws, justice-bred,
Shine hot beneath our tropic skies?
Would he, henceforth, deign ply the grace
Of his fair reign, Republic-wise,[2]
Charming our shores, from place to place,
That his sole scepter unifies?
Charles Dix, he![3] His Majesty,
God of our land's deliverance!
Let echo now repeat with me:
Long live Haiti! And long live France![4]

Often great monarchs choose today—
Favored scions of destiny!—
To play the perverse popinjay
And flay, with lightning cruelty,
Their hapless, hopeless subjects—nay,
Their victims! And yet ever we
Admire that king, habitué
Of battle, erstwhile enemy!
But as for a more generous one,
Proof to the disbelieving mind,
None but the kindly, worthy son
Of Henri Quatre might you find.[5]

A vile usurper, gone at last!
Scarce new king's brow lit bright the throne—
Avast, our fair shores' perils past!—
Than on our pardoned heroes shone

Que de ces rives protecteur,
Du beau pouvoir qui l'environne
Il détache un rayon vainqueur,
Qui charme le cœur et l'étonne.
À nos yeux encore éblouis
Il triomphe de tout obstacle;
Ce n'est qu'au fils de Saint-Louis
Qu'appartient un tel miracle.

1825

His grace munificent. Steadfast
Protector, standing staunch, alone,
A ray of triumph's light he cast
Upon charmed hearts, bewildered grown.
Before our gaze bedazzled, he
Bests every obstacle; for, thus,
None but a son of Saint-Louis
Would wreak such deeds miraculous.[6]

1825

Le monde a salué tes fils (Hymne à l'indépendance)

Le monde a salué tes fils,
Soleil, c'est aujourd'hui la fête!
Vois Haïti mêler le lys
Aux palmes qui couvrent sa tête.
Partage nos transports joyeux
En ce jour de réjouissance.
La France a comblé tous les vœux:
Vive Haïti! Vive la France.
Vive Haïti! Vive la France.

Le jour de gloire a lui pour vous;
Augustes ombres de nos Pères,
Venez célébrer avec nous
Nos destins si beaux, si prospères.
La France a scellé les efforts
De notre héroïque vaillance.
Chantez, chantez aux sombres bords:
Vive Haïti! Vive la France.
Vive Haïti! Vive la France.

Roule des flots plus orgueilleux,
Majestueuse Artibonite,
Toi qui, dans l'empire écumeux,
Avec fierté te précipite.
Que le murmure de tes eaux
Célébrant ce jour d'espérance,
Apprenne à dire à tes roseaux:
Vive Haïti! Vive la France.
Vive Haïti! Vive la France.

JEAN-BAPTISTE ROMANE

The world has hailed your sons (Hymn to Independence)[1]

The world has hailed your sons this day
Of days, O Sun! Haiti has spread
French lilies, in clustered array,
About her brow, palm-garlanded.[2]
Come share our lusty passion-fires
This day of joyful circumstance.
For France has bowed to our desires:
Long life to Haiti! Long live France![3]
Long life to Haiti! Long live France!

The day of glory shone for you:
O solemn Shades, come join with us
To offer praises thereunto
And fete a fate most prosperous.
France has affixed her seal about
Our heroes, poised in valiant stance.[4]
Sing! Sing! Let the dark shores ring out:
Long life to Haiti! Long live France!
Long life to Haiti! Long live France!

And you, Artibonite,[5] roll proud
Your waves, coursing majestically
As you dash, gushing in a shroud
Of foam-froth onward to the sea.
Let your fair waters, murmuring,
Join this day's hope-filled celebrants,
As all our reeds and rushes ring:
Long life to Haiti! Long live France!
Long life to Haiti! Long live France!

Allons aux pieds du grand Boyer,
Allons déposer nos offrandes;
La paix couronne ce guerrier
De ses immortelles guirlandes.
Ses constants et nobles travaux
Ont conquis notre indépendance;
Il a dit pour finir nos maux:
Vive Haïti! Vive la France!
Vive Haïti! Vive la France!

Salut, ô grand roi des Français
Toi qu'on vit couronné de gloire,
Enchaîner l'hydre des forfaits
Au char ailé de la victoire!
Ton front luit d'immortalité.
Nos fils, admirant ta clémence,
Diront dans la postérité:
Vive Haïti! Vive la France.
Vive Haïti! Vive la France.

Grand Dieu! Daigne agréer nos chants,
Tributs d'une sainte allégresse;
Que les liens les plus constants
De la paix nourrissent l'ivresse!
Que sur CHARLES et sur BOYER
Se répande ta bienvaillance!
Entends-les tous deux s'écrier:
Vive Haïti! Vive la France!
Vive Haïti! Vive la France!

1825

Come! At Boyer's feet[6] let us cast
Our tribute, as the warrior's head,
Wreathed about in a peace steadfast,
With deathless blooms is garlanded.
Our independence now we owe
To his noble inheritance;
His the decree ending our woe:
Long life to Haiti! Long live France!
Long life to Haiti! Long live France!

To you, French monarch, hail! All hail!
You, crowned with glory unprofaned,
Who fought the Hydra's bane and bale,
To victory's winged chariot chained!
Your brow will shine eternally.
Long will our children raise their chants,
Ever to praise your clemency:
Long life to Haiti! Long live France!
Long life to Haiti! Long live France!

Great God! Accept our songs this day,
Joy's sacred tributes sung for thee.
May peace ever embrace us, pray,
And feed our sacred ecstasy!
On BOYER and on CHARLES rejoice!
Pray shine on them thy countenance!
And hear them sing, both in one voice:
Long life to Haiti! Long live France!
Long life to Haiti! Long live France!

1825

Au loin, qui brille à nos yeux étonnés?

Au loin, qui brille à nos yeux étonnés?
Amis! c'est le pavillon de la France,
Haïtiens! ils sont donc arrivés
Ces jours tant promis à notre vaillance!
      Haïti! tu vas refleurir,
        Ton triomphe était infaillible;
      Savoir vivre libre ou mourir,
        C'est le secret d'être invincible.

Nos justes droits respectés, reconnus
Par Charles Dix, souverain philosophe,
D'un immuable sceau sont revêtus;
Vite à sa gloire essayons cette strophe:
      À Paris, le palais des rois
        Va donc être heureux et paisible;
      D'un peuple libre aimer les droits,
        C'est de régner, l'art infaillible.

Quoi, de trois mots le magique pouvoir,
Quoi, liberté, commerce, indépendance,
Au nouveau monde, offrant un doux espoir,
Avec l'ancien tressent son alliance.
      Raison, justice, d'applaudir
        À cet accord indestructible
      Qui sait vivre libre ou mourir
        Possède l'art d'être invincible.

Haïtiens! il est d'autres vertus
Que celles qui maîtrisent la victoire;
Jadis, n'a-t-on pas vu Cincinnatus

JUSTE CHANLATTE

What looms there, shining afar before our startled eyes?[1]

Friends! What looms there, shining afar before
Our startled eyes? It is the banner spread
Of our good French allies, come to our shore:
Ours, now, fair days awaited, heralded.
> Haiti, you bloom again; whereat
> Once more shall you taste victory.
> Live free or die:[2] the secret, that,
> Of man's invincibility.

Monarch-philosopher, the king Charles Dix,[3]
Has placed his royal seal upon our rights,
Never to falter, nevermore to cease.
Let our verse praise him, raise him to the heights!
> In Paris stands the palace: his
> Abode of peace and harmony!
> Love freedom! Such the fine art is
> Of king's infallibility.

Three magic words soon will empower you;
Three words: *liberty, independence, trade.*
In hope have they, 'twixt two worlds, Old and New,
With strands entwined, a fixed alliance made.
> Reason and justice glorify
> This pact that never rent shall be.
> He who would fain live free or die,
> Proves man's invincibility.

Haitians! More virtue is there, glorious,
Than but to savor battle's victory.
Did not the hero Cincinnatus[4] thus,

S'acquérir un nouveau genre de gloire?
> C'est peu que nos faits éclatants
> Aient retracé les fils du Tibre,
> C'est en fertilisant ses champs
> Qu'on se rend digne d'être libre.

Blonde Cérès! ah! daigne associer
À tes faveurs ce peuple qui t'en prie!
Par toi, tout naît, et son soc nourricier,
Sceptre du monde, en est l'âme et la vie.
> Qu'importe que nos faits brillants
> Aient retracé les fils du Tibre?
> Ce n'est qu'en labourant ses champs,
> Que l'on peut se maintenir libre.

Je te salue, illustre Président!
Le seul honneur pour toi, digne d'envie,
Et qui flatte ton vœu le plus ardent,
Est d'être utile et cher à ta patrie.
> Vis au gré de notre désir,
> Ton succès était infaillible;
> Savoir vivre libre ou mourir
> C'est le secret d'être invincible.

1826

Pursue in different wise his destiny?
          It matters not that, valor-bound,
          We retrace Tiber's progeny;
          Only in sowing rich the ground
          Is mankind worthy to live free.

Blond Ceres![5] Ah! Would that your favors grace
This race that plowshare-scepter wisely wields,
Bringing to life, in your sweet-souled embrace,
The bounty of their ever-fertile fields.
          What matters it that, valor-crowned,
          We retrace Tiber's progeny?
          Only in plowing rich the ground
          Does man remain unbound and free.

I hail you, O illustrious President![6]
The deed most worthy of your noble hand,
Most dear to your ardor beneficent,
Is to be loved and serve your fatherland.
          Thrive, guide our cause, I pray; whereat
          Once more shall you taste victory.
          Live free or die: the secret, that,
          Of man's invincibility.

1826

Le Lis un jour dit au Palmier (Le Lis et le Palmier)

Le Lis un jour dit au Palmier:
Oh combien la haine est cruelle!
Ami, quel charme d'oublier
Une trop funeste querelle!
De la puissante Liberté
Que j'orne aussi la plage hospitalière!
Charles, de cette Déité,
N'arbora-t-il point la bannière?

Oui, dit l'Arbre, soyons unis,
Noble fleur d'un monarque juste:
Qu'à jamais les palmes aux lis
Se joignent sur son front auguste!
Mes fils admirent les hauts-faits
Qui, de la France éternisent la gloire
Et, de l'immortel Béarnais,
Tous, ils chérissent la mémoire.

Mes fils, de l'illustre Boyer,
Bénissant la philanthropie,
Reprit la fleur: que l'olivier,
Aux palmes pour lui se marie!
Alors au monarque français
La Liberté présente une couronne,
Et toi, Boyer, la douce Paix
De ses guirlandes t'environne.

Fléaux du monde, conquérants,
Qu'entraîne une aveugle folie,
Prêtez l'oreille à mes accents,

PIERRE FAUBERT

One day, Lily to Palm says (The Lily and the Palm)[1]

One day, Lily to Palm says,[2] "Friend,
How charming it would be to let
Bygones be bygones, put an end
To hatreds, deadly strife forget!
For I, with doughty Liberty,
Would shade our gracious shores, like her! For I
Would do as Charles did.[3] Did not he
Bear that god's banner, hold it high?"

"Yes," says the tree, "let us be one;
You, just king's noble flower! Let now
Lily and palm in unison
Forever grace his august brow!
My scions prize his daring, pay
Him homage, France's glories sanctifying;
And of our deathless Béarnais,[4]
Cherish the memory undying."

"And mine," replies the Lily, "bless
Famed Boyer's proud philanthropy.
For him may palm-fronds' loveliness
In marriage join the olive tree!
Whereat will Liberty gird round
The fair French monarch's blessèd royal head,
And you, Boyer, with peace be crowned
And wreathed about, engarlanded."

Conquerors all! Earth's scourges, whom
Blind rage sweeps ever onward! Hear
My voice. Pray let us spell the doom

De Mars abhorrez la furie!
Que toujours Charles ou Boyer,
Dans vos discords vous serve de modèle:
Comme eux pensez que l'olivier
Est, des couronnes, la plus belle.

1826

Of Mars' bloodthirsty fell career!
May you, Boyer and Charles, who cease
Your warring ways, inspire tranquillity;
And may the olive wreath of peace,
Of all the crowns, the fairest be.[5]

1826

ANONYMOUS

Muse, à des chants nouveaux j'ai consacré ma lyre (*L'Haïtiade*, Chant premier)

Muse, à des chants nouveaux j'ai consacré ma lyre;
Viens embraser mon cœur de ton brûlant délire,
Imprime à mes accents une mâle fierté
Viens, Muse, et d'Haïti chantons la liberté.

C'est là que trop longtemps, d'un funeste esclavage,
Les enfants de l'Afrique ont ressenti l'outrage;
C'est là que tout un peuple aux regrets condamné,
A pleuré deux cents ans le malheur d'être né.
Là, méprisant ce Dieu dont les lois libérales
Dotèrent les humains de facultés égales,
Quelques faibles tyrans, séduits par leur orgueil,
Sur la liberté sainte étendirent le deuil.
Ils ne sont plus: le Ciel a puni tant d'audace,
Et d'éclatants effets ont suivi sa menace.

Au printemps douze fois empruntant ses couleurs,
L'univers rajeuni s'était paré de fleurs,
Et déjà douze fois, en sa marche insensible,
La terre avait tourné sur son axe inflexible,
Depuis ces jours de gloire où d'immortels exploits
À l'homme créé libre avaient rendu ses droits;
Ces grands jours où les Noirs, magnanimes esclaves,
Changeaient en fer vengeur le fer de leurs entraves;
Ces grands jours de triomphe où le sang des Colons,
Versé dans cent combats, arrosait leurs sillons,
Et que des fiers Anglais les dépouilles glacées,
Sur les mornes déserts languissaient dispersées.

ANONYMOUS

O Muse, now to new songs I tune my lyre
(*The Haitiade*, Canto 1)[1]

O Muse, now to new songs I tune my lyre:
Come, flame my heart with your mad passion-fire;
Let my voice, proud, with manly accents, ring;
Come, Muse, let us now Haiti's freedom sing.[2]

There it was that, in slavery's deathly reign,
Africa's children bore too long their pain.
There it was that a race—woeful, forlorn—
Wept for two hundred years for being born.
There, scorning God, whose generosity
Bestowed life's gifts on mankind equally,
Tyrants—few, weak, but prideful nonetheless—
Clad sacred liberty in mourning-dress.
Now are they gone! Their arrogance outspent,
By Heaven forewarned, reaped blazing punishment.

A dozen times the universe, in hue
Of flowering spring, bedecked itself anew,
And on its axis staunch, with not a sound,
A dozen times earth turned its silent round.
Since those days, glorious, when deathless deed
Earned man—born free, enslaved, and finally freed—
His rights...[3] Great days, when black men, noble-souled,
Beat to avenging blades their chains of old;
Great days triumphant when, in furrowed flood,
Planters, hundreds of times, fought, spilled their blood;
When the proud English carcasses—bare, chill—
Lingered, abandoned, on each barren hill.

Les pas d'un ennemi ne souillaient plus ces bords,
Et la paix souriait à d'illustres efforts.
Les vainqueurs généreux, oubliant leurs disgrâces,
D'un préjugé funeste avaient proscrit les traces;
Soumis au même Dieu, comme aux mêmes douleurs,
Ils jugeaient les vertus et non pas les couleurs.
Alliés par le sang aux races étrangères,
Ils venaient de former un grand peuple de frères;
Ennoblis par la gloire ils étaient tous égaux
Et servaient leur pays l'un et l'autre rivaux.
Dans le temple des lois des magistrats fidèles,
De l'équitable honneur gardaient les étincelles;
Dans les temples sacrés des prêtres vertueux
Faisaient monter au Ciel leur encens et leurs vœux;
Tout, d'un Dieu créateur, annonçait la présence,
Et de sa main propice éprouvait l'influence.
Sur les champs où la mort avait porté ses coups,
S'étendait en festons le pampre aux fruits si doux;
Sur d'immenses débris les roses purpurines
Cachaient d'un vain orgueil les pompeuses ruines.
L'instrument du travail, fardeau si douloureux,
Lorsqu'il devait nourrir un maître rigoureux,
N'était plus que léger dans cette main flétrie
Du soldat citoyen qui sauva sa patrie.
Tout inspirait l'oubli des humaines fureurs;
Tout de la haine aveugle abjurait les erreurs,
Et de la liberté pratiquant les maximes,
Pardonnait aux bourreaux en maudissant les crimes.

Du suprême pouvoir par le Ciel investi,
TOUSSAINT dictait des lois aux peuples d'Haïti.
Ce guerrier généreux trahi dès sa naissance,
Dans de honteux liens traîna sa longue enfance.

No longer did a foe's vile, fulsome trace
Sully the peace that smiled upon this place
And on its lofty aims; the conqueror,
Quick to forget old woes, stood firm before
The remnants of a brutal practice fell.
Subjects of one same God, subject as well
To the same human pains, men looked within
The man, beyond the color of his skin,
To judge his virtue; and, by blood allied,
They formed a race of brethren, side by side.
Glory-ennobled, all strove equally
And served their land in friendly rivalry.
In the law's temples honest judges fanned
Justice's sparks to life with even hand;
In sacred temples priests of virtue praised
Heaven with vows in clouds of incense raised;
All bespoke God, one being omnipotent,
As all witnessed his power benevolent.
Over the fields where death had dealt its blows
Vines in sweet-fruited garlands gently rose;
Roses of crimson spread the countryside
Hiding the pomp, laid waste, of vapid pride.
The hoe—burden so heavy when it fed
The cruel, slave-driving master—now, instead,
Weighed ever lightly in the withered hand
Of soldier-citizen who saved his land.
Everything sought to make mind rise reborn,
Forget Man's madness, blind hate's sins foresworn,
And with the maxims wrought of freedom's teaching,
Forgive the hangmen whilst their crimes impeaching.

Heaven-endowed with power supreme, it was
TOUSSAINT whose tongue decreed the Haitians' laws.[4]
Warrior valorous—betrayed, pursued—
He trudged through youth in shameful servitude.

Son cœur, foyer brûlant des plus nobles désirs,
Respirant pour la gloire était mort aux plaisirs.
Époux tendre, ami sûr, esclave sans faiblesse,
Ennemi de l'orgueil comme de la bassesse;
L'âme libre toujours, quand ses bras enchaînés
Aux plus vils des travaux se montraient résignés;
De toutes les vertus que flétrit l'esclavage,
Aux yeux de ses tyrans il offrit le partage.
Bientôt un cri de guerre enflammant sa valeur,
Il unit ses efforts aux efforts du malheur,
Et de ses compagnons les mains victorieuses,
Cueillirent sur ses pas des palmes glorieuses,
Maintenant d'un grand peuple heureux libérateur,
Il en devient le père et le législateur.
Un pacte auguste et saint, qu'a dicté la prudence,
Des enfants d'Haïti fonda l'indépendance;
Et ce pacte bientôt, à l'ombre des autels,
Restera consacré par des vœux solennels.

Déjà le jour a lui; le soleil sans nuage,
Des volontés du Ciel annonce le présage;
Les vents soufflent à peine et les flots balancés,
S'agitent mollement l'un sur l'autre pressés.
La terre a bu les pleurs que l'aurore naissante
Verse au calice d'or de la fleur languissante;
Les oiseaux fendent l'air, leur brillantes couleurs,
Sur un fond tout d'azur semblent tracer des fleurs;
Le ruisseau doucement coule sur la verdure
Et l'écho répond seul au torrent qui murmure.

Du lambi tout à coup les sons retentissants,
Fixent près d'un héros les Noirs reconnaissants.
Vers les plaines du Cap leurs cohortes s'avancent,

His heart burned but for glory, not one whit
For worldly pleasure, dead indeed to it;
True friend and tender husband, slave who never
Faltered; foe of the haughty, base; soul ever
Free, even when, in shackles bound, resigned,
He stooped to labors of the vilest kind.
To tyrants he displayed the panoply
Of all those virtues flayed by slavery.
But soon his valor rang with cries of war:[5]
He joined its pains to pains endured before—
New efforts to the woes of old—and those
Who followed, with triumphant hands arose
To pluck the palms of glory in his path.
Now, liberator in war's aftermath,
Great nation's father and lawgiver he;
A holy pact that his sagacity
Set firmly forth, became the very base
On which the independent Haitian race
Was founded: pact that, altar-consecrated,
With solemn vows, will long stand venerated.

Already day shines forth; the cloudless sun
Bespeaks Heaven's desires: in unison.
The waves break softly each on each; the breeze
Blows scarce a ruffle on the swaying sea's
Expanse... The earth has drunk the tears, long-drawn,
From languid bloom's gold chalice that new dawn
Lets fall... Birds rend the air; bright-hued, they seem
To trace flowers on the azure fair... The stream,
Flowing over the greensward, mutters by:
Only the echo murmurs its reply.

Suddenly, at the conch-shell's blaring sound,[6]
The thankful Blacks from all sides gather round
Their hero... Toward Le Cap their troops advance

Le front orné de fleurs, les vierges les devancent;
Par de pieuses mains les autels sont parés;
Le feu brûle l'encens dans des trépieds dorés;
Les apôtres du Christ, soumis à la loi sainte,
Du parvis radieux peuplent l'auguste enceinte;
Le signe précurseur du salut des humains
Réfléchit du soleil les rayons incertains;
On entonne des chants, et les chœurs angéliques
Dans les hauteurs des Cieux répètent ces cantiques.
Un panache flexible aux vents abandonné
Signale à tous les yeux le héros incliné;
Il invoque l'appui de l'arbitre suprême,
Qui protège le juste et lance l'anathème;
Il l'appelle à témoin des nobles sentiments
Qui vont être soumis à la foi des serments.
Il monte une cavale à la France enlevée;
Sa fougueuse valeur fut longtemps éprouvée.
Ses pieds frappent la terre et ses ongles d'airain
Dans son impatience en déchirent le sein.
Les vents ont dispersés sa crinière flottante,
L'écume sort à flots de sa bouche sanglante;
Le mors qui l'importune excite son horreur,
Et son sang généreux bouillonne avec fureur.
Sur le sein du héros se dessine et se joue
L'écharpe aux trois couleurs que la victoire avoue;
Ses regards imposants, sur la plaine étendus,
Y cherchent ses rivaux dans les rangs confondus.
Ils arrivent: d'abord, fiers de leurs longs services,
Marchent ces vieux guerriers couverts de cicatrices;
Que de fois au milieu du plus sanglant combat,
Au péril de leurs jours ils ont sauvé l'État!
Christophe les conduit; soldat infatigable,

Over the plains.[7] Brows decked in elegance
Beflowered, maidens march, leading the way.
Their pious hands strew many a fair bouquet
About the altars, and in gilded stands
Incense burns... On the church-front statue bands
Of Christ's apostles, bound by holy writ,
Shine on the august precinct exquisite;
Sun's timid rays reflect its glorydom,
Sign of mankind's salvation sure to come...
Voices rise up, the Heavens' height inspires
Hymns intoned by celestial angel choirs.[8]
A fluttering plume, wind-blown over the air,
Draws all eyes to the hero bowed in prayer;[9]
The succor of the judge supreme he seeks,
Protector of the just, who curses wreaks
When wreak he must, and begs him hear the oath
Whose noble sentiments he will be loath
To violate... He mounts a mare, at length—
Filched, indeed, from the French!—whose feverish strength
Has long been proven: hooves impatient pound,
Brazen-clawed; rip the bosom of the ground
Beneath; mane floating in the wind, a flood
Of foam spews from her lips awash in blood,
Abounding, as, recalcitrant, she pits
The power of her flesh against the bit's
Detested steel... Upon the hero's breast
Waves the three-colored sash of triumph's quest;
Casting his dominating gaze far, wide,
He seeks his rivals in the ranks, beside
Their men... Now here they come: proud of long years
In noble service, doughty cavaliers,
Old and scar-covered, on the march... How many
Times, in the bloody heat of battle, any
And all would save the state, at risk of life
And limb! Christophe,[10] the dauntless, leads them, rife

Christophe dans son cœur nourrit un vœu coupable,
Dès ses plus jeunes ans l'orgueil ambitieux
Lui rappela des droits perdus par ses aïeux.
Indigne de ses fers, comme un tigre en furie,
Il regretta vingt ans le ciel de sa patrie.
Mais depuis qu'arrachée à son joug détesté,
La terre d'Haïti conquit sa liberté,
Il a conçu l'espoir de l'asservir encore;
Ainsi doit s'étancher la soif qui le dévore.

Entraînés à leur tour par leurs coursiers fougueux,
Six mille cavaliers montrent leur front poudreux;
Ils agitent dans l'air de longues javelines
Et suivent en tremblant les pas de Dessalines.
Dessalines! Mortel qu'une funeste horreur
Détermine à la haine et pousse à la fureur!
Le plus farouche orgueil se peint sur son visage;
Des guerriers ses égaux il attend l'humble hommage.
C'est en vain qu'il voila les replis de son cœur,
Son langage superbe est celui d'un vainqueur.
Indocile au devoir, avide de puissance,
Son esprit se refuse à toute obéissance.
Il doit venir le jour où, souillant ses lauriers,
Il fixera sa place au rang des meurtriers,
Et qu'altéré de sang, dans son horrible joie,
De son propre pays il aura fait sa proie.

À la voix de Clerveaux, dix mille vétérans
Orgueilleux de leur chef, marchent aux seconds rangs.
Ce héros a conquis, par sa haute sagesse,
Le tribut de respect qu'on porte à sa jeunesse.
Du faste de l'Europe il fuit l'éclat trompeur:

With guilty thoughts, on base ambition bent;
Christophe himself, whose prideful youth was spent
Remembering the lost rights of his race
And of his roots, wild tiger on the chase,
Shamed by his shackles, yearning—for a score
Of years—to know his fatherland once more;
And who, with Haiti now unyoked and free,
Enjoying the sweet fruits of liberty,
Dreams again to enslave her—no mere whim!—
And quench the thirst for power devouring him.

Dust-browed, there follow some six thousand strong:
Stout cavaliers swept fervently along;
Spears, javelins poised, lunging with quivering tread,
Behind brave Dessalines they plunge ahead.
Dessalines![11] Mortal man whose unabated
Horror would lead to frenzied hate ill-fated!
Savagemost pride shines on his face, and he
Demands his warrior-equals' fealty
And their humble obedience... In vain
Would he attempt to veil his heart, constrain
Its innermost desires! His haughty tongue
Reveals the conqueror; his mind, unstrung,
Untamed to duty, thirsts for power—his own!—
Answers to none but to himself alone!
The day will come when, fouling free men's thanks,
Laurel-conferred, jeering, he joins the ranks
Of hateful killers drunk on blood; that day
When his own land becomes his fateful prey.

Ten thousand more, veterans all, march proud
To take their orders from Clerveaux, unbowed
By age, who, wise beyond his youthful years,
Has earned the admiration of his peers.[12]
Turning his back on Europe's luxury,

C'est un autre Bayard, sans reproche et sans peur;
Gédéon vient après; l'estime de l'armée
Est le prix glorieux qu'obtient sa renommée.
Fidèle compagnon de ses jeunes rivaux,
Injuste envers lui-même, il vante leurs travaux;
La seule ambition qui flatte sa grande âme,
C'est d'embraser les cœurs d'une céleste flamme,
D'inspirer aux soldats que séduit le repos,
Cet amour du pays qui produit les héros.
Il commande en ce jour la cohorte sacrée
Que sa valeur guerrière a toujours illustrée;
Trois fois elle a vaincu, trois fois par ses efforts,
D'Haïti l'avarice a dû purger les bords.

Moïse avec orgueil suit une noble trace
Son front majestueux, où respire la grâce,
Décèle un noble saint qui se voue aux combats.
Toussaint, dès le berceau, le reçut dans ses bras;
Il l'adopta pour fils, né d'une sœur trop chère,
Sur sa timide enfance il sut veiller en père.
L'âge a développé dans ce cœur généreux,
Des vertus qu'un héros appelait par ses vœux;
Jeune, superbe, fier, indocile et sauvage,
Époux de Tellésile, il la forme au courage;
Il prétend que la gloire unie avec l'amour,
De myrte et de laurier le couronnent un jour.

Tellésile, en naissant, à sa mère arrachée,
Aux regards des mortels vécut longtemps cachée;
Esclave d'un Colon, dont les fougueux désirs
Souriaient en secret à l'heure des plaisirs,
Heure trop lente, hélas! pour son impatience,

"Sans peur et sans reproche," new Bayard[13] he...
Following him comes Gédéon, whose fame
Bestows the prize of glory on his name.
Young rivals' boon companion, quick to sing
Their deeds, he scorns his own; only one thing—
One sole ambition—moves his soul: to fire
Men's heart with heavenly, burning flame, inspire
His troops to spurn repose, to heed the call
Of love of country and be heroes all.
On that day will his famous godly band
Shine once more in his soldierly command;
Thrice victory is theirs; thrice, by their toil,
Undone are they who covet Haiti's soil.

Next in distinguished line Moïse is seen
Leading his men,[14] he of majestic mien,
His worthy head held high, whose virile grace
Bespeaks the noble blood of warrior race
To combat born. Toussaint's own nephew, he—
His much-belovèd sister's progeny—
Was at his birth adopted as his son,
Raised by his foster father to fear none
And naught! At length, the hero's influence
Wrought in the child the strength of confidence:
Young, haughty, proud, unbridled, he would feel
A spouse's passion for fair Tellésile,
Shaping her heart to his, hoping that love
And fame would form the myrtle crown thereof.

Tellésile, babe from mother wrenched, long hidden
From human eyes, a planter's slave, was bidden
To do his will when fleshly urge might smile
In secret on his dalliances... But while,
Impatient, he would wait for her to keep

Cette jeune beauté pleurait dans le silence;
Elle attendait la mort et non le déshonneur...
Mais un Dieu tout-puissant veillait à son bonheur:
Le triomphe des Noirs découvrit l'humble asile
Où mourait dans sa fleur la jeune Tellésile.
Moïse l'entrevit, et, pénétré d'amour,
Osa solliciter le plus tendre retour:
Il l'obtint; et bientôt un heureux hyménée,
Sous les yeux maternels unit leur destinée;
Par l'amour embellis, leurs destins, désormais,
Coulent dans les douceurs d'une innocente paix.

D'un coursier castillan, Tellésile maîtresse,
Sans le secours du mors tempère la vitesse;
Le carquois africain contient ses javelots;
Son bras agite l'arc, instrument des héros;
Son casque aux crins dorés, où le zéphir se joue,
Avec des nœuds d'airain sous son menton se noue,
La dépouille d'un ours ceint et presse ses flancs;
Elle promène au loin ses yeux étincelants,
Et, fière de l'époux digne objet de sa flamme,
Des plus nobles désirs elle nourrit son âme.

Télémaque, suivi de mille fantassins,
Rend grâce au Dieu puissant qui remplit ses desseins.
Citoyen vertueux, guerrier plein de noblesse,
Il avait préparé ce grand jour d'allégresse;
Admis dans les conseils, son éloquente voix
S'y montra l'interprète et le soutien des lois.
Affaibli par son âge, il chérit sa patrie,
Et porta cet amour jusqu'à l'idolâtrie.

His lustful trysts, silently she would weep
And wait for death, rather than suffer, thus,
Shame at his loathsome hands lascivious...
But God omnipotent with watchful eye
Would bring her solace; and when, by and by,
The triumph of the Blacks disclosed the shed
Where, flower in youth's bloom, she spent her dread
And dying days, Moïse chanced to catch sight
Of her and, deep-impassioned, hoped she might
Return his love... She did. And soon they were
United, she to him and he to her,
With blessings motherly; their sweet fates thence
Flow, love-adorned, in peaceful innocence.

Tellésile, reins a-slack, plunges ahead,
Spurring on her Castilian thoroughbred,
African quiver on her back, and lo!
Brandishing high the hero-soldier's bow.
Her gold-plumed helmet, knotted on her chin,
Buckled in brass, wafts in the wind; the skin
Of flayed bear girds her loins, and as she plies
A distant gaze—pride flashing in her eyes—
On her most worthy mate, her love's desire
Surfeits her soul with yearning's noblest fire.

Old Télémaque,[15] commanding fifty score
Foot soldiers, follows, giving thanks before
Almighty God for virtuous aims fulfilled.
Staunch citizen, warrior noble-willed,
Long waiting for this joyous day, it was
He, with his eloquence, who framed the laws
Adopted in the councils. Age-worn, he
Turned love of country to idolatry.

Beauvais marche après lui, ce héros, dès longtemps
A marqué sa valeur par des faits éclatants.
Aux rives de la France, empressé de s'instruire,
Il a pu sur son cœur prendre un suprême empire;
Son esprit étendu par de constants efforts
A pu de la science embrasser les ressorts:
Il est homme d'État, il est homme de guerre;
Son bras, plus d'une fois, funeste à l'Angleterre,
Honora son pays qu'humilia l'orgueil,
Terre où tant de guerriers trouvèrent leur cercueil.

Les vaillants escadrons qui sauvèrent le Môle
Obéissant aux preux dont ils font leur idole.
Inginac est son nom, sa devise est l'honneur,
Au sort de l'infortune il lia son bonheur;
Consultant de Thémis les augustes maximes,
Il voua sa jeunesse à des devoirs sublimes;
Par la guerre troublé dans sa veille assidu,
À sa terre natale Inginac fut rendu.
Le glaive arma ses mains, et la gloire des armes
À son cœur généreux offrit de nouveaux charmes;
Maintenant, il soupire, et ses pressentiments
Comptent dans l'avenir d'affreux événements.

Marion, noble fils d'une mère étrangère,
Précède les lanciers armés à la légère;
Son front audacieux atteste ses exploits,
De ses propres soldats il a fixé le choix.
Au jour d'un grand péril, tous, d'une voix commune,
Du brave Marion suivirent la fortune.

Bonnet, que la vaillance eut le droit d'enflammer,
Sent naître un noble orgueil qu'il cherche à réprimer.
Il marche sur les pas d'un héros qu'il admire,

Next, Beauvais marches hither, hero long
Known for fine deeds of valor stout and strong.
Burning for knowledge, heart and head he turned
To France's shores, and thereupon he learned
To take science's measure—venturesome,
Determined—and with constant pluck to plumb
Her depths... Statesman and soldier, oftentimes
He parried pompous England's haughty crimes
Against his nation's honor; land where death
Claimed many a gallant warrior's final breath.

The troops that saved Le Mole[16] from siege obey—
Nay, worship—him whose valor won the day;
Inginac is his name, honor his sign.
He felt misfortune served the fate divine
That forged his happiness: Themis's sage
Precepts and counsel, from his earliest age,
Fashioned his love of duty justly wrought.
Troubled, observing from afar, war brought
Inginac home; once in his native land,
Glory's charms stirred his breast: with blade in hand,
Sighing, he knows the frightful happenings—
The woes, the pains—the future surely brings.

Leading the light-armed lancers, noble son
Born of a foreign mother... Such an one
Is Marion, he whose brow audacious shows
His feats, and who each of his soldiers chose;
Who, when great peril threatened, by their choice,
Threw in their lot with Marion, with one voice.

Bonnet, courage-impassioned, would repress
His well-earned flames of noble haughtiness.
With admiration for his hero, while

Et sur de mâles traits brille un touchant sourire;
Les hussards généreux, aux combats exercés,
Sur des coursiers ardents suivent ses pas pressés.

Des derniers rangs enfin arrive la phalange.
Quel chef doit commander ce glorieux mélange
Du sang des opprimés et du sang oppresseur?
Du magnanime Ogé, courageux successeur
Un guerrier a paru; son âme est éclairée;
Par la religion sa foi fut épurée.
Né du sang de l'Europe et fruit d'un chaste amour,
Au sein d'une créole il a puisé le jour;
Il a vu s'écouler l'âge heureux de l'enfance
Au milieu des plaisirs qui flattent l'innocence.
Plus tard, son cœur, nourri des plus purs sentiments,
D'un orgueil généreux connut les mouvements;
Il adora la gloire, et, devançant son âge,
Des plus mâles vertus recueillit l'héritage.
Son œil, où respirait une fière valeur,
Ne refuse jamais des larmes au malheur.
Son sourire exprimait la douce bienveillance,
Et des plus tendres vœux annonçait l'alliance.
Sur un hongre indocile, avec grâce élancé,
Son corps majestueux, mollement balancé,
Du coursier indomptable embrassait la surface.
Et rappelait aux yeux des guerriers de la Thrace.
Ce preux, c'était Rigaud; illustre et respecté
Ce nom sera l'orgueil de la postérité.

Jaloux de faire aimer des pouvoirs légitimes,
TOUSSAINT marche entouré des guerriers magnanimes
Dont les sages conseils, éclairant tous ses pas,
Préviennent l'arbitraire et ses noirs attentats.

He follows in his wake, a tender smile
Breaks on his manly face... Brave horsemen, bred
For war, press on as he plunges ahead...

A final phalanx ends the march. Who may
The chieftain be, commanding this array,
This blood of the oppressed and the oppressor?
A warrior had arisen, brave successor
To the magnanimous Ogé;[17] unstained,
Indeed, was he, and ever had remained
Pure in his faith, enlightened in his soul.
Europe's blood and love of a chaste Creole
Had formed in him the fruit of life. Days spent
In pastimes' simple pleasures innocent
Had marked his youth. Later, his heart, well fed
On the most pure of passions, will have led
To noble self-esteem... Not yet grown old,
He worshiped glory's virile virtues bold.
Nor did his eyes' valorous spirit fail
To shed tears when misfortune might prevail.
Rather, a smile complaisant would express
His feelings born of gentle tenderness
On an unbroken gelding, restless breed,
His form majestic, one with his fierce steed,
Swayed at each gallop with an easy grace
That called to mind the valiant knights of Thrace...
No other than Rigaud![18] This stalwart's fame,
Through years untold, will glorify his name.

And so, TOUSSAINT, eager in word and deed
To spread the love of righteous power, will lead
To war his worthies; they whose counsels light
His way against fate's hazards dark as night.

Là s'offre Pétion, guerrier que sa clémence
Égale au Dieu propice en qui l'être commence;
Sa grande âme a souffert des maux de son pays;
Il pleure ces guerriers par le malheur trahis;
D'un tribut de regrets il honore leur cendre,
Mais c'est à les venger qu'il veut un jour prétendre.
S'il se tait, son silence enchaîne tous les cœurs;
S'il a parlé, tout cède à ses accents vainqueurs;
Son front toujours serein, son regard tutélaire,
Signalent des vertus l'auguste sanctuaire.
Un sentiment d'amour se peint dans tous ses traits,
Et ses prodigues mains dispensent les bienfaits.

Près de lui son émule et son rival en gloire,
Boyer, jeune et vaillant, sourit à la victoire.
C'est le fier Antiloque auprès du vieux Nestor,
Télémaque attentif aux conseils de Mentor.
Sous un habile maître, il apprend l'art suprême
De régler ses penchants, de se vaincre soi-même,
D'écarter de son cœur un dangereux poison,
D'appliquer sa constance à mûrir sa raison.
Ce jour, ce jour de gloire, à son âme charmée,
Dans son éclat divin s'offrit la renommée.
Il contemple ravi son front prestigieux,
Et s'enflamme aux éclairs qui partent de ses yeux.
Tout à coup d'un héros il révèle l'audace,
Au faîte des pouvoirs le temps marque sa place;
Son esprit a percé l'ombre de l'avenir,
Il a vu les chemins que Dieu semble aplanir;
Il pressent la grandeur des devoirs qui l'attendent,
Et se forme aux vertus que ces devoirs demandent.

Thereat Pétion appears,[19] whose kindness vies
With God's himself, source of all being. War-wise
And weary, his great soul has keenly felt
The many sufferings to his nation dealt.
He weeps those warriors woe-betrayed, and pays
Tribute unto their ashes with his praise,
Sign of the vengeance that he yearns to wreak.
Silent, he binds all hearts; and should he speak,
His tone triumphant conquers all. His brow
Serene, his godly gaze, appear, somehow,
Altars of virtue pure; love marks his face,
And his prodigious hands bestow his grace.

Close by him comes Boyer[20]—gallant youth—one
Much like Antilochus, old Nestor's son.
Or like Telemachus, young protégé
Of Mentor, he of counsel sage;[21] Boyer,
Who smiles on victory, knows the fine art
Of reining in the yearnings of his heart,
Keeping it free of poison perilous,
Ever his reason strengthening... And thus,
Today, this day of glory, war's renown,
Resplendent and divine, descends, lights down
Upon his head, charming his soul. And there,
Entranced, he contemplates the noble air
Of his fair laureled brow; passion-flamed, he
Sees his eyes flash with lightning!... Suddenly,
With hero's grandeur, at his powers' height,
He stands forth... Time, in everlasting light,
Marks his eternal place: his spirit can
Pierce through the future's shades, foresee God's plan,
The road laid clear before him, and the great
Duties magnificent that stand in wait;
Virtues that take his measure, form his very
Being... He spurs his extraordinary

D'un coursier généreux Boyer presse les flancs:
Il embrase les airs de ses naseaux brûlants;
Son orgueil indompté, son ardeur belliqueuse
Secondent de ses pas la fougue impétueuse.

Non loin du fier Boukman on distingue Magni,
Borgella, Théodat, Blanchet, Panayoti,
L'inflexible Romain, le généreux Chanlatte,
Et l'intrépide Éloy, l'émule de Villate:
Tous enfants de la guerre; ils doivent à leurs bras
Les titres glorieux qu'honorent leurs soldats.

Les magistrats, couverts de simarres antiques,
Occupent du parvis les gradins magnifiques.
Là siège, révéré, d'Imbert, dont la vertu
Fut tant de fois propice au malheur abattu;
D'Imbert, riche en savoir, riche en expérience,
Et dont la modestie embellit la science;
D'Imbert dont les conseils par l'honneur inspirés,
Comme ceux de Caton sont toujours éclairés.
Près de lui, jeune encore, nourri dans la sagesse,
Avide des conseils, trésors de la vieillesse,
Se montrait Colombel, lui, qu'un Dieu de bonté
Forma pour honorer la sainte humanité.
Ses yeux où respirait une grâce infinie,
Par de fréquents éclairs dévoilent le génie;
Sur un front généreux, la modeste pudeur,
De son âme céleste annonçait la candeur.
Salut, salut! ô toi dont la vertu profonde,
D'un glorieux espoir flattait le Nouveau-Monde!
Mais, qu'ai-je dit, hélas! où vais-je m'égarer?
J'exalte une vertu que nous devons pleurer.

Mount's stalwart flanks, presses ahead... The steed's
Nostrils, a-fire, enflame the wind; war's deeds
Echo his every pace... He gallops bold,
In tune with Boyer's passions uncontrolled.

There, too, arrogant Boukman and Magni,
Steadfast Romain, Blanchet, Panayoti,
Borgella, Théodat, upright Chanlatte,
Fearless Eloy, the rival of Villate... [22]
Battle-bred minions, honored one and all,
Who earn their soldiers' glorious clarion-call.

On lavish tribune-stands raised off the ground
Before the church, in long, antique robes gowned,
The magistrates watch. Much revered, d'Imbert—
Hero of woe-betrodden souls—sits there
Amongst the ranks; d'Imbert,[23] experienced,
In knowledge rich, who, much praised—nay, incensed!—
Adorns his talents with his modesty.
D'Imbert, whose verdicts, honor-wrought, could be
Compared to Cato's,[24] for in truth so sage
Were they... And next to him, in youth's sweet age,
One bred on wisdom, much a-thirst for his
Wise counsel, treasure of his years. Such is
Young Colombel,[25] by a good God designed,
An honor paid to holy humankind.
Oft would his gracious manner infinite
Flash genius from his eyes with lightning lit;
On a broad, ample brow, modesty-graced,
Shone, limpid, pure, a soul divinely chaste.
Hail, hail! O you, whose virtue deep, unbounded,
Gave the New World a glorious hope, new-founded!...
Ah, but I stray. What have I said? No more
May I praise him we ought be weeping for,

Voyez-vous ce vaisseau qui, bravant les orages,
Du royaume des Francs va chercher les rivages?
Sur son fragile bord Colombel est monté...
Il fuit loin d'Haïti, par les vents emporté.
Dieux puissants! protégez ces voiles blanchissantes,
Enchaînez le courroux des vagues frémissantes;
Pendant un jour serein, que du ciel le plus pur
Dans le cristal des flots se reflète l'azur!
Ministre d'un héros, à sa gloire fidèle,
Colombel, des amis le plus parfait modèle;
Colombel, dont le cœur était resté Français,
Portait au roi Louis l'olive de la paix...
O regrets! ô douleur! la mort, au front livide,
Balance dans les airs une faulx homicide;
Les flots, en mugissant, s'élancent jusqu'aux cieux.
Un gouffre est entr'ouvert et s'offre à tous les yeux.
Les nochers ont pâli; Colombel, immobile,
A tourné vers le Ciel un visage tranquille:
Un sentiment divin brille dans tous ses traits.
Étranger par son âme aux humains intérêts,
Il cède au Dieu puissant, qui créa tous les mondes,
Et descend résigné dans l'abîme des ondes.
Tout périt: c'en est fait, et Colombel n'est plus!
Déplorable victime! au séjour des élus,
Lieux saints où la vertu brille de tous ses charmes,
Accueille le tribut de nos pieuses larmes!

Les vieillards d'Haïti, des marches de l'autel,
Portent leurs vœux ardents jusqu'aux voûtes du Ciel,

Alas!... Alas! His grace, his virtue... See
That boat braving the tempest, fearlessly
Sailing off to the Frankish shores? See how
Colombel stands upon her fragile bow,
Leaving behind his Haitian land? Wind-tossed,
His bark plows on and on... But oh, the cost!
Powerful gods! Protect those white-spread sails!
Chain the waves' trembling fury! Let the gales
Grow calm, serene... Let the dawn gently ply
The crystal sea, against pure-azured sky!
Serving his hero's glory, Colombel—
Minister, friend—knew and performed full well
Friendship's demands. For he it was who bore—
A Frenchman still—unto the royal shore
Of King Louis,[26] the olive branch... But oh!
Bitter the grief, bitter the pain, the woe!
Pallid death swings his scythe in murderous wise...
The waters rise, fall, groan, reach to the skies,
Unleashed... Above the chasm-like abyss,
Motionless on the waters' precipice,
Colombel stands amongst the boatmen, grown
Fearsomely pale, as he and he alone
Turns Heavenward his countenance... No fright,
No fear disturb its peace; naught but a light
Divine shines thereupon; human concerns
Are his no more. And so, resigned, he turns
To God, creator of all things, and goes
Plunging into the deep... O woe of woes!
All is lost!... Colombel! Forever you
Will dwell amongst the chosen retinue!
There, midst the virtues of your sainted peers
Receive the tribute of our pious tears.

The Haitian elders, at the altar shrine,
Lift up their prayers unto the vault divine,

Et le peuple à genoux, qu'un doux espoir éveille,
À la voix de son Dieu semble prêter l'oreille.

Le héros va parler; son front est découvert,
Ses regards dans les cieux cherchent le Roi qu'il sert.
Le glaive est dans ses mains, il s'élance et s'écrie:
"Généreux compagnons, orgueil de la patrie;
Peuple, de qui l'amour m'offre un rang glorieux,
Écoutez les serments d'un cœur religieux:
Je jure, au nom du Ciel, dont je crains la colère,
De maintenir vos lois, de gouverner en père;
De m'oublier toujours pour ne songer qu'à vous.
Si je vous trahissais... De votre honneur jaloux,
Frappez... et que la mort, expiant vos injures,
Aux bords du précipice arrête les parjures:
Le pacte qui nous lie est un pacte sacré;
Tremblez que par vos mains il ne soit déchiré.
Mille devoirs, hélas! inconnus aux esclaves,
Des fiers républicains sont les nobles entraves.
Respectez ces devoirs; la liberté jamais
N'imita la licence et n'eut soif de forfaits.
Libres d'un joug funeste, il faut tout craindre encore:
Vos tyrans sont punis, mais l'orgueil les dévore;
À l'horrible vengeance ils sont abandonnés;
Ils regrettent le sol où leurs enfants sont nés.
Même au sein de la paix il faut prévoir la guerre,
Et veiller à cette heure où s'endort le tonnerre.
Pour moi, que tant de vœux portent au premier rang,
Peuple régénéré! je vous dois tout mon sang.

As, hopeful, common folk kneel, and appear
Waiting the very voice of God to hear.

The hero is about to speak;[27] head bare,
Gazing at Heaven as if seeking there
The king he serves, dagger in hand, he stands
Out from them all, calls, "You, O fatherland's
New pride, esteemed and faithful friends! You who
Bestow on me love's glorious rank! To you
I swear, by my faith and in Heaven's name—
Heaven, whose wrath I fear... Here, I proclaim
To govern by your laws and, fatherly,
Ever to think of you, never of me!
Should I betray you... Ah! Then, honor-bound,
I pray you slay me, strike me to the ground
To expiate my faithlessness before
It casts you down instead! Forevermore
This pact betwixt us is a sacred one.
Tremble lest by your hands it be undone,
Destroyed... A thousand duties slaves know not
Redound to proud republicans, whose lot
Is bound to the respect for obligations
Imposed by liberty. Nor ought free nations
Turn liberty to license: freedom's folk
Must shun crime once the dreaded, deadly yoke
Of servitude falls free. Your tyrants may
Have been defeated, but still feared are they,
By arrogance devoured, on vengeance bent.
They miss their children's land. And you, intent
On peace, and living in its bosom blest,
Beware the battle-thunder's silence, lest,
Sleeping, war reawaken. As for me,
O race reborn, whose unanimity
Makes me your chief, to you I owe my all—
My very blood, shed at your beck and call;

À ce titre du moins vous pourrez reconnaître
Que je suis votre chef et non pas votre maître."

Ce discours, accueilli par d'unanimes vœux,
Excite les transports d'un peuple généreux.
Le clairon retentit, la loi fondamentale
A reçu des serments qu'un prodige signale,
Et les cœurs des guerriers, noirs enfants du désert,
Pour fêter ce grand jour forment un doux concert.

Salut! Fille du Ciel, salut! liberté sainte,
Du malheur sur nos fronts viens effacer l'empreinte.

Messagère de paix, défends à nos esprits
L'odieux souvenir d'un si funeste esprit;
Ton aspect glorieux répand sur la nature
L'éclat éblouissant d'une lumière pure;
Il agrandit notre âme, et sur ces tristes bords,
De la reconnaissance excite les transports.
Telle aux regards flattés, l'aurore matinale,
Sème du pourpre et d'or la rive orientale,
Et du vaste horizon nuançant les couleurs,
Prodigue la rosée au calice des fleurs.
Telle une jeune vierge à l'amour asservie,
D'un époux adoré charme l'heureuse vie;
Sa douce voix l'éveille au bruit de ses concerts,
Et ses regards confus s'échappent en éclairs.

Salut! Fille du Ciel, salut! liberté sainte,
Du malheur sur nos fronts viens effacer l'empreinte.

Après des temps de deuil, le siècle est arrivé;
Les tyrans sont connus et leur masque est levé.
La France en proclamant des vérités sublimes,
Rendit tous les humains à leurs droits légitimes:

Whence be it known that, by common accord,
Your leader am I, yes, but not your lord!"

This speech before the multitude was heard
With generous acclaim, and straightway stirred
Black souls... The desert's children gather round;
The trumpet blares its miracle of sound.
All vow to keep the law... Whence, they rejoice,
Praising this day of days, all in one voice.

Hail, Heaven's daughter! Sacred freedom! Come
Cleanse our brows of our wretched martyrdom.[28]

Herald of peace, let our minds now stand free
Of deathly scorn's vile, hateful memory.
Your glory spreads its brilliant luster pure—
Far, wide, through nature's realm—bright cynosure;
Expands our soul, and on this hapless shore
Spawns ecstasies of gratitude therefor.
Just as the dawn, caressed with looks of thanks,
Strews gold and crimson on its eastern banks,
And blending the horizon's changing hue,
Lavishes bloom corollas with its dew.
Just as young maiden, heart in thrall to love,
Delights adoring mate with charms thereof;
Her sweet voice wakes him with its melodies,
Her gaze, obscure, flashes strange mysteries.

Hail, Heaven's daughter! Sacred freedom! Come
Cleanse our brows of our wretched martyrdom.

Mourning-times past, at last dawns a new day!
The tyrants stand revealed, unmasked are they.
Proclaiming truth sublime, France has returned
Man to the rights that centuries had spurned,[29]

Elle brisa le joug qu'un insolent pouvoir
Imposa par la force au nom d'un saint devoir;
L'égalité des droits, si longtemps méconnue,
Aux regards des mortels se montra toute nue;
Une voix protectrice apprit à l'Univers,
Que pour le crime seul Dieu prépara des fers.

Salut! Fille du Ciel, salut! liberté sainte,
Du malheur sur nos fronts viens effacer l'empreinte.

Doux champs de la patrie où dorment nos aïeux;
Soleil dont les rayons brillaient plus radieux;
Ténébreuses forêts, dont les retraites sombres,
À la faiblesse en pleurs refusèrent leurs ombres;
Cabane hospitalière où l'ineffable paix
Berça nos premiers ans perdus dans les souhaits;
Lieux chéris, toit paisible où notre âme entraînée,
Serra du doux hymen la chaîne fortunée;
Sol brûlant de l'Afrique, accueille nos adieux;
Nos cœurs ont triomphé d'un sort injurieux.
Libres d'un joug cruel, sur la terre où nous sommes,
Le fer nous a placés au rang des autres hommes;
Nos bras ne servent plus à d'ignobles travaux,
Et, lassés d'obéir, nous marchons leurs égaux.

Salut! Fille du Ciel, salut! liberté sainte,
Du malheur sur nos fronts viens effacer l'empreinte.

Ainsi chantaient les Noirs: les derniers feux du jour,
De la nuit libérale annoncent le retour,
Et le peuple, oubliant de funestes alarmes,
S'abandonne au repos et savoure ses charmes.

1827–28

Smashing the yoke that power's insolence
Forged in the name divine of providence.
Equality of rights, so long ignored,
Stood bare, in naked truth, to men restored.
Fair, guardian voice informed the Universe:
"Chains are God's wage for crime, not mankind's curse."

Hail, Heaven's daughter! Sacred freedom! Come
Cleanse our brows of our wretched martyrdom.

O fatherland's sweet fields where sleep our dead,
O sun, whose rays shone brilliant overhead;
You, forests shadowed dark, whose somber glades
Chased tearful weakness from their gentle shades;
You, cabin warm and welcoming, where calm
Beyond description cradled us in balm
Of childhood dreams... O cherished home, peace-blest,
Where marriage-bonds enlaced us, breast to breast;
O burning soil of Africa! Now hear
Our hearts' farewell. They triumphed over drear,
Fell destiny... Yokeless, victorious,
In this our land, where fate had driven us,
Saved by the sword, no more men's slaves are we,
But by their side we march, equal and free!

Hail, Heaven's daughter! Sacred freedom! Come
Cleanse our brows of our woeful martyrdom.

So sang the Blacks; the daylight's last flames burn,
Announcing once more freedom-night's return.
The people, putting by life's baleful woes,
Give way to restful charms of sweet repose.

1827–28

CORIOLAN ARDOUIN

Les Betjouanes

Comme une fille demi nue (La Danse)

Comme une fille demi nue
Laisse les ondes d'un bassin,
La lune que voile une nue
Sort de l'océan indien.

Joyeuse, la mer sur la grève
Vient soupirer avec amour;
Le pêcheur en sa barque rêve
À ses gains ou pertes du jour.

Au loin les brunes Amirantes
Avec leurs santals, leurs dattiers,
Brillent sur les eaux murmurantes
Ainsi que l'île des palmiers.

Spectacle ravissant! nombreuses
Comme les étoiles des cieux,
Les Betjouanes gracieuses
Dansent à fasciner les yeux!

Voyez, à l'éclat de la lune,
Étinceler leurs bracelets;
Oh! qu'elles sont belles chacune!
Admirez-les, admirez-les!

Les sons du tambour retentissent
Et vont dans la forêt bien loin
Se perdre; les lions rugissent
Aux alentours, mais c'est en vain.

CORIOLAN ARDOUIN

The Bechouans

Like a maid . . . in near-nakedness (The Dance)[1]

Like a maid stepping from a pond,
Standing forth in near-nakedness,
Rises the moon, with cloud-veil donned,
From Indian Ocean's dark recess.

Joyous, the sea sighs lovingly
Against the strand. The fisher muses,
Dreamily, in his bark, as he
Thinks what he takes and what he loses.

Yonder, the brown-hued Amirantes[2]
Gleam on the murmuring waters, calm,
In date-and-boxwood elegance,
Like the isles of the coco-palm.

Ravishing sight! The Bechouan[3] belles,
Numerous as the stars on high,
Dance through the night, casting the spells
That grace and fascinate the eye.

Look! See what beauty they possess,
Bangles a-gleam with moonbeams' fire!
Ah! What a wealth of loveliness!
Admire each one! Each one admire!

The tom-tom's notes, beating, repeating
Their muffled tones[4]... Again, again...
And deep into the forest fleeting...
Round about, lions roar—in vain.

La Betjouane se balance,
Recule, vient, recule encore;
Mais cette fois elle s'élance
Et plane au-dessus du *Sotor;*

Et les mains battent en cadence,
Et mille harmonieuses voix,
Douce musique de la danse,
Se prolongent au fond des bois.

Dansez jeunes filles d'Afrique!
Tandis que vous chantez en chœur.
Dansez! la danse est poétique;
La danse est l'hydromel du cœur.

C'est le son du tambour (Chant de Minora)

"C'est le son du tambour," dit-elle.
"Que m'importe à moi le tambour,
Qu'importe à la lionne une ombre fraîche et belle
Si le lion n'est alentour!

"Apprends-moi, mon fleuve limpide,
Apprends-moi, mon bleu Koûramma,
Sous quels cieux ton onde rapide
A vu l'amant de Minora.

"Il est parti malgré mes larmes,
Il est parti son arc en main;
A-t-il trouvé la mort? a-t-il trouvé des charmes
Ingrat! sur quelque sol lointain?

"Désormais errante et pensive,
J'irai m'exiler au désert.

The Bechouan maid—now to, now fro—
Sways, swings her haunches... With a bound,
Leaps in the air and seems to go
Gliding above the *sotor*'s[5] sound.

Hands clap in cadence to the chants
Of countless sweet-voiced harmonies,
And the lush music of the dance
Joins with the woodland mysteries.

African maids, dance ceaselessly,
Singing together, each her part,
Dancing the dance of poetry.
Dance, the sweet nectar of the heart...

The drums (Song of Minora)[6]

"The drums," she moans. "What matter they
    To me? What fortune can betide
The lioness, spying a fine, fresh prey,
    Without her lion by her side?[7]

"Tell me, Koûramma[8]—limpid, blue—
    Tell me, stream flowing on and on,
    Beneath what skies above have you
    Seen where Minora's love has gone?

"He left despite my tears! Ah, me!
    He left with trusty bow in hand
Has he found other charms?—Oh, infamy!—
    Or lies he dead in distant land?[9]

"In woe's despair I ponder my
    Distress, wander I know not where.

Le malheur m'a touchée, et pauvre sensitive,
    Je ferme mes feuilles à l'air!

    "Apprends-moi, mon fleuve limpide,
    Apprends-moi, mon bleu Koûramma,
    Sous quels cieux ton onde rapide
    A vu l'amant de Minora."

Puis, suivant du regard le fleuve dans la plaine,
Elle contemple encore son cours majestueux,
Lui, si calme et si bleu, lui dont l'onde sereine
A vu tant de climats, passé sous tant de cieux.

Baignons-nous! (Le Bain)

    "Baignons-nous! baignons-nous," dit l'une,
    Et toutes ont dit: "baignons-nous!"
    Les feux paisibles de la lune,
En se mêlant aux flots, rendent les flots plus doux.

    Et c'est Minora la dernière
Qui laisse de ses reins tomber le beau santal,
Comme l'astre des nuits, reine brillante et fière,
Attend que chaque étoile ait montré sa lumière
Pour faire luire au ciel son globe de cristal.

    Le Koûramma gémit d'ivresse
En entendant glisser sur ses ondes d'argent,
    Ces vierges que dans sa vieillesse,
Il ose encore aimer comme aime un jeune amant.

    Le nénuphar et les mimoses,
Étendant des deux bords leurs guirlandes de fleurs
    Se confondent avec ces roses [. . .]

Helpless, the frail mimosa-flower am I,[10]
My petals closed unto the air.

"Tell me, Koûramma—limpid, blue—
Tell me, stream flowing on and on,
Beneath what skies above have you
Seen where Minora's love has gone?"

Then, as her eyes follow his course serene,
She contemplates the stream who, in his time—
Calm, blue, flowing majestically—has seen
So many a sky, so many a far-off clime.

Let's bathe! (The Bath)

"Let's bathe! Let's bathe!" Cries one, and soon
All of them raise the shout: "Let's bathe!"
Gentle beams, glimmering from the moon,
Go shimmering softly, and the billows swathe.

Minora bares her loins, lets fall
The fragrant santal-leaf; and, moon-clad, she—
Like heaven's bright queen!—stands waiting until all
The stars, each one, cast off the darkling pall,
And let the crystal orb shine radiantly.

The Koûramma, old though he is,
Welcomes with blissful shudders of delight,
Into those silvered waves of his,
Maids he dares lust for, as young lovers might.

Lotuses and mimosas spread
Between his banks, with roses garlanded [. . .][11]

Mais tandis que nageant, ainsi qu'une Syrène,
La Betjouane fend les flots,
S'y plonge et laisse à peine
Balancer son corps sur les eaux,

Un bruit lointain s'élève;
Il s'éteint. Est-ce un rêve?
Le bruit s'élève encore et de nouveau se perd!
La Betjouane timide
Abandonne toute humide
Le fleuve qui s'en va plus limpide et plus clair.

Fuyez, filles timides (Les Boschismens)

Fuyez, filles timides,
Fuyez de toutes parts!
Les Boschismens avides
S'élancent. Leurs regards
Sont des regards d'hyène;
Ils viennent, vagabonds,
Par les chemins de plaine,
Par les chemins de monts!
Tout en eux est farouche.
De misérables peaux
Les couvrent [. . .]
Ils bondissent de joie,
Quand par hasard leurs yeux
Tombent sur quelque proie [. . .]
D'une ivresse infernale
Tout leur être est saisi,
Lorsque du sang qui coule
Colorant leurs cheveux,
Ces barbares en foule
Mêlent des cris affreux

But as the comely Bechouan[12] belle goes swimming—
      Beauteous as a Siren fair—
      Now diving, and now scarcely skimming
      The waters—lissome, debonair,

      Far-off, a noise is heard... It dies...
      A dream?... Again it seems to rise,
And dies again!... Alarmed, the Bechouan maid
      Steps from the water, wet, afraid...
Limpid, the river flows in peaceful wise.

Flee, timid maidens! (The Bushmen)

      Flee, timid maidens! Flee
      Wherever fly you may!
      The Bushmen,[13] on a spree,
      Are hunting you today!
      Hyena-eyed, their gaze!
      Over the plain, the hill,
      They roam. Random the ways
      They wander at their will! [. . .]
      Wild and uncouth, they wear
      Vile skins. And when, perchance,
      They spy a victim fair,
      Fit to be seized, they prance
      And dance their hellish rounds [. . .]
      Blood in their hair, deep red,
      Beastly barbaric sounds
      Blend, evil-spirited,

Aux cris d'une victime,
Singeant ses mouvements,
Et conviant au crime
Tous leurs petits enfants [. . .]
La Betjouane écoute: un bruit lointain s'élève
Encore et retentit. Ce bruit, était-ce un rêve,
Ou le simoun impur qui tournoyait dans l'air?
En vain Minora fuit et dans le bois se perd [. . .]
Et comme sous son aile, un vautour brise et ploie
Le cou frêle et blanc du ramier,
Les cruels Boschismens en ont fait une proie
Qu'ils destinent au négrier [. . .]
Adieu, les nuits d'ivresse!
Adieu, son du tambour,
Récits de la vieillesse
À la chute du jour,
Promenade rêveuse
Le long du fleuve bleu,
Et la tonnelle heureuse
Et le culte du dieu
Qu'adorait leur jeunesse
Dans les bois d'alentour!
Adieu, les nuits d'ivresse
Adieu, son du tambour!

Le vent soufflait (Le Départ du négrier)

Le vent soufflait; quelques nuages
Empourprés des feux du soleil,
Miraient leurs brillantes images
Dans les replis du flot vermeil.
On les embarque pêle-mêle;
Le négrier, immense oiseau,

With victims' cries. Outsprung,
Their aping limbs, as they
Even invite their young
To help lay low their prey [. . .]
The Bechouan hears a sound... An echo... Soon
Hears it again... A dream? The foul simoon[14]
Whirling about the air?... Minora flees
Into the wood—in vain!—among the trees! [. . .]
And like the vulture with the dove, whose frail
    Neck yields beneath its conquering wing,
Brutish, the Bushmen mark her, without fail,
    To join the slave ship's trafficking [. . .]
        Ecstatic nights, farewell!
        Farewell, the tom-tom's sound,
        Tales the old men would tell
        As dusk fell on the ground,
        Stroll by the river, dreaming
        By its blue waters, streaming...
        And in the trees spread round,
        Sacred, the rites' *tonnelle*,[15]
        Bower where gods would dwell,
        Worshiped in youth, spellbound!
        Ecstatic nights, farewell!
        Farewell, the tom-tom's sound!

The wind was blowing (The Departure of the Slave Ship)

        The wind was blowing; clouds—here, there,
        Tinged with the sun's deep crimsons, golds
        Ablaze—gazed at their ruby glare
        Mirrored in furrowed ocean folds.[16]
        Into the slave ship, claws spread wide
        Like hungering bird with wings outspanned,

Leur ouvre une serre cruelle,
Et les ravit à leur berceau!

L'une, le front sur le cordage,
Répand des larmes tristement;
L'autre de l'alcyon qui nage
Écoute le gémissement;
L'une sourit dans un doux rêve,
Se réveille et soupire encore,
Toutes en regardant la grève
Demandent son aile au Condor.

—Minora, quel exil pour ton cœur et ton âge!
Son œil réfléchissait le mobile rivage:
Elle était sur la proue: on dirait à la voir,
Toute belle, et des pleurs coulant sur son visage,
Cet ange qui nous vient dans nos rêves du soir.

C'en est fait! le navire
Sillonne au loin les mers;
Sa quille entend l'eau bruire
Et ses matelots fiers
Aiment sa voile blanche
Qui dans les airs s'étend
Et son grand mât qui penche
Sous le souffle du vent.
Car à la nef qu'importe
La rive qui l'attend?
Insensible, elle porte
Et l'esclave et le blanc!

1835

Pell-mell, one herded them inside,
Ravaged, wrenched from their cradle-land.

Her brow against the rigging, one
Weeps her sad tears; another hears
The low moan of the halcyon,[17]
Soaring the deep; one, smiling for
Her dream of far more gentle things,
Awakes, sighs... All, turned toward the shore,
Would beg the Condor for its wings.[18]

—Minora, heart so young! What dire exile
For you! The land, quickly receding, gleamed
There in her glance. And at the bow she seemed—
Beautiful maid, tears streaming all the while—
To be that angel that our nights have dreamed.

Done! Now the ship, wind-blown,
Plows through the distant deep;[19]
Her keel hears the waves groan,
As, proud, her sailors keep
Fond watch on her white sails
Billowing in the air,
And her main mast, that gales
Bend to their will. For where
She goes concerns her not—
Cold and unfeeling, quite—
Caring never a jot
That she bears slave and white![20]

1835

Quand le ciel se dorait d'un beau soleil couchant (Pétion)

I

Quand le ciel se dorait d'un beau soleil couchant;
Quand il voyait le soir aux brises d'Orient,
Jeter les premiers plis de son écharpe noire,
Et qu'au pied du palmier quelques soldats assis,
Quelques vieux compagnons d'infortune et de gloire,
     Contaient leurs peines, leurs soucis;

Il s'approchait alors, toujours pensif et sombre,
Recueillait leurs aveux, se mêlait à leur nombre,
Et parlait à chacun comme à son propre enfant.
Puis, il s'en retournait triste et mélancolique,
Puis, quand la nuit venait, il la passait, rêvant
     Aux destins de la République.

Et son cœur palpitait, et son front incliné,
Dans ses deux mains tombait, de rides couronné.
Oh! que d'illusions dans son âme bercée!
Le présent trop étroit ne peut le contenir,
Et sa pensée alors, sa sublime pensée
     Vole au devant de l'avenir!

II
     Ainsi, lorsqu'au doux bruit des voiles,
     Aspirant le parfum des mers,
     Le nautonnier voit les étoiles
     Briller et flotter dans les airs,
     Il rêve une lointaine plage
     Que ses yeux ne verront jamais!
     Car bientôt la voix de l'orage

When the sky donned the setting sun's fine golds
(Pétion)[1]

I
When the sky donned the setting sun's fine golds;
When, on the air, it shook free the first folds
Of its black sash, amid the Orient's breeze;
When, at the palm tree's foot, old soldiers sat
Exchanging woes and bitter memories,
      Or no-less-glorious feats thereat;[2]

He would approach, pensive, bowing his head,[3]
Would join them there, listen to what they said,
And speak to each, their very father seeming;
Then, sad and deep in melancholy, he
Would return and, come night, would spend it dreaming
      Of the Republic's destiny.

Head in his hands, his brow with wrinkles crowned,
Thinking, musing... Oh! How his heart would pound
With plans, ideas, lulling his soul to sleep!
Scarce could the present hold his dream sublime,
Too vast! And so his thought would ever keep
      Winging off to a future time!

II
      Just so, the helmsman stands, inhales
      The fragrant sea-scent, as he sees
      The stars—amid the murmuring sails—
      Floating, flickering in the breeze;
      Like him, he dreams of darkling shore
      That he will never see! For soon
      The tempest's blast will, with a roar,

Réveille ses sens inquiets;
Bientôt le souffle de la brise
Cède aux fureurs de l'ouragan,
Bientôt c'est la nef qui se brise
Sur les écueils de l'océan.

III

C'est le mal qui triomphe et le bien qui s'exile!
C'est l'immense volcan de la guerre civile
Éclairant notre nuit de son funèbre éclair!
Avides de son sang qu'ils ne peuvent répandre,
Ce sont des insensés qui voudraient que sa cendre
  Fût jetée aux brises de l'air!

Hélas! en vain sa fille, ange du ciel venue,
Montrait à ses regards son enfance ingénue!
Comme un astre pâli se plonge à l'horizon,
Il abîma son cœur en des flots d'amertume,
Et lorsqu'après sa mort on écarta l'écume,
  On vit le désespoir au fond!

1835

Turn the breeze to a wild simoon,
A huge and furious hurricane
Unleashed with force beyond belief,
Lashing his bark—again, again—
Smashing it on the rockbound reef.[4]

III

Evil triumphant! Good prevails no more!
Vast, the volcano of the civil war
Flames in our dark night with its deathly glare![5]
They who thirst for his blood, but thirst in vain,
Would satisfy instead their lust insane
    And cast his ashes on the air!

Alas! His daughter—angel heaven-sent—
In vain as well, would spread her innocent
Youth... [6] Like the moon, grown pale, sinking between
The waves, he drowned his heart in the foul tide.
And when, in death, the foam was swept aside,
    Naught but his deep despair was seen.

1835

Hélas! je me souviens de ce jour (Mila)

I

Hélas! je me souviens de ce jour que mon père
Me dit la mort si triste et l'existence amère
De Mila, la pauvrette, éteinte avant le temps!
Je me souviens encore de cet ange des champs!
Sa démarche était simple, et son âme aussi douce
Que la lune qui dort un beau soir sur la mousse.

"Quand le vent du matin
Fait balancer les cannes,
Et m'apporte au jardin
L'odeur des frangipanes,
    Ce vent me dit:
    'Fille d'Angole,
    Le beau créole,
    Ta chère idole,
    Dieu l'a béni!
    Dieu l'a béni!'

"Sur ma maison de paille,
Quand le soir un oiseau
Chante petit et beau,
Pour mon cœur qui tressaille,
    L'oiseau me dit:
    'Fille d'Angole
    Le beau créole,
    Ta chère idole,
    Dieu l'a béni!
    Dieu l'a béni!'

CORIOLAN ARDOUIN

Oh! I recall that day (Mila)[1]

I

Oh! I recall that day my father said
That Mila, who the bitterest life had led,
Before her time had died, poor thing![2] Ah yes!
I recall all her rustic tenderness!
Simple her angel's gait, her soul like dozing
Moonbeams lighting the moss, gently reposing.

"When blows the breeze at morn[3]
It sways the sugarcane,
And to my garden borne,
The scent of frangipane
Has this to tell:[4]
'Angola belle,
Your Creole swain—
Your deity!—
God blest is he!
God blest is he!'

"When on my thatch, at night,
Warbles a bird, then, oh!
How my heart, with delight,
Trembles a tremolo!
Hear the bird tell:
'Angola belle,
Your Creole beau—
Your deity!—
God blest is he!
God blest is he!'

"C'est Osala que j'aime!
Dieu, soyez son appui,
Et répandez sur lui
Votre bonté suprême!
Et Dieu me dit:
'Fille d'Angole,
Le beau créole,
Ta chère idole,
Je l'ai béni!
Je l'ai béni!'"

Mila laisse dormir les herbes sous sa houe,
Et sur elle se penche et rêve doucement,
Et regarde le vent qui joue
Avec la canne au loin, comme eût fait un amant.

Oh! que de fois, Mila, la colombe plaintive
Enivre de ses chants la vallée attentive,
Quand l'écho trop ingrat à ses accents d'amour
La trahit, la découvre aux griffes du vautour.

II
Mila, c'est une esclave, et la naïve angole
Appelle Elbreuil "mon maître." Ainsi qu'une créole
Elle est belle, Mila! c'est la fleur du jardin.
Oh! qui pour la cueillir ne tendrait pas la main!
Sa beauté, doux rayon, flamme divine et pure,
N'attend pas pour briller l'éclat de la parure:
C'est l'étoile des nuits aux feux plus scintillants
Lorsqu'un nuage obscur l'entoure de ses flancs.

Lorsque Mila chantait sa chanson ingénue,
Elbreuil n'était pas loin; et, ravi, l'âme émue,
Le colon écoutait: la brise lui porta
Les paroles d'amour et le nom d'Osala.

"Osala is my love!
Pray, God, make his heart glad,
And shower from above
Blessings, a myriad!
        Said God: 'Mark well,
        Angola belle:
        Your Creole lad—
        Your deity!—
        Is blest by me!
        Is blest by me!'"

Mila lets sleep the grass beneath her scythe,[5]
Leaning upon its shaft in musing fashion,
    Watching the breeze play with the lithe
Stalks of cane, yonder, with a lover's passion.

How often, Mila, has the plaintive dove
Betrayed herself with cooed echoes of love,
The victim of the valley's bliss, because
She fell, discovered, to the vulture's claws!

II
Mila... A slave-girl, she. Angola belle,
Childlike, fair as a Creole demoiselle,
She calls Elbreuil "my master"! Who would be
Loath to reach out his hand and pluck her free,
That garden flower! Sweet flame, pure, divine,
That needs no jewel, no gem, to make it shine:
Star in the black skies glimmering, despite
The cloud's flanks shrouding round in dark of night.

As Mila sang her simple, artless air,
Elbreuil, close by, knew bliss beyond compare.
The settler listened: on the breeze there came
Sweet words of love... but with Osala's name.

Retenant ce nom, il s'avance.
Il la voit sous un ciel brûlant,
Travaillant avec patience.
D'abord son langage est d'un blanc:
C'est une pitié qui vers elle
Le conduit.—Puis changeant de ton,
Il lui dit qu'elle est la plus belle
De toute l'habitation!

Elle est la fleur de la colline!
L'oiseau chantant sur le palmier!
Son âme est la blanche aubépine!
Sa voix est la voix du ramier!

Mais c'est vainement qu'il la presse,
Le maître ne peut la fléchir,
Car de son cœur elle est maîtresse.
Le Colon se sentant rougir,
De fuir promptement se hâte,
Et craignant qu'à l'œil de Mila
La rougeur de son front n'éclate,
Par un sentier, non loin de là,
S'éloigne et disparaît.
                              Une noire pensée,
Maintenant qu'il est seul, de son cœur élancée,
S'imprime sur ses traits; de mille éclairs ses yeux
Scintillent et sa bouche en un sourire affreux
Se ride. Il est muet de honte et de colère.
Silencieux, il marche en regardant la terre.
On dirait le démon du séjour infernal
Rêvant profondément et ne rêvant que mal.

III

C'est la cloche argentine
Qui sonne le repos;

He hears the name, tucks it away,
Draws near and sees her patiently
Laboring in the heat of day,
Speaks, first, the white man's way. Says he,
Pity it is that brings him there...
But soon a flattering declaration
Tells her she is most passing fair
By far of the entire plantation.

She is the hillside flower! And she,
The bird singing atop the palm!
The hawthorn white her soul must be!
Her voice, the ring dove's cooing calm!

But she bends not one whit before him,
Deaf to the fawning words he speaks;
And as the more she would ignore him,
A blush will paint the master's cheeks
And brow. Whereat, fearing her eye
Might see his flushed embarrassment,
Spying a path that ran nearby,
He turned and, straightway, off he went,
Into the distance...
                Now... alone he wanders,
And as he goes a foul design he ponders.
Spawned in his heart and leaping forth, it marks
His features; from his eyes a thousand sparks
Go darting... With a lip-contorting smile—
A sneer of shame and anger—like a vile,
Fell, hell-born demon, silent, he goes dreaming,
Downcast his eyes, and naught but evil scheming.

III

        At the bell's silvered call,
        Beside the river's flood,

Tout le troupeau rumine,
Couché près des ruisseaux.
Le soleil monte et brille
Au plus haut point des cieux;
L'onde ardente scintille,
Éblouissant les yeux.
Le rossignol soupire!
À cette heure du jour,
C'est la vivante lyre
Du cœur et de l'amour.

À cette heure venez, venez aussi l'entendre,
Esclaves malheureux. Son nid est sur vos toits!
Ce chantre aimé du ciel ne sera pas moins tendre
  Si l'esclave écoute sa voix.

Osala, c'est ce beau, c'est ce jeune créole
Qui s'avance en sifflant, à travers le vallon:
Le bonheur un moment brille aux yeux de l'angole
  Et s'épanouit sur son front.

Il arrive. "Voilà," dit-il, "ma tendre amie,
Quelques fruits et des fleurs que je t'apporte, prends.
Oh! j'ai beaucoup souffert, mais ma peine est finie,
  Car je te vois et je t'entends."

Tous deux obéissant à la douce nature
Se parlèrent de l'âme à l'ombrage des bois,
Et doutèrent ensemble en leur ivresse pure
  Qu'on s'aimât comme eux autrefois.

"Ce soir, lorsque la lune au haut de la colline
Montera," disait-elle, "Osala chantera
Quelques-uns de ces airs que sur sa mandoline
  Il fit pour sa bonne Mila.

The flock rests, one and all,
Musing, chewing their cud.
The sunlight burns the sky,
Aflame; the waters run
Their course, go dazzling by,
Bright in the morning sun.
The nightingale, above,
Sighs the day's hours along!
The lyre of hearftfelt love
Comes to life in his song.[6]

Poor slaves! He rests upon your roofs! Draw near,
I pray... Give ear to his heaven-blest throat's
Delights! No less a joy is he to hear
    When mere slaves listen to his notes.

Osala is this young Creole lad who
Whistles his way across the vale... Oh, how
Happy the glance that Mila, come there too,
    Flashes brightly about her brow.

 "Ah! There she stands," says he, "my gentle love!
Here! Take these fruits and flowers... Let me rejoice
In my heart's passion! Gone the pain thereof,
    For you I see, and hear your voice."

In the wood's shade they share their souls' sweet troth,
Each with the other, and—quick to obey
Nature's tender demands therefor—as loath
    To think one ever loved as they.

"Tonight, when climbs the moon in opaline
Path up the hill, Osala will be there,
Singing and strumming on his mandolin
    Airs meant for me, his Mila fair.[7]

"Et moi je te dirai quelque histoire natale
Comment on sait dompter le lion le plus fier,
Et puis je dépeindrai la brise si fatale
        Aux habitants du Grand-Désert.

"Doux pays de l'Afrique, oh! que je t'aime encore!
Pour le tigre et le blanc, Dieu fit un même cœur!
Plus je vis avec eux et plus je les abhorre!
        Pour eux l'or, pour nous la douleur!"

Osala répondit: "Mila, pourquoi ces larmes?
Au lieu de tant gémir, adorons-nous plutôt!
Tous mes chagrins s'en vont, quand j'admire tes charmes,
        Garde tes pleurs pour mon tombeau!"

Il dit, et l'embrassa timide et palpitante!
La vie est le Sarah, l'amour, c'est l'oasis
Où l'on voit à l'abri de l'arène inconstante,
        Flotter le duvet des épis.

IV
Deux heures ont sonné, l'esclave aux champs revole!
        Non, il n'a point d'ailes, le temps,
        Lorsqu'il sépare deux amants!
        Quand viendra le soir qui console?

C'est mourir que d'attendre! oh! quand viendra le soir
        Où tous deux ensemble au manoir
Ils pourront se bercer d'une douce parole?
Où Mila contera quelque histoire d'Angole,
Où le tendre Osala, de son naïf accent,
        Et des sons de sa mandoline,
Montera saluer au haut de la colline
La lune chère aux monts, leur couronne d'argent!

"And I shall tell you tales brought from my land,
Of how the haughtiest lion is laid low,
And how, in the Great Desert, gusts of sand
    Deal death about as tempests blow.

"I love you, Africa, just as before!
God gave the whites a tiger's heart! In vain
I live with them, yet still loathe them the more!
    For them, their gold; for us, our pain!"

Answered Osala: "Mila, why those tears?
Come, let us love, rather than drone our doom!
Before your charm, all my grief disappears.
    Pray save your weeping for my tomb!"

He kissed the trembling maid, shy as you please:
Life—the Sahara;[8] love—oasis spring,
Where shielded from the shifting sands, one sees
    Grains, soft as down, go fluttering...

IV
Two o'clock tolls. The slave girl flies, returning
    To the fields! Flies? No, time has no
    Wings when it treats true lovers so!
    When will night come to calm their yearning?

The waiting is like death! Oh, when will night
    Come to the manse, wherein they might
Speak soft, sweet words to cradle them therein?
When Mila will recount tales that had been
Brought from Angola; and with childlike sound,
    Plucking the strings, Osala will
Go climbing high, to hail upon the hill
The moon, dear to the summit, silver-crowned!

Que béni soit le ciel! et toi, Mila, respire.
Regarde le soleil derrière les dattiers
Qui s'en va dans la mer. La pauvrette! un sourire
A couru sur sa bouche, et les rayons derniers
De l'astre dont le disque à l'océan se noie
Quoique tièdes, chez elle ont allumé la joie.

V

      Hélas! on voit du haut du ciel
Briller des astres d'or la lumière lointaine!
     Hélas! déjà la nuit est dans la plaine!
Et d'où vient qu'Osala, sous le toit paternel,
Se fasse désirer. Pauvre Mila! son âme,
Qui ce matin encore était toute gaîté,
      Par mille chimères de femme
Augmente les douleurs de son sein agité:
"Marie a les yeux noirs, Marie a les dents blanches,
    Et le serin qui chante entre les branches
Chante encore moins bien qu'elle; et le jeune roseau
Qui plie au gré des vents sa taille obéissante
      La balance moins élégante
      Qu'elle en marchant, son corps si beau!
Et les hommes! comment à leur vaine parole
      Se fier un moment?
Les filles à leur cœur sont ce qu'est une yole
Aux flots qu'elle ne peut qu'effleurer seulement!"

Vous diriez à la voir toute pâle et songeuse,
S'éloignant de ses sœurs qui l'entendaient gémir,
Vous diriez que Mila, naguère calme, heureuse,
     Pressentait un sombre avenir!

VI

Oh! laissez-la pleurer! Lui que sur cette terre
Elle aime plus qu'on aime une sœur ou son frère,
     Osala, son amour,

Blest be the sky! And you, Mila, breathe deep.
Mark well the sun behind the date trees, sinking
Into the sea. Poor child! A smile will keep
Playing upon her lips, as the last-blinking
Rays from the disk, dipping into the bowl,
Cooling now, light joy's fires within her soul.

V

    Alas! One sees high in the sky
The distant stars shine in their glittering gold!
    Alas! The shades of night enfold
The plain, whereat Osala, by the by,
Dwells in his father's house. Much yearned for, he
Casts in poor Mila's breast much misery!
    Her soul, so gay this morning, now
Prey to a thousand female jealousies,
Torments her suffering bosom: "Ah! I vow,
No teeth as white, no eyes as black!... Marie's
Are whiter, blacker... And the little bird
Chirps tunes that are, by far, less gladly heard
Than hers! And the young reed that lithely sways
Before the breeze, and every gust obeys,
    Has not her grace, so lissome she!
Ah, men! How can we trust their word? For we
Are as the bark is to the wave: we only
Graze it, then sail our way, alone and lonely!"[9]

One would say, as her sisters saw her pale,
Faraway look, quitting their side... Yes, one
Would say Mila mourned her life, now undone—
    A life of cheerless, dark travail.

VI

Oh! Let her weep! The one she loves above
All else, more than one loves one's family,
    Osala, her dear love,

Il languit maintenant bien loin; sa longue chaîne,
Car Elbreuil l'a voulu, sillonne une autre plaine
Où courbé sur le sol, jamais il n'entendra
Les jardins retentir du nom de sa Mila!

Et Mila fut jadis la couronne d'Angole!
Aujourd'hui voyez-la! rêveuse et triste folle,
        Partout elle porte ses pas,
Sans cesse commençant une chanson créole
            Qu'elle n'achève pas!

Oh! c'est pitié de voir une amante en délire!
Compagnes de Mila, cachez-lui donc vos pleurs!
Mère, et vous son vieux père, et vous, ses tendres sœurs,
Couvrez d'un voile épais le mal qui vous déchire!

Elbreuil, vois ta victime! Une main sur le cœur,
Ses beaux yeux noirs levés vers le ciel, elle est morte,
Oui, morte avant le temps, et morte de douleur!
        Et voici qu'on l'emporte
        Sans bruit, sans une fleur.
Sa famille, un vieux prêtre accompagnent sa bière
            Au prochain cimetière;
        Et dans la fosse le cercueil
        Est bientôt couvert par la terre.
Puis pour elle chacun a dit une prière
Tout haut, en maudissant tout bas le nom d'Elbreuil.

1835

Languishes now afar. For Elbreuil, he
Has had him sent, in chains, mercilessly,
To plow in distant fields, there to remain,
Bent low, nor hear his Mila's name again![10]

Mila! She who was once Angola's pride!
Look at her now! Despondent, flown her wit,
    She wanders here and there, wild-eyed,
Would sing a Creole air, but soon must quit,
        Too mad to finish it!

How pitiful to see a maid so true
Witless with love! O friends of Mila, pray
Hide your sad tears! Old parents, sisters, may
Thick veils conceal the anguish racking you!

Elbreuil, look at her! Hand upon her breast,
Her beautiful black eyes heavenward turned,
Lifeless she lies, in death untimely earned,
    Your victim, much the mournfulest!
    Flowerless, noiselessly they bear
Her off—her kin, an old curé—to where
        The churchyard stands. And they
    Cast earth upon her coffin, say
A prayer aloud to honor her in death—
And curse Elbreuil the while, under their breath...

1835

C'est là qu'il est tombé (Le Pont rouge)

I

C'est là qu'il est tombé dans toute sa puissance
Celui dont le bras fort conquit l'Indépendance!
Que lui faisaient à lui sa gloire et son grand nom?
Sous son pied d'Empereur il foula cette gloire,
Et du sang fraternel il a tâché l'histoire
    De notre révolution!

Pourtant il était beau quand, tirant nu son glaive,
Il s'écria: "ton jour, ô liberté, se lève!"
Cri de lion qui fit tressaillir les déserts!
Cri sublime! Et soudain de vils troupeaux d'esclaves
Deviennent des guerriers qui brisent leurs entraves
    En s'armant de leurs propres fers!

II

    Le Blanc disait: "Toussaint expire,
    L'aigle est tombé dans nos filets!
    Rage impuissante! Vain délire!
    Ils redeviendront nos sujets!
    Et nous rirons de leur défaite,
    De leur orgueil, de leur espoir!
    La liberté n'était point faite
    Pour l'homme qui porte un front noir."

III

Dessalines apparut superbe, grand, immense!
Lui-même les pendit à l'ignoble potence,
Qu'élevèrent pour nous leurs criminelles mains!
C'était pitié de voir la terreur de leurs âmes!
Pâles, on les prenait sous des habits de femmes,
Et leurs têtes tombaient à paver les chemins!

CORIOLAN ARDOUIN

There did he fall (The Pont-Rouge)[1]

I

There did he fall in all his power, he
Whose mighty, conquering arm had set us free!
But what cared he for his great name, his story!
Beneath his Emperor's heel,[2] he crushed its fame
And with his brothers' blood covered with shame
        Our revolution and its glory![3]

Yet how comely he was when, blade raised bare,
He cried: "O liberty, your dawn shines fair!"[4]
A lion's cry, that shook the deserts round them!
Cry sublime! And at once slaves' ragged bands
Turn warriors, freed; and now their smashing hands
        Brandish the chains that once had bound them!

II

        The white man said, "Toussaint lies dying!
        Mad is their fury!... Futile!... Vain!...
        The eagle in our net came flying!
        Soon will they be our slaves again!
        And laugh we shall at their defeat,
        Their hopes, their arrogance! I vow,
        Freedom was not meant to be meet
        For man who bears a black-skinned brow!"[5]

III

Then Dessalines, superb, appeared, stood tall!
He hanged them from the gibbets, one and all,
That their crime-sullied hands had raised for us![6]
How pitiful their anguished souls, each one!
Hiding in women's garments—pale, undone—
Their heads, like paving-stones, fell copious!

Oh! s'il voulut détruire après son propre ouvrage,
Si contre des écueils sa barque fit naufrage
Et qu'il s'ensevelit sous un triste linceul,
C'est qu'il faut que d'un ciel la clarté se ternisse,
Que le flot se mêlant au sable se brunisse,
C'est que la pure gloire appartient à Dieu seul.

1835

Oh! If he let his work thus come to grief,
If his bark smashed against the rock-bound reef,
And if he, in a woeful shroud has lain,
Remember that sky's brightness must die down,
That waters clear cloud to a brackish brown,
That glory pure is none but God's domain.[7]

1835

Dessalines!... À ce nom, amis, découvrons-nous!

Dessalines!... À ce nom, amis, découvrons-nous!
Je me sens le cœur battre à fléchir les genoux
Et jaillir à ce nom un sang chaud dans mes veines.
Demain, quand le soleil reluira sur nos plaines,
Quand son disque demain ira de ses rayons
Réveiller l'harmonie et l'encens de nos monts,
Qu'au bruit de la fanfare et de l'artillerie
Le peuple saluera le jour de la Patrie,
Suspendez vos plaisirs, recueillez votre cœur,
Songez à nos héros, songez à l'Empereur!

Quand cet aigle africain parut sur nos campagnes
On dit avoir senti tressaillir les montagnes,
Vu ployer leurs sommets comme un noble coursier
Qui fléchit et reçoit son royal écuyer,
Et tout à coup le sol osciller sous les maîtres,
Les repoussant partout comme ennemis et traîtres.
À voir l'aigle promis que longtemps il rêva,
D'un seul cri, d'un seul bond l'esclave se leva,
Et, surprenant l'impie au milieu de ses fêtes,
Rompit son joug de fer contre ses mille têtes.

Et ce peuple nouveau qui d'esclaves naquit,
Fier des libertés que sa force conquit,
Dédaigne de s'asseoir autour des mêmes tables
Pleines encore de vins et de mets délectables,
Cette orgie insultait à ses mille douleurs;
Le vin était son sang et le pain ses sueurs.
—"Purifions le sol des péchés de l'impie,"
Dit le peuple, et la torche alluma l'incendie,

IGNACE NAU

Dessalines!... At that name, doff hats, my friends![1]

Dessalines!... At that name, doff hats, my friends![2]
My heart pounds in my bosom, my knee bends,
And I feel, coursing hot within my veins,
My very blood. Tomorrow, on our plains,
When the sun's disc, with darting brilliancies,
Wakens our mountain-incense harmonies;
When we, to trumpet's patriotic blare
And proud artillery's loud boom, prepare
To fete this day,[3] pray turn your heart and mind
To Dessalines, and heroes all, enshrined!

African eagle![4] When, fierce-spirited,
He first appeared, the mountains, it is said,
Would quail and quake; and lofty summits bent
Their heads to earth, like mounted steer, intent
On shaking off vile masters, cast aground
By flouting cavalier routing them round.
When slave perceived the eagle—promised bird
Long dreamt—he fell a-howl and undeterred
Upon the blithely feasting foe, and broke
Against a thousand heads the iron yoke.

Whence this new people, born of slaves, and proud
Of its fresh-conquered liberties, unbowed,
Disdains the felons' tables still replete
With delicacies, wines. Nor will it eat
The orgy relics of its slavedom's pains:
Wine is its blood; and bread, sweat's cruel remains!
"Come," cry the people, torch divine held high.
"Let us the sinners' land now purify!"[5]

Et Jean-Jacques, semblable à quelque esprit de Dieu,
Dicta l'indépendance à la lueur du feu!...

Écoutez... le canon! La montagne en tressaille
Comme autrefois de joie au son de la bataille!
—Oh! demain le soleil se lèvera plus pur
Et plus majestueux dans sa courbe d'azur!
L'oiseau nous chantera des chants d'amour encore,
La voix de nos forêts redeviendra sonore,
Et nos fleuves taris jailliront en torrents,
Et nos lacs rouleront des flots plus transparents,
Et toi, peuple héroïque, et toi, mon beau génie,
Demain vous saluerez une ère d'harmonie!...

1839

Fire spread, as Jean-Jacques, speaking in God's name,
Forged independence, lit by freedom's flame![6]

Listen! The cannon!... Hear the mountains shake,
As before, joyful in the battle's wake.
Unblemished, lo! tomorrow's sun shall rise
In its majestic sweep through azure skies![7]
The birds once more shall sing of love; the trees
Shall fill our forests with deep harmonies.
Our arid riverbeds shall gush and pour;
Our lakes shall, crystalline, shine shore to shore.
And you, heroic folk, and you, my pen,
Shall hail an era, blessèd once again!...

1839

Qu'ils sont délicieux tes jours de liberté!
(Au Génie de la patrie)

Qu'ils sont délicieux tes jours de liberté!
Comme il est pur ton ciel, firmament enchanté
Où le plus beau soleil du haut de sa coupole
Couronne nos cités d'une ardente auréole
Et promet l'abondance et la paix à nos champs!
Merci! femme aux yeux noirs, toi, l'objet de mes chants,
Merci, pour ces bienfaits!—cher et mâle Génie
Dont le sein allaita ces fils de la Patrie
Héros aux bras de fer dont jamais les grands cœurs
N'ont tressailli de crainte aux canons destructeurs.

C'est à toi maintenant que s'attache ma Muse,
Elle que la douleur aujourd'hui désabuse!
Ma pensée erre en vain de désir en désir,
Mon cœur n'a plus de cœur où trouver un soupir;
J'ai des rêves brûlants, des songes où mon âme
Doute presque du ciel à cause de la femme.
Ah! j'ai souffert assez; j'ai le cœur labouré
Et j'ai le front meurtri comme ton sein sacré
Lorsque tes fils, luttant contre la tyrannie.
Tombaient en te nommant dans leur triste agonie.

Oh! oui; j'ai bien souffert de la femme que Dieu
Créa pour nous aimer toujours en ce bas lieu!
La femme! hélas!—vois-tu l'oiseau dans ses caprices
Qui chante et va chercher de nouvelles délices
En ses migrations de climats en climats,
Oubliant les gazons qu'hier encore ses pas
Ont foulés, l'atmosphère où ses ailes soyeuses
Ont dans ses jeux tracé des spirales joyeuses?

IGNACE NAU

Oh, the delight of your days freedom-spent!
(To the Spirit of the Fatherland)[1]

Oh, the delight of your days freedom-spent!
How pure your sky, your charm-wrought firmament,
Where, high in zenith-cupola, sun rings
Haloes about our towns; where my verse sings
Your beauty, black-eyed mistress mine! As you,
Spirit[2] of peace-borne crops' abundance, who
Suckled—for all your manly grace!—those bold
Fatherland stalwarts,[3] brash heroes of old,
Whose hearts held fast, unflinching, as the air
Bellowed before the cannons' blast and blare...

Today, Spirit, you seize upon my Muse's
Soul, she whom grief lays bare and disabuses!
In vain my thoughts go wandering through desires'
Domain—fro, to... No more the heartfelt fires
Of woe churn sighs that burn the air! Now I
Dream dreams of flame, and I would fain decry
Heaven itself because of Woman! Yes,
Heart raked, brow racked, as in your sons' duress,
They scarred your breast when, dying valiantly,
They called your name: foe of fell tyranny!

Alas! It is for Woman that I know
Heart's pain; she whom God fashioned here below
To love us! Woman... Yes... Look! See the bird,
Chirping, flitting capricious, undeterred
From bough to bough, from joy to joy, forever
Seeking new, still untried delights, and never
Content with yesterday's fair grasslands, where
Her silken wings, swirling her here and there,

C'est ainsi qu'elle fuit en vous laissant le cœur
Vide d'affections, incrédule au bonheur.

Et c'est le doute alors qui vient poser son prisme
Entre le monde et vous; et puis le Fatalisme
Vous berce entre le ciel et l'aveugle Destin,
Il ébranle le cœur et quand la foi s'éteint...
Oh! quelle perspective! où donc est l'espérance?
Cependant, à travers tant d'écueils, de souffrance,
Malheur, cent fois malheur à qui doute de Dieu!
Mes rêves, mes pensées, sont des charbons de feu,
Mon front bout sous leur flamme... oh! hâte-toi Génie;
Oh! viens sauver mon cœur de l'athéisme impie!

Non! j'en jure par toi, d'angoisse et de douleurs
Tu n'accables jamais, tes chauds adorateurs!
Non! non!—et si contr'eux il surgit dans la vie
Quelques hommes méchants, aimant la calomnie,
Envieux de la gloire et du bonheur d'autrui,
Fatigués de croupir dans un monde sans bruit,
Et dont la haine enfin, par la critique infâme,
En ternissant leurs jours les blesse et les diffame,
Quand leurs yeux sont fermés dans la nuit du tombeau,
Alors toi seul, Génie, allumant ton flambeau,

Et voilant ton front triste, et l'âme désolée,
Tu viens t'agenouiller seul à leur mausolée!
Sur tes lèvres leurs noms n'ont plus rien de mortel
Et leur cher souvenir, ainsi qu'un arc-en-ciel,
Brille au fond de ton cœur, et tu transmets leur gloire
Et, leurs humbles vertus au creuset de l'histoire.
Puis, un jour la Patrie, oubliant leurs malheurs,
Éternise leurs noms, environne d'honneurs

Bore her off!... So, too, are you—loveless—left
Heart-sore, evermore happiness-bereft!

Whereupon Doubt, with his dour cynicism.
Places his lens before you... Fatalism
Cradles you, lulls you 'twixt blind Destiny
And heaven's design... Faith yields to blasphemy
As heart's strength fades. Where now is hope? Gone? Fled?
And yet, from reef to reef, squall-buffeted,
Woe unto you a hundredfold if you
Doubt in God's grace! My flaming dreams sear through
My thought, my brow boils hot!... Come, Spirit! Bless
My heart! Make haste! Save it from godlessness!

No! I swear by your name that never would
You flout your worshipers with victimhood.
No, no!... And should they feel the wrath of some
Vile souls who seek to heap opprobrium
Upon their heads—men ignominious,
Jealous of others' glory, envious
Of others' joy, who crawl through muck, intent
On soiling them with tongues malevolent—
Then for the sightless victims of death's gloom,
You, Spirit, kneel alone and grace their tomb,

Lighting your torch! Your sad brow veiled, your breath
Mutters their names, now mute no more in death,
And their dear memory—like a rainbow spread
Over the breadth of heaven, vast overhead—
Flares in your heart's deepmost recess, and you
Pour into history's eternal brew
Their glory and their humble virtues. Then,
The Fatherland, one day, surrounds these men

Le seul asile enfin où leur triste poussière
A trouvé la justice et la paix sur la terre.

Réveille-toi, Génie, et ranime les cœurs
De tes jeunes enfants croupis dans les langueurs
D'un coupable repos où la honte et le vice,
Où la mollesse, hélas! font naître l'injustice
Et germer dans leur sein la vile lâcheté,
La triste ingratitude au regard déhonté!
Étouffe dans leurs cœurs l'orgueil et l'égoïsme,
Ramène leurs pensers au saint patriotisme,
Pour qu'aux jours de danger surgis à l'horizon
La nation s'ébranle et marche à l'unisson!

Et toi, le cœur rempli d'extases et de joie,
Tu guideras leurs pas dans cette immense voie
Où l'humanité marche et poursuit son destin
Jusqu'à cet horizon dont Dieu seul est la fin.
Et puis tu verseras dans le sein de nos femmes
La constance et l'amour, céleste encens des âmes,
Surtout le souvenir trop sacré des bienfaits...
Ô songes! ô désirs d'union et de paix!
N'est-il pas temps d'éclore? et jusqu'à quand, Génie,
Réaliseras-tu ces rêves d'harmonie?

Voici.—Moi, j'eus hier de douces visions
Où mon cœur un instant bercé d'illusions,
Pressentit les beaux jours promis à ma Patrie.
—Entouré dans le ciel d'une foule chérie
De héros, compagnons de ses premiers combats,
Intrépides martyrs, attachés à ses pas,
De son mol édredon d'azur et de nuage
Pétion, arrêtant ses regards sur la plage
Où son peuple vainqueur erre libre aujourd'hui
Et projette bien loin son éclat et son bruit,

With honor, and, forgetting cares, woes past,
Bestows just peace unto their dust at last.

Awake, Spirit! Renew the hearts of those,
Your children, languishing in guilt's repose,
Nourished by vice, and shame, and idleness,
That spawn injustice and—alas! no less—
Cowardice in their breasts, and strip their glance
Of its once grateful homeland radiance!
Stifle hearts' haughty selfishness; restore
Feelings of sacred Fatherland once more,
So that, when danger looms, each mother's son,
Stirring awake, may march in unison![4]

And you, heart filled with thrill-borne ecstasy,
Shall guide their steps through the immensity
Where marches humankind unto its fated
Goal: the horizon God alone created.
There shall you pour into fair Woman's breast
A loving constancy—soul incense-blest—
And make our dreams forever mindful of
God's boons: our dreams of union, peace, and love.
Is it not time, Spirit, to favor us
With unity, long-dreamt, harmonious?

Lo! Hear my vision!... Yesterday, I seemed
To see in dream my Fatherland redeemed,
As had been promised, and it cradled me
In sweet illusion... Midst a panoply
Of heroes, martyrs, faithful to his cause,
There, in clouds' azured eiderdown, there, was
Pétion aloft, gaze cast upon the beach,
Where, free, his conquering people, each with each,
Roams today in its new-won liberty
Heralding loud its brilliant destiny;

Dit:—"Bénis soient mes fils et toi, leur terre sainte
Que mes pas ont foulée, où j'ai bu mon absinthe,
Où j'ai laissé ma gloire et mon nom immortel
Et bâti seul une aire à mon peuple éternel.
Ma couvée est éclose aujourd'hui pour ma gloire!
Oh! mon Dieu, soutenez dans l'air son aile noire
Trop faible maintenant pour franchir d'un essor
Et d'un vol assuré l'espace que le sort
A mis entr'elle, hélas! et ces peuples du monde
Resplendissants d'éclat et de gloire profonde.

  "Prends ton casque, ô Génie, où flotte un noir cimier
Plus noble que la flèche au front de mon Palmier,
Va t'asseoir sur les pics de nos vertes montagnes,
Et, de tes regards d'aigle embrassant nos campagnes
Et l'immense archipel, du haut de tes gradins
Veillent sur nos enfants et leurs jeunes destins;
Que ton front couronné des foudres de l'orage,
Superbe et menaçant, éloigne du rivage
Où dorment nos cités la guerre et le fléau,
Et laisse croître en paix le peuple en son berceau."

Je le vis ceindre alors ton front d'une auréole
Et ses mains rattacher en plis sur ton épaule,
L'étendard rouge et bleu qu'il suivait aux combats:
Je vis s'agenouiller à tes pieds ses soldats,
Et, tes puissantes mains sur leurs fronts imposées,
Comme aux champs on voit l'aube épandre ses rosées;
Sur ces jeunes martyrs des révolutions
Tes lèvres murmurer des bénédictions;
Puis, d'un vol tu revins vers la terre bénie
Que ton cœur lui promit de veiller, ô Génie!

1839

And he said, "Blessèd be my sons and their
Sacred soil where my feet have trod, and where
I've drunk my absinthe-draft of glory, and
Built, alone, for my race, its deathless land
Eternal! Now my brood of hatchlings springs
To life!... God! Lift them on their weak black wings—
Too weak to bear them in their flight through space's
Realm, which fate placed between them and those races
Peopling the earth in splendor limitless,
Bespeaking haughty glorydom's noblesse!

 "O Spirit, don your black-plumed helmet, yet
Nobler than Palm-tree's dart-shaft coronet.
Go sit atop our mountains green... View wide
The scene spread vast below you, eagle-eyed,
And the great archipelago... From your
Perch, guard our children, keep them safe, secure.
Chase off, from our shores' cities, slumbering,
War's curse... With storm-fierce brow—proud, menacing—
Let pestilence and woe forever cease,
And let our people, cradled, grow in peace."

I saw him wreathe a halo round your head,
And his hands drape the standard, blue and red,
That he followed in battle, loosely bound
About you.[5] And I saw kneel to the ground
His faithful soldiers, at your feet, as you
Laid on their brows your mighty hands, like dew
On dawning fields. And, Spirit, I could hear,
Muted, your blessings on each cavalier—
Young, martyred—as you flew to earth and swore
To guard his sacred homeland evermore...

1839

ANONYMOUS

Mon père, j'aime à voir ces champs et leurs coteaux

Le Fils

Mon père, j'aime à voir ces champs et leurs coteaux
S'ondoyer à nos pieds et confondre leurs flots
Aux flots lointains des mers: le soleil qui se voile,
Au couchant, tel qu'un peintre incliné sur sa toile,
Achève de dorer ce tableau ravissant
De fleurs et de verdure et d'ondes palissant
Sous les ciels gris du soir—Quelle étendue immense!
C'est le digne berceau de notre indépendance;
Jamais la liberté n'eut fait éclore ailleurs,
Mieux qu'en ce vaste sol son arbre aux doux couleurs!
Berce-toi sur tes flots ô mon île enchantée,
Fille de l'occident si belle et si vantée!
Laisse aux vents palpiter tes immenses forêts,
Tes montagnes coiffer de vapeurs leurs sommets,
Tes fleuves s'élancer au fond de ces montagnes
Pour aller de leurs flots inonder tes campagnes.
Ton soleil brille encore, ton cri est encore pur
Et l'espoir te sourit à travers son azur.
Oh! qui pourra compter ces moments qui vont naître
Et répandre sur toi la joie et le bien-être?
Qui pourra limiter ton progrès incessant?
Jusqu'à quand dira-t-on à ton peuple puissant:
—"Arrête! C'est ici le terme de ta gloire,
Voici le dernier jour qui clora ton histoire."
Mon père, il est des jours que Dieu garde pour nous
Où jamais le soleil n'aura brillé plus doux!
Quand l'orage soudain s'est versé sur la terre,
Quand les vents déchaînés, dans leur folle colère,
Ont effeuillé les bois et remué les eaux,

Father dear, how I love to cast my glance over these hills and fields[1]

The Son
Father dear, how I love to cast my glance
Over these hills and fields, whose broad expanse
In gentle ripples rolls; whose brooks and rills
Join in the waters' flow that floods and spills
Into the sea beyond.[2] I love to see
The setting sun, cloud-veiled, and happily
Stand, like a painter at his canvas bent,
Before his gilded scene magnificent;
Who, with his final brushstrokes sows a few
More flowers, more green; who daubs a bit of blue
Above the waves beneath his pale-gray sky
Of eventide... Art spread before my eye!
Cradle of independence! Vast! Nowhere
Did freedom's budding tree sport hues more fair!
Charmed isle! Lie lulled and rocked over the water,
You, the West's beautiful and vaunted daughter!
Let the winds stir your woodland deeps, enshroud
Your summits, hurl your torrents gushing proud
Down from the mountains! Still your cry rings true;
Still your sun burns majestically; and through
The azure, hope still smiles on you. Who can
Count all the joyous moments that will span
Your destiny? Who will dare limit your
Limitless progress, or shout: "No! No more!
Glory lasts but a day! Now is yours done!..."
No, father! God rewards us with a sun
That oft-times shines for us alone; and when
Vicious winds strip the trees, churn the seas, then

L'azur qui reparaît à travers les lambeaux
Des nuages brisés, dispersés dans l'espace,
Est bien plus pur, lavé par l'orage qui passe:
Le jour est plus limpide et le gazon plus vert,
Le roseau se relève et s'agite dans l'air.

Le Vieillard
Les Révolutions, surtout aussi sanglantes
Que celle que nos bras sur nos plages brûlantes
Ont accomplie, hélas! germent toujours mon fils,
Pour le bonheur futur du peuple et du pays.
Nos milliers de soldats qu'a dévorés la guerre
Certes feront éclore un jour de leur poussière
Des siècles d'avenir, de paix et de grandeur!
Conserve donc l'espoir qui brille dans ton cœur,
Car, vous tous, vous avez, enfants, une patrie;
L'on vous a fait des jours de liberté chérie,
Des jours où, rassemblés dans vos libres foyers,
Vous repassez nos temps de guerre et de dangers.
Ose-t-on aujourd'hui frapper à vos demeures
Et la verge à la main, disposant de vos heures,
Vous traiter par les champs, comme des bestiaux,
Haletant tout le jour sous de rudes travaux?
L'Empire est effacé, de même le Royaume,
La République est seule à côté d'un seul homme!
Quiconque, mon enfant, parce qu'un jour ou deux
Le ciel est incertain et le temps hasardeux,
S'afflige dans son cœur, tremble et se désespère,
Doit être rejeté quand la chose est prospère.
Viens: laissons le soleil s'en aller sous les eaux;
Laissons la nuit en paix rallumer ses flambeaux;
Assis tous deux aux pieds de ces tombes chéries
Que le temps cache aux yeux sous les herbes fleuries,
Remontons seul à seul jusqu'au premier martyr
De notre liberté—lui qui nous fit sentir

Grow calm; when azure once again peeks out
Through ragged, jagged clouds strewn roundabout,
More pure the light cleansed by the sudden gale,
Greener the grass; and lo! the reed—slight, frail—
Once more stands tall, soft-swaying in the air.[3]

The Old Man
Know this, my son. When Revolutions flare,
Searing our beaches with the blood of war—
Like the one not long past that drenched our shore—
It is but to assure the happiness
Of those who follow us, nor more nor less.
Our myriad souls, war-swallowed—blessèd dead—
Will, at length, from their dust, sprout strength, and spread
Long centuries of grandeur and of peace.
Wherefore be stout of heart and never cease
To hope; for you, our children, now live free
In a land of our own, at liberty
To congregate and ruminate upon
War and past perils of a woebegone,
Grief-ravaged race. Would one dare now, this day,
Pound on your dwelling place, cart you away,
Switch in hand, to the fields, there to command
That, beastlike, you obey and work the land,
Panting, day-long, at toilsome labors? No!
Gone now Empire and Kingdom! Here below,
No rule but the Republic, thanks to one
Man's reign... [4] If such there be—when fair the sun,
At last—who groans despair and moans distress,
Bemused by one or two days' fickleness,
Let him begone! Rather, let us stand by
And watch our sun dip in the evening sky
Beneath the waves; let peaceful shades of night
With heavens' torches once again flare bright;
And let us sit, we two, before these tombs—

Qu'il était temps déjà de laver cette plage
Des mille iniquités de l'impie esclavage;
Oh! oui, mon fils, parlons de l'immortel Ogé
Lui que chacun de nous a mille fois vengé.
—Je ne sais quelle date il aborda la plage;
Mais débarquant tout seul un jour sur le rivage,
Il adressa, d'abord ses premiers vœux à Dieu,
Baisa le sol béni; puis, tout ardeur, tout feu,
Il s'élança soudain et laissant les campagnes
Il disparut bientôt au milieu des montagnes.
Au premier cri de guerre incessamment jeté,
Quelques cœurs, vrais soutiens de notre liberté,
Répondirent, mon fils, d'une voix solennelle.
Oh! quelle heure, quel jour de mémoire éternelle!
Et dans leur dévoûment, oubliant leur repos,
Ils fuient se ranger à l'ombre des drapeaux,
Et tous dirent: "Marchons, marchons contre les traîtres,
Qu'ils sachent aujourd'hui qu'il n'est donc plus de maîtres!"
Le sein gonflé d'orgueil, d'espérance et d'ardeur,
Ce bataillon naissant fut tout d'abord vainqueur:
Mais l'ennemi, honteux de sa prompte défaite,
Fort et grossi, revint l'artillerie en tête.
Plus aguerri que nous et surtout plus nombreux.
Il écrasa bientôt nos hommes courageux,
Mais dépourvus de tout, hors la seule espérance
Qu'il approcha enfin le jour de délivrance!
Peu, suivis de leur chef, gagnèrent les ravins
Et purent s'échapper chez leurs humbles voisins.
Mais tout à coup saisis par un ordre suprême
En secret émané du Gouverneur lui-même,

Sacred and dear—that time, with grave-strewn blooms,
Conceals from sight. Here let us venture through
Our past, returning to that martyr who—
The first—declared that it was meet for us
To purge these shores of the iniquitous
Myriad ills of slavery!... Ogé[5]
His name, hero immortal, who that day—
I know not when—set foot upon our shore,
To be avenged a thousand times and more!
Offering his first prayers to God, he bent
Low, kissed the hallowed ground; then—vehement,
Enflamed—went mountainside and disappeared...
As shouts of war broke forth, there volunteered
Many stout hearts, my son, who solemnly
Responded: bastions of our liberty!
Oh, that day! Oh, that hour! Engraved within
Eternal memory! Brave souls begin
Our march against the foe, all banners flying,
Summoning them to war. And they, replying,
"Come, let us march against the traitorous band!
Show them that now no masters rule this land!"
Breasts puffed out, proud, hope-fired, the troop, a-strut,
Cuts down the shamefaced foeman, routed... But
The latter swells his ranks, returns, behind
Artillery in battle stance aligned.
More numerous they than we, more war-inured,
His victory was easily assured;
For naught had we, indeed, save for the mere
Hope that in time were we to persevere,
Deliverance was ours! Defeated then,
The chieftain and a handful of his men
Take flight through many a mountain-pass ravine,
Beyond the border, and, betwixt between,
Find refuge with their humble neighbors;[6] whence
The Governor himself[7]—His Eminence!—

Ils furent poursuivis, jugés et condamnés,
Et livrés aux colons, avilis, enchaînés...
Infortunés! mon Dieu! leur courage sublime
Avait anticipé sur le jour où le crime
De l'esclavage impur dût être enfin puni,
Où le maître, à son tour, traqué partout, honni,
Dût se sentir frappé de peur et d'anathème!...

Le Fils

Oh! mon Dieu, pourquoi donc, votre bonté suprême
Avait-elle permis que ces infortunés
Dans leur noble début fussent abandonnés,
Jetés à la merci des maîtres intraitables?
Eh! dans vos jugements, décrets impénétrables,
Seigneur, que vouliez-vous?

Le Vieillard

                                        Il voulait que le sang
De ces premiers martyrs arrosât, mon enfant,
Ce sol prodigieux, et qu'aussi leurs souffrances
Fîssent dans tous les cœurs germer des espérances
Où l'esclave énervé pût toujours retremper
Son courage affaibli, pour surprendre et frapper
L'impie insoucieux qui, dans ses jouissances,
Méprisait l'humble serf, oubliant ses souffrances.
L'on brisa sur la roue, hélas! le grand Ogé,
Dont le seul crime était d'avoir donc outragé
Les blancs en demandant l'ÉGALITÉ de l'homme,
La LIBERTÉ pour tous.—C'était là le fantôme
Qui se dressait sans cesse aux yeux de nos tyrans,
Qui troublait leurs plaisirs, leurs songes enivrants,
Et glaçait tout le sang qui coulait dans leurs veines.
Dès ce jour, quand l'esclave, accablé sous ses peines,
Béchait le sol, on dit qu'il s'arrêtait parfois

Orders that they be seized and judged, and sent
Back, in chains, to their masters' punishment.
Dear God! The wretches thought the day had come
To pay for slavedom's wrenching martyrdom;
When masters might be tracked and—roles reversed!—
Live in the throes of horror, terror-cursed!...

The Son
Good God! How can it be that such as you,
A being of kindness infinite, should do
Nothing to save these sorry souls, undone,
Bowed to their evil masters' will, each one?
What was the sense of our heartless decrees,
O Lord?

The Old Man
                The sense, my son? It was that these
First martyrs' blood enrich our blessèd land;
That every heart that bore the impious brand
Of slavery's dark sin might see the bright
New bloom of hope, and that each victim might
Renew his flagging breath, and find the strength
Therein to wreak a just revenge!... At length,
The great Ogé dies, broken, on the rack;
His one and only crime—alas, alack!—
A crime passing appalling (or so thought,
Indeed, the outraged white!) was that he sought
EQUALITY and LIBERTY for all!
Liberty! Ever-present phantom-pall
Outspread before our tyrants' eyes, confuting
Pleasures and joys, dulling desires, and muting
Passionate dreams, as blood froze in their veins.
From that day forth, when, bent beneath his pains,
His chains, the slave—hoeing the land—would seem

Et semblait écouter comme un son, une voix,
Comme un vague soupir, une plainte jetée
Jusqu'à lui, pauvre serf! par la terre agitée,
L'esclave se troublait. Revenu des travaux,
Seul assis dans sa case, en rêvant à ses maux,
Il songeait aux soupirs échappés de la terre.
—"O mon cœur, disait-il, il est dans ce mystère
Quelque chose de Dieu! prions, mais attendons...
Bientôt l'heure du ciel surprendra les colons!"
Il priait, il fumait pour alléger ses peines,
Pour oublier une heure et le poids de ses chaînes
Et l'amer souvenir des maux du lendemain.
Dieu venait d'arracher de sa puissante main
La page où, jour par jour étaient gravés les crimes
Des maîtres insolents, le nombre des victimes
Dont sans cesse le sang, remonté vers le ciel,
Aux pieds de Christ brûlait en encens éternel.
Le rayon, l'air, le son, tout, tout dans la nature
Rapportait jusqu'à lui, soit quelque forfaiture,
Soit le dernier soupir d'esclaves assommés.
Tous les crimes enfin étaient pleins, consommés!
Et le grand jour promis où l'esclave intrépide
Devait rompre ses fers, marchant d'un pas rapide.
Les montagnes partout exhalaient de leur sein
Des soupirs inconnus et tressaillaient soudain.
Sous les pieds des colons les champs tenaient à peine;
Une agitation dans l'air, vague, incertaine
Annonçait au pays quelque renversement
Dont l'instant approchait, terrible, incessamment...
L'horizon rougissait sous le vif incendie,
Les pics s'illuminaient et leur crête rougie
Reflétait sur les champs une sombre lueur
Dont le livide éclat saisissait de terreur
L'infortuné colon qui, malgré sa détresse,
Osait encore lui-même enfouir sa richesse.

To pause a moment, stand, as in a dream,
Listening to the troubled earth heave low,
Soft moans, meant for his ears; whence he would grow
Troubled as well! Then, when day's toils were through,
Alone in his hut he would muse anew
On earth's mysterious sounds. "Ah me, how odd,
Those voices! Doubtless they must come from God!
Thus shall I pray. And wait. For soon disaster
Fell must, most surely, fall upon the master!"
So pray he did. And with a pipeful, he
Would smoke and put aside the savagery
And wretchedness the morrow's dawn would bring...
God, with his hand, mighty and chastening,
Had from the book of life ripped out the page
Of masters' every sin, thus to assuage
The victims with their haughty blood, that rose,
Wafted on smoking incense, as their woes
Burned aloft to the Christ, forevermore.
Sound, air, light... Everything in nature bore
Witness to battered slaves' last-gasping sigh,
Rising, midst endless crimes, to him on high,
Yearning for promised times when, striding free,
The slave would burst the bonds of slavery!...
Suddenly, mountains shook, and everywhere,
From their deep bosoms, strange sighs rent the air.
Beneath the settlers' feet the very land
Began to crumble, and they scarce could stand
Unmoved; a sense of doom—vague but profound—
Rumbled its message to the country round:
The moment was at hand, approaching, when
Vast, boundless change would rule the fate of men...
Red, the horizon flared; the summits shone,
Flame-crested, cast a somber glare upon
The fields; and there, the settlers, pale with fright,
Dare yet amass their ill-starred wealth, despite

Ivre aux cris de la guerre et de la liberté,
L'esclave s'ébranlait de colère agité…
Ah! mon fils, laissons-là ces pages affligeantes
Où l'esclave lava ses peines outrageantes,
Sa honte et ses douleurs en des ruisseaux de sang.
Oublions sa colère et voyons-le, puissant,
Auprès de ses foyers, aussi calme à cette heure
Aussi doux et paisible assis dans sa demeure
Qu'il était intraitable en ces temps orageux
Où sa main immolait ses maîtres dédaigneux.
Les voilà, ces soldats, ces hommes intrépides
Dont le sabre brisa de maîtres trop avides
Le régime de fer, de crimes et d'orgueil.
Regarde autour de toi, jette donc un coup d'œil
Sur ces quelques vieillards, les seuls qui t'environnent;
Ils penchent vers le sol leurs têtes qui grisonnent,
Et leurs corps affaiblis demandent aujourd'hui
À leurs jeunes enfants un soutien, un appui
Pour raffermir leurs pas chancelants sur la terre
Qu'ils ont, hélas! bénie, eux, de leur sang naguère.
Ah! je vous ai perdus, chers enfants, mes soutiens,
Je vous ai vu tomber, mourir, vous mes seuls biens!…
À peine si je puis retrouver votre place
Tant de ses nœuds pressés la vigne vous enlace!
Tant les vertes saisons ont jonché votre croix
De débris amassés de feuilles et de bois.

Le Fils
Mon père, ils sont tombés et morts pour la Patrie,
Ils ont tous deux offert à l'Éternel leur vie
En offrande agréable afin qu'il pût bénir
Et le pays naissant et son grand avenir.
Lorsqu'après les combats, cette longue souffrance,
L'on vint à proclamer enfin l'Indépendance,
Mon père, oh! quel moment! Quel jour d'enivrement.

Their imminent distress. Drunk on the cries
Of war and liberty, the slaves arise...
But no, my son! Let us discuss no more
Those pages streaming with the blood, the gore
Of servitude's demise![8] Cleansed now slave's shame
And pain! Let us forget his wrath, the blame
Heaped on his master's head as, freed now, he
Dwells in a peaceful, sweet tranquillity,
Calm as was violent, then, the storm and stress
Of vengeance wreaked on slaver's wantonness...
There too, the soldiers—heroes brave and bold—
Whose sabers slashed the master's iron hold
Of arrogance and greed... See? Let your glance
Dwell on those few old men, in head-bowed stance—
Those who live yet—beneath their crowns of gray,
With bodies weak, who seek their sons today
To guide their halting, faltering footsteps, lest
They stumble on the soil their blood once blest...
Lost to me now as well, two sons! O you,
My only strength, my only bulwark, who,
Fallen in battle, leave me succorless...
Scarce can I find your resting place: vines press,
Profuse, about you; spring's thick grasses green,
Mosses and leaves, caress your cross, unseen!

The Son
They fell, my father, so that with their death
Our race might live; they gave their final breath
To the Eternal, ever-vigilant,
That he, unto our newborn nation grant
His blessing for endless prosperity.
When, battles done, after dire misery,
We proclaimed Independence, at long last,
O days of revelry! Proud, the sun cast

Que le soleil a dû lancer du firmament
Des rayons éclatants! ô! comme la nature
A dû soudainement paraître belle et pure
Et se montrer aux yeux de ce peuple vainqueur,
Nation désormais, dans toute sa splendeur!
C'est pourquoi je tressaille au grand anniversaire,
Quand j'entends le canon annoncer la lumière
De ce jour immortel où le peuple enchanté
Jura de maintenir toujours sa liberté!
Sonnez, cloches, sonnez dis-je, au haut des églises,
Pur encens des autels remontez sur les brises,
Et vous prêtres chantez nos doux remercîments;
Vous canons, prolongez vos retentissements
Mêlés au chant du cor que le peuple accompagne,
Et que vos bruits, portés de montagne en montagne,
Rappellent en ce jour au dernier habitant
Qu'il avait juré, lui, de vivre indépendant!...

1839

Brilliant rays from the heavens on high! Oh, how
Suddenly all of nature, here and now,
Seemed pure, unblemished; and our land—fresh, new—
Resplendent with our heroes' derring-do!
My father, that is why I tremble, why
I shudder at this festive hour. For I
Remember—as the cannons glorify
The dawning of that day immortal, when
Victory graced our people, free again,
Who swore, hearts high, that ever would they be
Staunch guardians of their precious liberty!
Toll, toll you steeple-bells. Toll, peel, and ring,
As in the sky the incense, billowing,
Rises up from the altars, on the breeze;
And you, O priests, chant now your litanies
Of thanks. You, cannons, thunder long and loud,
Bellowing to the notes this people proud
Sounds on the horn of victory! I pray
Your booming voice, summit to summit, may
Touch every soul, remind them that they swore
To live free and unchained forevermore!...

1839

PIERRE FAUBERT

Persécutés sur ce rivage

Persécutés sur ce rivage,
Sans pays dans le monde entier,
Nous n'avons que notre courage;
Il faut nous y réfugier!
L'heure enfin sonne où notre race
Ne doit plus vivre pour souffrir;
Au rang des peuples prenons place,
Ou sachons noblement mourir!

Partout l'homme, au nom de *Patrie,*
Sent d'orgueil tressaillir son cœur;
Partout, cette image chérie
Le console au sein du malheur;
Et nous seuls, nous, pleins d'énergie,
Un nom si beau nous fait rougir!
Ah! conquérons une patrie,
Ou sachons noblement mourir!

Oui mourons, et que l'esclavage
Ne souille plus ces lieux riants;
Ce ciel pur, cette heureuse plage
Ne sont point faits pour des tyrans:
Un jour, consacrant notre audace,
La grande voix de l'avenir
Dira: pour affranchir leur race,
Ils ont su noblement mourir.

1842

PIERRE FAUBERT

Harried, we stand upon this shore[1]

Harried, we stand upon this shore,
Country-less, over earth's breadth, length.
Courage is ours, but little more:
Be it our refuge and our strength!
At last the hour tolls when our race
Need not live but for suffering, dying:
In this world let us take our place,
Or nobly let us die for trying![2]

Man's heart, throughout the earth outspanned,
Pounds proud whenever he will hear
The cherished phrase "My Fatherland,"
Whose image calms woes bleak and blear.
We blush before its beauty's powers,
Though strong our hands, our dole defying.
Ah! Let a fatherland be ours,
Or nobly let us die for trying!

Yes, let us die lest slavery's hand
Sully yet more these smiling shores;
This pure sky and this happy strand
Shine not for tyrant conquerors!
One day a booming voice on high
Shall sing our praises, glorify
The liberators' deeds, and cry:
"Nobly they vied, and died for trying."

1842

Du Dieu des opprimés célébrons la puissance!

I

Ogé

Du Dieu des opprimés célébrons la puissance!
　　Il a comblé notre espérance:
　　Devant nos drapeaux triomphants,
　　Ils ont fui, ces lâches tyrans!
　　Du bienfait que ta voix implore,
　　Ô mon pays, voici l'aurore:
　　Oui, l'astre de la Liberté
Luira bientôt dans ton ciel enchanté!

Chœur

　　Du bienfait que ta voix implore,
　　Ô mon pays, voici l'aurore:
　　Oui, l'astre de la Liberté
Luira bientôt dans ton ciel enchanté!

II

Ogé

Vous qui traînez encore les fers de l'esclavage,
　　Pour vos maux quel heureux présage!
　　Vous le voyez, vos oppresseurs
　　Peuvent rencontrer des vainqueurs!
　　De Dieu la foudre toute prête,
　　Commence à gronder sur leur tête:
　　Oui, l'astre de la Liberté
Luira bientôt dans ton ciel enchanté!

Chœur

　　De Dieu la foudre toute prête,
　　Commence à gronder sur leur tête:
　　Oui, l'astre de la Liberté
Luira bientôt dans ton ciel enchanté!

1842

All praise his power, the God of the oppressed!¹

I

*Ogé*²

All praise his power, the God of the oppressed!
      Our hopes, our prayers are heaven-blest:
      Fled, now, the craven tyrant band
      Before our banners, thrashed, unmanned.
      O land of mine, bright dawns the morn
      Of boon long, long implored, now born:
      Yes, soon the star of Liberty
Shall light your skies' enchanted panoply!

Chorus

      O land of mine, bright dawns the morn
      Of boon long, long implored, now born:
      Yes, soon the star of Liberty
Shall light your skies' enchanted panoply!

II

Ogé

For you who bear slavery's shackles yet,³
      Welcome, this omen, and well met!
      To your oppressors, Requiem!
      Others rise here to vanquish them.
      God's thunder spreads its fear and dread,
      Ready to rumble round their head:
      Yes, soon the star of Liberty
Shall light your skies' enchanted panoply!

Chorus

      God's thunder spreads its fear and dread,
      Ready to rumble round their head:
      Yes, soon the star of Liberty
Shall light your skies' enchanted panoply!

1842

PIERRE FAUBERT

Je suis fier de le dire, ô négresse, je t'aime (La Négresse)

Je suis fier de le dire, ô négresse, je t'aime;
Et ta noire couleur me plaît; sais-tu pourquoi?
C'est que nobles vertus, chaste cœur, beauté même,
Tout ce qui charme enfin, le ciel l'a mis en toi.

Je t'étonne? Eh bien écoute, rare femme:
Qu'est-ce que la vertu, sinon le dévouement?
Et la beauté, sinon le doux reflet de l'âme
Qui radieux et pur, sous nos traits se répand?

Or, d'une absurde erreur, innocente victime,
Mire-toi dans cette onde, aux feux naissants du jour;
Et vois comme tes yeux sont beaux du don sublime,
Source de dévouement, et que l'on nomme amour!

Oui, tu sais bien aimer! Qu'importe qu'on t'abreuve
De ces chagrins amers qui sont pis que mourir?
D'un amour vrai, dis-tu, la souffrance est l'épreuve:
Épargnez-le, Seigneur, et faites-moi souffrir!

Oh! Combien tu souffris! Que je fus égoïste,
Moi blanc! Et l'on prétend que je suis plus que toi!
Mais au risque, être pur, que ton cœur s'en attriste,
Je te dirais toujours: tu vaux bien mieux que moi.

Quand la blanche Élina, que partout on admire,
Malgré tant de serments me retira sa foi;
Quand la fortune enfin cessa de me sourire
Qui donc se ressouvint d'un ingrat? Ce fut toi.

PIERRE FAUBERT

Proudly I say, "I love you," negress mine (The Negress)[1]

Proudly I say, "I love you," negress mine.
Your blackness strikes my fancy. Know you why?
Heaven endows your being with virtues fine:
Beauty, chaste heart, fair gifts to please thereby.[2]

Do I surprise you? Woman rare, give ear:
For what is virtue but a loyal creature's
Heart? What is beauty but a soul sincere,
Spreading its radiance pure beneath our features?

Come, look here on dawn-waters' flashing fire;
Gaze at yourself, innocent victim of
Errant caprice; see how your eyes conspire,
Bestowing that devotion we call "love."

Yes, skilled in love are you! What matters it
That you are steeped in mortal misery?
Suffering proves love true, not counterfeit!
Spare it, dear Lord; let me the victim be![3]

How deep your woe! And oh, how selfish I,
A white, whom they declare your better far![4]
No, hear me. Sadly though your heart deny:
You, pure soul, you, so much my better are!

When fair-skinned Elina—admired by all—
Breaking her every oath, would cruelly end
Our troth; when frowning fortune cast its pall,
Whose kindness buoyed my worthless heart? Yours, friend!

Vainement j'attendis, au jour de la détresse,
Amis que je crus vrais, amantes, même ceux
Dont j'adoucis les maux; mais alors, ô négresse,
Comme un ange gardien tu parus à mes yeux.

"Courage!" me dis-tu; "courage! voilà celle
Qui n'aima que toi seul, et qui revient t'offrir
Le tribut dédaigné d'un amour trop fidèle;
Que l'oubli soit son lot; mais cesse de souffrir!"

Adversaires, amis, vous tous que l'honneur guide,
Accueillez ce récit, car c'est la vérité;
Et que partout enfin la justice préside
Seule au destin de l'homme, avec la liberté!

1842

In my distress I waited—but in vain!—
For comrades I thought true; for lovers too,
Even those I assuaged, calmed in their pain...
None! Guardian-angel negress, none but you!

 "Be brave," you said. "Here stands the only one
Who loved you truly, you alone! I bring
Scorned tribute of a faithful love undone.
Forget her, and pray cease your suffering!"

Enemies, friends... All of you, honor-bound,
Believe these lines, for true they are, I swear.
At last may Justice spread her reign around,
Man's destiny be freedom everywhere.

1842

PIERRE FAUBERT

Frères, nous avons tous brisé le joug infâme (Aux Haïtiens)

Frères, nous avons tous brisé le joug infâme
        Qui trop longtemps courba nos fronts;
Jaunes et Noirs, brûlant d'une héroïque flamme,
        Nous avons vengé nos affronts;

Et le Dieu juste et fort couronnant notre audace,
        Noir ou Jaune, à l'égal du Blanc,
A pu se dire enfin: "J'ai créé pour ma race
        Une patrie avec mon sang."

Oh! pour nous tous alors quels beaux jours! À nos braves
        La vieille Europe applaudissait;
Et ce peuple oppresseur de millions d'esclaves,
        Au bruit de leurs fers frémissait.

"Bravo!" disaient Granville, Wilberforce, Grégoire,
        Et tant de généreux amis!
"Bravo! Mais voulez-vous compléter votre gloire?
        Noirs et Jaunes, soyez unis.

"Votre tâche est immense; hélas, combien de frères
        Qu'opprime encore l'iniquité!
Eh bien, vous sécherez tant de larmes amères,
        En honorant la liberté.

"Oui ne l'oubliez pas, amis; votre vaillance
        Vous a faits à moitié vainqueurs;
Désormais vos vertus et votre intelligence
        Combattront mieux vos oppresseurs."

PIERRE FAUBERT

Brothers all, we have now that foul yoke broken (To the Haitians)[1]

Brothers all, we have now that foul yoke broken
    That bowed our brows to tyranny;
Mulattos, Blacks... Heroes enflamed, awoken,
    We have avenged our infamy.

A just, strong God has crowned our bold endeavor.
    Blacks and Mulattos, like the White,
Can say, "My fatherland is mine forever;
    Land that my blood bought, set aright."

Oh! What fair days were ours! Old Europe rained
    Her cheers upon us; huzzahs rang;
And states where slaves by millions lie enchained
    Shuddered to hear their shackles clang.[2]

"Bravo!" cried Granville, Grégoire, Wilberforce,[3]
    Noble friends whom your feats delighted.
"Bravo!... But to complete your glory's course,
    Blacks and Mulattos, stand united!

"Immense, your task! How many brothers lie
    Sore oppressed by the tyrant's shame!
How many the bitter tears you yet must dry,
    Waging just war in freedom's name.

"Forget not, friends. Your brave accomplishments
    Made you victors by half! And so,
Now must your virtues and intelligence
    Complete your task against the foe."

Pourtant jusqu'à ce jour la Discorde implacable
    T'agite encore, beau pays;
En ton sol enchanté, Pactole inépuisable,
    S'abreuve du sang de tes fils.

Que n'ai-je en ce moment, ô mon île chérie,
    La sainte éloquence du cœur!
Tous bientôt, désarmés au seul nom de patrie,
    Gémiraient d'une telle erreur.

Quoi! divisés lorsque, tout près de votre plage,
    Mulâtres et Noirs sont proscrits!
Quand cette République, appui de l'esclavage,
    Rêve, avide, à vos champs fleuris!

Haines, dissensions, et ce vautour rapace
    Dans votre ciel planant déjà
Pour mieux perpétuer les maux de votre race,
    S'apprête à fondre sur Cuba!

Oh! par tous ces guerriers qui, pères magnanimes,
    Ont tant souffert pour leurs enfants;
Par tant de sang versé, tant de nobles victimes,
    Haïtiens, serrez vos rangs!

Anathème éternel à la guerre intestine,
    Fléau de toute nation:
Des Hongrois désunis, l'éclatante ruine
    Assez haut vous crie: "Union!"

"Union!" mot bien vieux, frères, mais mot sublime;
    Ah! qu'il pénètre chaque cœur!
Dieu même nous le dit, Dieu qui, dans l'homme, estime
    L'âme seule et non la couleur.

1850

And yet, O land of Plenty,[4] your rich soil
      Until this very day must be
Blood-soaked by dogged Discord's moil and broil,
      Wrought by your warring progeny.

Would I possessed, O blessèd, cherished isle,
      A tongue to chant the heart's travail!
All those whom homeland's fair name might beguile,
      Would moan their error, weep and wail.

What? Still divided, when, so close to you,
      Blacks and Mulattos' doom is sealed!
When slavery rules that Republic, who
      Covets your every flowering field!

Hatreds, dissensions!... And that vulture goes
      Sweeping your sky, vile predator;
Nevermore to let sleep your race's woes,
      Ready to swoop on Cuba's shore![5]

In the name of those fathers, they who bled
      To save their children, gave their all;
Those valiant victims, warriors lying dead...
      O Haitians, close your ranks! Stand tall!

Civil strife! Deadly scourge of every nation!
      Curse never-ending! Listen! Hear
Hungary's disunited devastation[6]
      Cry the word "Union!" in your ear!

"Union!" Old word, my brothers, but divine:
      Let all hearts etch it deep within!
God wills it so; God who, in his design,
      Judges Man's soul and not his skin.

1850

APPENDIXES

HÉRARD-DUMESLE

Voyage dans le nord d'Haïti
(Voyage in the North of Haiti)

Hérard-Dumesle's 1824 narrative of his travels around the North of Haiti after the fall of the Christophe monarchy contains the earliest-known transcription of the "Oath of the Cayman Woods" (Serment du Bois Caïman), in both a French version, which is integrated into the text of a longer poem, and a Creole version that appears separately at the bottom of the page. *Voyage in the North of Haiti* echoes the French orientalist travel narrative style of meditations on history triggered by the sight of ruined monuments. This poem appears in chapter 9, "Ruins' Revelations: A Sketch of the Historical Tableau of the Haitian Revolution," which marks the first, or among the first, uses of the expression "the Haitian Revolution." Hérard-Dumesle prefaces this poem about the dramatic events of the August 14, 1791, nocturnal reunion of insurrectional leaders (slave drivers, house servants, spiritual or group leaders, and maroons) with a prose description of the longer continuum of insurrectional events in the North, beginning with the alleged plot to poison French plantation owners and planters in 1854 by Makandal. The poem then fuses the different revolutionary moments together through the use of the name "Macanda" (Makandal), as if different leaders and rituals all formed part of one longer ceremonial launching of the Haitian Revolution.

An asterisk appears in the poem at the point where the priestly orator speaks to the throng in the simple words of the forebears:

Bondié qui fait soleil, qui clairé nous enhaut,
Qui soulevé la mer, qui fait grondé l'orage,
Bon dié la, zot tandé? caché dans youn nuage,
Et la li gadé nous, li vouai tout ça blancs faits!

Bon dié blancs mandé crime, et part nous vlé bienfets
mais dié lá qui si bon, ordonnin nous vengeance;
Li va conduit bras nous, la ba nous assistance,
Jetté portrait dié blancs qui soif dlo dans gié nous,
      Couté la liberté li pale cœurs nous toùs.

A literal translation might read:

God who makes the sun that lights us from above,
[God] Who raises up the seas, who makes the storm rage,
God is there, do you hear? hidden in a cloud,
And there he watches us, he sees everything the whites are
    doing!
The God of the whites orders crime, and wants nothing good
    for us,
But the god there who is so good orders our vengeance;
He will guide our arms, he gives us assistance;
Throw down the portrait of the god of the whites who is
    thirsty for the tears in our eyes,
Listen to liberty, it speaks in all of our hearts.

The "Oath of the Cayman Woods" originally introduces
"Bondié" ("the good lord" or "bondieu") as the name for God,
and then separates the term into two syllables ("bon dié la," "the
good lord over there"), followed by distinction from the god of
the whites (dié blancs) and a return to a different god—"dié la
qui si bon" (the god there who is so good). The Vodou priest
seems to gesture to different spheres of the stormy night sky,
where an electrically present familiar god contrasts with the
god of the whites. The icon of the god of the whites stimulates
the production of tears, perhaps through empathy with Christ's
crucifixion, but also through the cruelty with which, as a Western
European god, he appears associated.

Summary of *L'Haïtiade* (*The Haitiade*)

Canto 1 opens with a first-person evocation of the Muse of poetry and an address to the Muse and the people of Haiti: "Chantons la liberté" (Let us now Haiti's freedom sing). Divine intervention ("le merveilleux chrétien") will assist the Haitians in their noble cause. The narrative then shifts to an omniscient third-person narrator. Identification of 1802 as the starting point of the narrative in Canto 1 (the dates are all approximate: the poem does not contain any specific dates) is indicated by the periphrastic expression that the earth had turned twelve times on its axis since the Haitian saga began (1790–91). An impartial tone is introduced from the start: the French, the Haitians, and those of mixed race all form "un grand peuple de frères" (a race of brethren, side by side). Peace, freedom, and tolerance are celebrated. Toussaint is shown as he was when leading his people in peace time (1800–1802). The major participants in the battle and their troops are present, as if summoned to attend a reenactment. Some, notably Pétion and Boyer, are eulogized. Others—in particular Christophe and Dessalines—are criticized for their ambition, cruelty, and tryannical acts. Of diverse racial backgrounds and both sexes, the cadre of respected, committed Haitians is reunited as they were in battle. Toussaint speaks. He warns of possible danger ahead brought about by "vos tyrans" (your tyrans), the bitter, prejudiced colonists. He defends the harsh but necessary measures he has had to impose to assure prosperity and productivity. At the end, four repetitions occur of the refrain "Salut! fille du Ciel, salut! liberté sainte,/Du malheur sur nos fronts viens effacer l'empreinte" (Hail, Heaven's daughter! Come/Cleanse our brows of our wretched martyrdom). Evoking the time in 1825 when Haiti and France were reconciled, the narrator states that the trauma of the past must produce conciliation, not further conflict or bitterness. At the end of Canto 1, two voices are heard: that of the omniscient narrator who states, "Ainsi chantaient les Noirs" (So sang the Blacks), and a first-person voice that evokes childhood memories of Haiti.

Canto 2 picks up at the chronological point at which Canto 1 began. A divine messenger visits Toussaint. He reveals the evil intentions of the French led by Napoleon and promises God's help to the Haitian people. Toussaint prepares for battle. In France, preparations are made for an invasion. The names of the French ships and the principal French participants are identified. They have been summoned to battle. The fate of Toussaint's sons (identified as Isaac and Telephe) is deplored. A tragic fate awaits the combatants who undertake this mission. Pauline (the sister of Napoleon and wife of the expedition leader, Leclerc) celebrates in music the bravery and glory of France and its revolutionary past, accompanied by the French troubadour Oscar.

In Canto 3, the omniscient narrator recounts God's scorn for France's plan to attack the freedom of the Haitians and condemns the French to die at sea. Eloa, "le génie de la France" (the spirit of France) intervenes and argues that their intentions are good. God relents, saying that they can live but his wrath will be upon them if they try to reimpose slavery. But God is not the only one concerned. Satan dredges up from Hell the worst figures, including former tyrants, and they set off for Haiti.

Canto 4 recounts Toussaint's reactions when the French expedition carrying his sons arrives (February 1802). Their preceptor, Coisnon, is depicted as perfidious: he assures Toussaint that the French are honorable and have no intention of reimposing slavery. Speaking in his own voice, Toussaint reveals that he is not deceived. His wife, Mopsa, deplores the fate of her family. Battle ensues between the French and Haitian armies, in which Toussaint, Dessalines, and Christophe are all engaged. The omniscient narrator does not take sides, referring to the "deux peuples généreux" (two generous peoples). But his comments on the respective valor of Christophe, Dessalines, Pétion, and Boyer show a political bias from within Haitian politics in favor of the South, particularly of Boyer. Above all, Toussaint's valor is celebrated. A shift to the first person at one point—"Mais déjà des Français j'entends les cris perçants" (But already I hear the piercing cries of the French)—celebrates the bravery of the French warriors, who are victorious and force Toussaint to sign a treaty (May 1802). The omniscient narrator deplores the fate of the Haitians and points an accusatory finger at the betrayers of Toussaint, who, defeated but virtuous, is reunited with his family.

Canto 5 shifts the focus to Leclerc and his wife, Pauline, whose unprincipled and immoral behavior is condemned. Erotic descriptions are given of the women of color who tempt and form unions with European men. In some cases, they are virtuous, such as the native-born mixed-race Elma, but the outcome of such unions will nonetheless be tragic. Pauline is depicted as the devil's emissary. Dreaming of glory she leads her husband astray. The uxorious Leclerc violates the noble intentions of France, determining to capture Toussaint. The narrator deplores the betrayal of Toussaint and the grief of his family. Toussaint is arrested and imprisoned in France (August 1802), but God sets things right. Leclerc is doomed to contract a fatal illness (September 1802), while Pauline must suffer alone in France. Satan intervenes, using the beautiful women of Haiti as bait to entrap and doom the French soldiers, who, distracted by love, lay down their arms. Even virtuous couples such as Elma (mixed race) and Oscar (European) are doomed.

Canto 6 begins with the arrival of Toussaint in France (July 1802), which is praised as a wonderful country despite the crimes against the Haitians that have been committed. The horror of imprisonment is evoked, not only for Toussaint but for other victims of Napoleon's wrath. The company of the imprisoned general Mallet alleviates Toussaint's solitude. Toussaint then takes narrative control and attests to the horrific events, recounting to Mallet the saga of his country's recent history, which begins with an angel sent by God alighting to speak to them. The angel announces that Ogé will lead the way. Ogé arrives (October

1790), intending to end injustices by colonialists. He speaks to the oppressed and encourages them to rise up. The French, led by the dissolute d'Hespel, march off to suppress the uprising. The Haitians win, but then a ferocious return of French fighting power occurs. This time Azémar leads the French troops. Ogé's valor is celebrated. But despite his courage, Satan uses his powers to shore up the French forces, and Ogé's soldiers flee. Azémar and the French soldiers are inclined to be merciful, but the colonists are brutal and vindictive. Ogé is captured, tortured, and put to death. The colonists argue for independence in order to be free of abolitionist pressure from the French and to have the power to continue to oppress blacks: they are nefarious forces opposed to the more beneficent French. Satan, who is behind the colonists, sends his evil archangel Astaroth to reestablish their authority. Astaroth prods peace-loving Haitians like Grégor to resume battle. They perform atrocities against the colonists at Satan's bidding.

Canto 7 continues the narrative of the battles. The colonists' brutality is deplored but so too is that of the massacring blacks. Grégor sets an example of compassion in saving an elderly colonist. The colonists pursue the blacks with ferocity. Grégor rallies forces to retaliate and burn Le Cap (August 1791). Toussaint declares that the Haitians' vengeance was warranted: it was a "juste retour du sort" (fate's just response). France grants citizenship to free blacks and persons of color (April 1792) and sends Civil Commissioners Léger-Félicité Sonthonax and Étienne Polverel. The focus shifts to perfidious England, at war with France (February 1793) and motivated by the desire to take over Haiti (September 1793). An Englishman, Dobson, offers Grégor his country's support in order to turn him away from France and incite the blacks to fight. Satan is behind the offer, which the blacks accept. The well-intentioned Sonthonax is outwitted by the British, who support the blacks in their massacre but intend to reenslave them when the battle is over. Toussaint evokes his brothers, their hopes at the time, and the victories they achieved together, driving out the English (1794–95) and defeating the colonists. France was threatened by their victories, and divisiveness was sown among the Haitians, but they remained victorious. Toussaint reigned (1796–1802) over Saint-Domingue. Toussaint ends his narration by stating that all was well until he was captured (June 1802). Mallet, his prison companion, commiserates and blames Napoleon, whom he vows to punish if he is ever released. Toussaint dies (April 1803).

Canto 8 deplores at length the evils of colonial rule. The first-person narrator presents the horrors he has seen. In an attempt to defeat the blacks after Leclerc's death, Napoleon sends the French general Rochambeau (March 1803). Dessalines and others gather to defeat the French. Toussaint appears from beyond the grave to encourage the Haitian warriors. He reminds them that God is on their side and that the French will be laid low by disease. He looks into the future and sees tyrants in Haiti's future: he names Dessalines and emphasizes his acts of brutality. Finally Pétion ends the tyrannical phase of Dessalines's reign, which characterized Christophe's as well. An encomium for Boyer follows. Satan has received his reward in the number of those who died; the English have been chased away; France has come to accept the outcome of the uprisings; Haiti has gained and retained its freedom. The narrator, speaking in the voice of a Haitian survivor, hails the celestial spirit of freedom—"fille du ciel" (heaven's daughter)—and asks her to erase the horrible memories of oppression and violence.

ANONYMOUS

Quand sur les habitants (Chant patriotique)

Quand sur les habitants du coupable univers
L'Éternel eut versé les flots de la vengeance,
Dans leurs vastes bassins il replaça les mers
Et d'un monde nouveau concevant l'espérance:
"Sem, l'Asie est à vous: Dans ces climats heureux
Que le soleil naissant dore de sa lumière,
Un jour doivent régner des peuples belliqueux,
Législateurs du monde et maîtres de la terre.
C'est là que le sauveur promis à vos aïeux
Brisera sous ses pieds le serpent orgueilleux!
Vous, Japhet, l'Occident sera votre partage;
    Longtemps vos fils dans leurs sombres déserts
    Ne connaîtront qu'une vertu sauvage,
Longtemps ces cœurs altiers languiront dans les fers
Et porteront le joug d'un honteux esclavage:
        Mais sur les bords où le Jourdain
        Promène obscurément son onde,
        Bientôt brille un rayon divin
        Qui dissipant la nuit profonde
        Où sommeillait le genre humain
        Doit éclairer au loin le monde.
Pour toi, fils criminel, qui n'a pas respecté
    De ton vieux père la faiblesse,
Toi qui n'as pas rougi d'insulter sa vieillesse,
    Je maudis ta postérité!
Dieu dit que sa fureur sur nos têtes coupables
    Pèse encore après trois mille ans;
Grand Dieu! quand finiront vos décrets redoutables?

ANONYMOUS

Once the Eternal (Patriotic Song)[1]

Once the Eternal, with avenging hand,
Had punished Man, denizen of a world
Guilt-ridden; once he had the flood unfurled,
He spread the seas once more over the land
Newborn, hope-filled, saying: "Shem, unto you
I bestow Asia; there the sun's rebirth
Each day gilds her fair clime. In time there, too,
Shall reign in war the masters of the earth;[2]
Lawgivers, welcoming the savior who,
Long promised to your ancestors, will trample
Beneath his feet the haughty serpent vile.
And to you, Japhet, I bequeath the ample
 West, where your sons shall, all the while,
  In their grim wilderness, know naught
  But savage ways: days anguish-fraught
As they, though proud of heart, languish unfree,
Bowed by the shameful yoke of slavery.[3]
 But soon, by Jordan's banks, where flow
 Its somber waters, there will shine
 A brilliant ray, and it will—lo!—
 Sweep away with a power divine
 The sleep of mankind—dark, profound—
 And cast its light the vast world round...
Now, as for you, foul son, last of the three,
Who scorn your father's feeble age, and would
Unblushing, flout him in your cravenhood,
 A curse on your posterity!"
This did God say. Three thousand years have passed,
 And yet his curse upon our head
Weighs heavy still. Great God! How long must last

Punirez-vous toujours les malheureux enfants
Des crimes de leur père?
Hélas! du Dieu vengeur l'implacable colère
Depuis ce jour fatal
A livré mon pays au cruel Dieu du Mal:
Et le génie affreux, de ses ailes funèbres
Enveloppant ce monde malheureux,
A dérobé la lumière à nos yeux,
A jeté devant nous un voile de ténèbres.
En vain Carthage sur nos bords
Voulait fixer les arts et leurs nobles conquêtes.
En vain ses soldats dans leurs ports
Bravaient Rome, le temps, la mer et ses tempêtes;
En vain de ce vaste univers
L'Afrique un jour fut la maîtresse
Et des trésors de cent peuples divers
Elle augmenta sa gloire et sa richesse:
Dieu l'ordonnait, et Carthage au cercueil
Pleure aujourd'hui sa gloire et son orgueil;
Sa gloire s'est évanouie
Comme ces vains ruisseaux
Qui vont perdre leurs eaux
Dans les sables brûlants de l'inculte Syrie!
Terre à jamais maudite, il ne te reste plus
Que de vains souvenirs, des regrets superflus!
Si quelques fois au bruit des flots et de l'orage
Se mêlent dans les airs quelques chants imparfaits
D'une lyre sauvage,
Ce n'est point pour vanter les dons ni les bienfaits
D'un Dieu qui nous punit et d'une terre avare
Dont les trésors secrets
Refusent de nourrir une race barbare:
Mais des combats les sanglantes horreurs,

Your rage? Must father's sins be visited
   Upon his children innocent?
      For since that deathly day,
The vengeful God, with wrath impenitent,
      Has bent us to the sway
Of Evil's god![4] Alas, my people! See
How that fell spirit, dolorous of wing,
   The wretched world enveloping,
Has veiled our eyes in dark obscurity.
   In vain did Carthage, on our shores,
Foster the arts, make her their noble home!
   In vain her doughty conquerors
Braved sea, storm, time itself, and challenged Rome!
   In vain was Africa, back then
The mistress of the universe: her men
Sacked treasures of a hundred different races,
Adding wealth to her exploits valorous.
God willed it so... Today, Carthage embraces
   Naught but her tomb, and, piteous,
      Laments with copious tear
A pride and glory vanished now, like those
      Streams, brooks, whose water flows
Down to a trickle, only to disappear
In savage Syria's burning desert sand...
   Now nothing is your lot, O land
Forever cursed! Naught but vain memories,
Regrets... And if, betimes, the wind-swept seas
Blend to their gales the halting airs from some
      Untamed and artless lyre,
It is not to raise an encomium
   To gifts of wrathful God, whose ire
Punishes still, or praise the treasures hidden
   In lands unyielding, boons forbidden
To nourish a barbaric race. It is,
Rather, to sing our horror-ridden fights

Un amant massacré dans les bras d'une amante,
D'un farouche soldat les brutales fureurs,
    Le sang, la mort, le meurtre et l'épouvante...
        Voilà les lugubres concerts
        Qui troublent seuls la paix des airs.
        Voilà les nobles chants de gloire
Qui vantent du guerrier la cruelle victoire!
Et moi, je les maudis ces funestes combats
            Qui m'ont privé d'un père!...
J'étais jeune, et ne pus accompagner ses pas;
Captif, il est allé sur la rive étrangère,
Et parmi ses aïeux il ne dormira pas!
        J'ai vu l'Européen avide
L'enchaîner, lui ravir l'aspect du doux pays.
Loin des bords malheureux qui retenaient son fils
        Mon père a fui d'un vol rapide.
        Et moi, dans vos vastes déserts
        Fils orphelin, j'aurais pu vivre!
        Non, non; j'ai voulu le poursuivre
        Et le chercher de mers en mers.
Ah! je le cherche encore!... Peut-être au sein de l'onde
Le vaisseau ravisseur s'est-il enseveli,
        Peut-être dans un meilleur monde
Mon père de ses maux goûte le long oubli:
Mais non, j'ai vu souvent un vieillard vénérable
Briser un sol ingrat, l'arroser de ses pleurs,
Et, tremblant sous les coups d'un maître impitoyable,
Appeler vainement la mort ou des vengeurs;
        Loin des climats qui l'ont vu naître,

And feats; a lover massacred in his
Mistress' embrace; the brutish appetites
Of a crazed soldier: blood, death, terror... These
   Are the lugubrious melodies
   That, alone, stir the peaceful air.
   Such are the noble eulogies
That laud our glorious warriors brave and their
Bloodthirsty victories!... No, I decry,
I curse them all, these deadly struggles where
   I lost a father!... Young was I—
Too young to join him. Captive, he was taken
Off to a foreign shore. And I, forsaken,
Watched as the rabid European took
Him, chained, from his fair land, no more to look
Upon her beauty, nor to sleep among
The ancestors... In rapid flight they bore
   Him off to foreign climes, far-flung,
   And left me on this tragic shore
   In my vast wilderness! Ah, could
   I live in such dire orphanhood?
   No, no! Not so! And thus I followed,
Seeking the vicious ship from sea to sea...
   I seek it still. In vain! Ah me,
   Perhaps the villain-waves have swallowed
The vessel down; perhaps my father now
Knows a far better world; perhaps, somehow,
He revels in his ills' oblivion...
   Alas, no!... Often more than one
Venerable old man have I seen with hoe
In hand, breaking the hard, tear-spattered ground
As heartless master lashes, whips him round
About, and, in his voice, a tremolo
Calls for avengers, or for death, to come—
Unheard!—and save him from his martyrdom.
   Doubtless, far from his native land,

Sans doute, comme ce vieillard,

Mon père tremble sous un maître,

Et moi j'erre seul au hasard,

Sans pouvoir soulager sa chaîne

Ni fléchir d'un tyran la fureur inhumaine!

Cruels fils de Japhet, est-ce un plaisir si doux

De servir si longtemps le céleste courroux?

Craignez qu'un Dieu vengeur, pour punir tant de crimes,

Ne livre les bourreaux à leurs faibles victimes...

Mais où m'emporte ma douleur?

Une voix sur les mers profondes

A retenti jusqu'à mon cœur

Et proclame dans les deux mondes

Le nom sacré de liberté.

"Albion, superbe cité,

Toi, dont l'orgueil et l'avarice

Firent longtemps couler nos pleurs,

Nous oublions ton injustice.

C'est toi qui finis nos malheurs!

Comment le Dieu qui gouverne le monde

A-t-il conduit ce grand événement?

Naguère dans tout l'occident

Régnait une terreur profonde:

Un homme, un soldat sous ses lois

Voyait s'incliner tous les rois;

La France alors, l'Europe était captive.

Mais du char triomphal le Danube surpris

Contemple avec effroi les superbes débris

Like them, my father trembles too,
Suffering at a master's hand.
And I, ah woe! can little do
But wander, aimless, powerless
To lift the burden of his chains, or stay
A tyrant's inhumane ferociousness!
Cruel sons of Japhet! Do you yet today
Take pleasure in a wrath divine unspent?
Beware! Fear lest a God on justice bent
Yield up the executioners, in time,
To bear, at victims' hands, just punishment!...
But whither leads my pain? What voice sublime
    Pierces me to the very core,
    Echoing over the abyss
    Betwixt two worlds, from shore to shore,
    Over the sea? What word is this?
    "Liberty!" Sacred liberty!
    O Albion, you whose avarice
    And haughty pride so endlessly
    Caused bitter tears to flow! And yet,
    Despite your crimes, we must forget.
    For you it is who now propose
    An ending to our pains and woes!
How did the God of law omnipotent
Contrive to bring about this odd event?
    In days not long since past, there spread
    Throughout the West a somber pall
    Of terror: monarchs one and all
    In dread submission bowed the head
    And bent the knee to one man—one,
    A soldier, and whose will be done!
France and all Europe lay in thrall. But then
The Danube's banks, trodden by victory,
Gaze, rapt in awe, on war's grandiose debris.

Et épars aujourd'hui sur sa rive

La France est libre, et dans tout l'univers

Les pays ont brisé leurs fers.

Je te salue, ô belle France,

Dont le destin commande au reste des humains,

Reine des nations, et qui tiens dans tes mains

Leur esclavage ou bien leur espérance,

Je te salue! et toi, monarque généreux,

Dont l'exil avait fait le malheur de la terre,

Dont le retour a comblé tous les vœux,

Et fermé pour jamais le temple de la guerre,

Aux chants d'amour des peuples et des rois

Le sauvage Africain ose mêler sa voix,

Et, libre enfin, t'offrir son faible hommage.

Poursuis, noble Bourbon, achève ton ouvrage,

Ordonne à tes heureux vaisseaux

D'aller sur ce lointain rivage

Porter à des peuples nouveaux

Les arts, les trésors du génie,

Et ce langage dont les doux sons enchanteurs

Et la poétique harmonie

Ont jadis policé les mœurs.

De la Grèce et de l'Ausonie

Parle et dans leurs vieux monuments

Ta voix a réveillé ces ombres magnanimes,

Ces prêtres, qui jadis réparant tous les crimes

Des indomptables Castillans

Élevaient, sans soldat ces cités florissantes,

Ouvraient leur seins aux peuples abattus,

Et faisaient dire à ces hordes errantes

Il est donc partout des vertus!

De vos sacrés tombeaux, secourez la poussière,

Colomb et Las Casas,

L'humanité vous ouvre une nouvelle terre,

All through the universe, chains, once again,
    Fall, smashed... France too is free! All hail
To you, majestic land, born to prevail
    Over the rest of humankind!
    Queen of the nations, in your hand,
Man's slavery? Man's hope? Yours to command...
All hail to you, savior and king combined,
Most worthy ruler who, in exile, left
The world entire in pain and help-bereft;
But whose return, feeding our hopes once more,
Has now, forever, barred the shrine of war!
Africa's savage, too, dares add his voice
To paeans that the kings and people raise.
    Now, free at last, he may rejoice
And sing, dim though the notes, his song of praise.
Pursue your course, O noble Bourbon king![5]
Let your fair-favored ships go voyaging
Unto that distant coast, and take to those
New peoples the rich treasures of your arts—
    Creations of your hands and hearts.
And you, poetic tongue, whose harmonies
Enchant the ear, invest the social graces,
    As once they did in Greece and Italy's—
Or, as one said, "Ausonia's"—noble places;[6]
And which, intoned in monuments of old,
    Awoke those priests—good men and bold,
Mere shadows now—who, wiping clean the traces
    Of brash Castilians' crimes, raised high—
Unarmed and soldierless—fine cities, there
To pour their hearts' grief, and to save thereby
    These peoples beaten to despair,
Telling the errant hordes that everywhere
Virtues can thrive! Yes, you, Las Casas;[7] you
    Columbus! Shake the sacred dust
From your sarcophagi. Come! Now you must

Allez, suivez ses pas!
J'entends le vent frémir dans les voiles flottantes,
Le calme règne sur les eaux,
Dieu lui-même à travers les vagues écumantes
Dirige vos légers vaisseaux,
Vents empestés qui d'une mort soudaine
Avez souvent puni nos ravisseurs;
Ces étrangers sont nos sauveurs!
Aux accents de leur voix, l'Africain dans son âme
A senti s'éveiller les feux mal assoupis
De cette noble flamme
Dont les Grecs, les Romains brûlaient pour leur pays:
Les hommes ont ravi de leur molle indolence,
Et d'une faible main, inhabile aux travaux,
La vieillesse et l'enfance
Ont fait gémir le fer sous le poids des marteaux.
Déjà les sons divins d'une lyre magique
Font naître des cités, des temples, des remparts
Et du sein de l'Afrique
S'élèvent en chantant les Muses, les beaux arts,
Ô Foullepointe, et toi, doux fleuve du Zaïre,
Un jour peut-être, un jour le voyageur
S'arrêtera surpris de ta splendeur
Et dira: Dieu lui-même a créé cet empire!"

Ainsi ma voix, sur le luth des Français,
Soupirait les malheurs de la patrie absente,
Ainsi ma voix, faible et reconnaissante,
D'un peuple généreux célébrait les bienfaits.
Je ne suis qu'un barbare, et cependant j'admire,
Nouvel Anacharsie, les chants mélodieux

Follow humanity unto a new,
   An unknown land! I hear the gales
   A-shudder in the fluttering sails...
Calm lie the waters... God would seem to be
Leading your barks over the froth-foamed sea,
O tainted winds, who, with one reeking breath,
Often would blow our captors to their death!
   Foreigners are our saviors now!
Hearing their voice, the African—soul yearning
   For home, its noble flame still burning
      With fire unquenched—knows how
The Greeks and Romans felt when homeward sailing...
Wrenched from their indolence, with feeble strength,
      Ill-fit, their vigor failing,
Even the very old and young, at length,
Smash groaning chains with many a hammer blow.
Already notes divine—magic the strings
   Plucked on the lyre!—make cities grow,
   Ramparts and temples; and there springs,
Rising up from the bosom, yes, the heart
Of Africa, the Muses' glorious art:
O Foullepointe![8] And you, Zaïre, sweet river!
The traveler, one fine day, may stop and stand
   Gazing in disbelief, a-quiver,
   And will declare, amazed and awed:
This empire is the handiwork of God!"

Thus my voice, on the Frenchman's lute,[9] entunes,
Sighs for my absent country's sufferings.
   Thus my voice, weak but thankful, sings
Praise to a noble people's generous boons.
A mere barbarian I well may be,
But, an Anarchasis of latter day,[10]
No less do I admire the melody,
The dulcet chords, that they divinely play,

Et les divins accords des enfants de la lyre.
Comme eux, j'aurais voulu, d'un sol audacieux
Planant du haut des airs sur le céleste empire,
M'asseoir, noble convive, à la table des Dieux.
Mon cœur ne nourrit plus cette folle espérance,
Et déjà le vaisseau m'emporte sur les mers.
Je vais enfin revoir les champs de mon enfance,
Hélas! et je n'ai pas la palme des beaux vers!
Toi que j'aurais voulu choisir pour ma patrie,
Ô France, sur tes bords j'ai vu quelques beaux jours;
Mais mon cœur est aux lieux où commença ma vie,
Adieu, France, adieu pour toujours!

1823

These children of the lyre! Like them, did I
Aspire—sweeping a bold land from on high,
God's empire!—there to sit, an honored guest
At heaven's table, there with all the rest!
But no more does this hope, this folly vain
Feed my desire... Now the ship carries me
Homeward, to see my childhood fields again.
Ah! Had I but the gift of poesy!
My heart belongs where it woke to life's morn.
Farewell, France, where I fain would have been born,
Where many a happy day I spent... Now, never
    Shall I return: farewell forever!

1823

OSWALD DURAND

Quand nos aïeux (Chant national)

> Derrière la charrue, au travail résignée
> Marche à grands pas la liberté
> —Oswald Durand

I

Quand nos aïeux brisèrent leurs entraves,
Ce n'était pas pour se croiser les bras.
Pour travailler en maîtres, les esclaves
Ont embrassé, corps à corps, le trépas,
Leur sang, à flots, engraissa nos collines.
À notre tour, jaunes et noirs, allons!
Creusons le sol légué par Dessalines:
Notre fortune est là, dans nos vallons.
    L'indépendance est éphémère
    Sans le droit à l'égalité!
    Pour fouler, heureux, cette terre,
    Il nous faut la devise austère:
    "Dieu! le travail! la liberté!"

II

Quoi de plus beau que ces fils de l'Afrique
Qui, trois cents ans, dans tous les maux plongés,
Tournent leurs fers, leur carcan et leur trique
Contre la force et les vieux préjugés!
En bas, voyez! C'est la noble bannière
Cernant les noirs qui vont mourir là-haut...
—Non! Leur torrent, avec Lamartinière,
Descend fougueux de la Crète-à-Pierrot!
    Tout cela serait éphémère
    Sans le droit à l'égalité.
    Pour fouler, heureux, notre terre,

OSWALD DURAND

When our ancestors (National Song)[1]

> Behind the plow, to toil's demands resigned
> Freedom strides boldly on, apace.
> —Oswald Durand[2]

I

When our ancestors smashed their serfdom's chains,
It was not so that, slothful, we might lie
In idleness! The slaves embraced death's pains
So that, free, we might labor by and by.
Fertile our hills, drenched by their blood that flowed
Unstinting through our valleys' treasure! Thus.
In turn, blacks and mulattos, now let us
Toil in the soil that Dessalines bestowed!

> One day is independence won
> And lost, unless, as equals, we
> Tread earth with none cast low and none
> Cast high! Sing we in unison:
> "For God, our toil, our liberty!"[3]

II

What fairer sight is there to see than these,
Africa's sons, now turn their shackles, rent
At last—whip, lash that dealt dire punishment—
Against base crimes of threefold centuries!
Look! See the noble banner flying there
Round blacks destined for dying!... Ah! But no!
The torrent loosed by brave Lamartinière
Streams, hurtling headlong, from Crète-à-Pierrot![4]

> All would be lost, all that we won
> That day, unless, as equals, we
> Tread earth with none cast low and none

Il nous faut la devise austère:
"Dieu! le travail! la liberté!"

III

De Rochambeau les cohortes altières,
Quelques instants, suspendirent leur feu,
Pour saluer le héros de Vertières,
—Capoix-la-Mort, grand comme un demi-dieu?
Vers le progrès, crions comme ce brave:
"Noirs en avant! en avant!" Et bêchons
Le sol trempé des sueurs de l'esclave!
Nous avons là ce qu'ailleurs nous cherchons!

Sans quoi, tout devient éphémère;
Pas d'ordre et pas d'égalité!
Pour fouler, heureux, notre terre,
Il nous faut la devise austère:
"Dieu! le travail! la liberté!"

IV

Sang des martyrs dont la pourpre écumante
A secoué nos chaînes et nos jougs!
Chavanne, Ogé, sur la roue infamante,
Toi, vieux Toussaint, dans ton cachot de Joux;
Ô précurseurs, dont les dernières fibres
Ont dû frémir—vous les porte-flambeaux—
En nous voyant maintenant fiers et libres,
Conseillez-nous, du fond de vos tombeaux!

—Votre bonheur est éphémère;
Ayez droit à l'égalité!
Pour fouler, heureux, votre terre,
Il vous faut la devise austère:
"Dieu! le travail! la liberté!"

V

À l'œuvre donc, descendants de l'Afrique,
Jaunes et noirs, fils du même berceau!
L'antique Europe et la jeune Amérique

Cast high! Sing we in unison:
"For God, our toil, our liberty!"

III

Rochambeau's haughty troops,[5] one moment, hold
Their fire in tribute to Capoix-la-Mort,[6]
The valiant hero of Vertières... Brash, bold
Capoix-la-Mort, demigod conqueror!
Like him, let us cry: "Forward, black men all!"
This land is ours, to till, to hoe. Eyes set
On progress, ever standing staunch and tall,
On this, our soil long steeped in slavery's sweat!

      Else will we lose what we have won!
      Would we be equals? Then must we
      Tread earth with none cast low and none
      Cast high! Sing we in unison:
      "For God, our toil, our liberty!"

IV

Blood of our martyrs, spurting crimson, who
Shook off our shackles, yokes... Chavanne, Ogé,
Racked, broken... You, Toussaint, prisoned in Joux...[7]
See us now, risen strong and free! I pray—
Forebears all, you who trembled to your doom—
Light our way with your wisdom! Grant to us
Your counsel sage, torchbearers, from the tomb,
That this, our land, may long live prosperous!

      —In one day happiness is won
      And lost, unless, as equals we
      Tread earth with none cast low and none
      Cast high! Sing we in unison:
      "For God, our toil, our liberty!"

V

To work, Africa's sons! Your foes defy!
Mulattos, blacks... All in one cradle bred![8]
Old Europe, young America stand by

Nous voient, de loin, tenter le rude assaut.
Bêchons le sol qu'en l'an mil huit cent quatre
Nous ont conquis nos aïeux au bras fort.
C'est notre tour, à présent, de combattre
Avec ce cri: "Le progrès ou la mort!"
      A l'œuvre, ou tout est éphémère!
      Ayons droit à l'égalité!
      Nous foulerons, plus fiers, la terre,
      Avec cette devise austère:
      "Dieu! le travail! la liberté!"

1887

To swoop and sweep destruction on your head!
Our ancestors, in eighteen hundred four,
Waged war to win this land. Today we must
Toil, till it, fill the air with cries once more.
Her wealth be ours! "Progress! Or death... and dust!"
       To work! Lest all that we have won
       Be lost... Unless, as equals, we
       Tread earth with pride second to none,
       And sing we, proud, in unison:
       "For God, our toil, our liberty!"

1887

Notes

Introduction

1. See Fischer, *Modernity Disavowed*.
2. *Plato's Republic,* trans. Benjamin Jowett (Millis, Mass.: Agora, 2001), 95.
3. Nau, "De La Poésie native en général et incidemment de la poésie des naturels d'Haïti," 3.
4. See Martin Munroe, *Different Drummers,* for the key role of music in the Haitian Revolution, in the evolution of Vodou religion, and in the spread of Haitian ideas to other Caribbean and New World sites.
5. Amy Reinsel, "Poetry of Revolution," 9–10. Reinsel's dissertation focuses principally on Haitian poetry from the 1830s to the late 1890s.
6. We provide a free translation of the French motto "L'épée et les talents doivent n'avoir qu'un but/Que chacun à l'État apporte son tribut."
7. Alexandre Bonneau states that there were thirty-one journals in Haiti in the period 1804 to 1856: "Les Noirs, les jaunes et la littérature française," 133. Justin Emmanuel Castera notes the ties between early Haitian journalism and the forty-four papers published in colonial Saint-Domingue. For example, printers probably relied on the use of Saint-Domingan typographical machinery: *Bref Coup d'œil,* 81–86.
8. This list provides the beginning dates of the journals as documented by Castera, *Bref Coup d'œil,* 105–20.
9. "La Presse en Haïti." Writing in 1860, directly following the repressive regime of Faustin Soulouque (1847–59), Francingues argued that freedom of the press dated back to 1806 under Pétion and was only violated later in Haiti's history.
10. Nicholls, *From Dessalines to Duvalier,* 72–73.
11. See Jenson, ed., "The Haiti Issue."
12. We have found the following to be the most useful: Berrou and Pompilus, *Histoire de la littérature haïtienne,* Charles, *Les Pionniers de la littérature haïtienne,* Morpeau, *Anthologie de la poésie haïtienne,* Trouillot, *Les Origines sociales de la littérature haïtienne,* Vaval, *Histoire de la littérature haïtienne.*

13. Fischer, *Modernity Disavowed,* 205.
14. Although Haiti's leaders publicly opposed Vodou because of its potential for political instability, they privately retained faith in native religious beliefs: see Desmangles, *The Faces of the Gods,* 45.
15. Fischer, *Modernity Disavowed,* 50, 53. In *De l'égalité des races humaines* (1885), Anténon Firmin deals directly with the Egyptians as regards concepts of race. For the meaning and history of Haitian Vodou, see Ramsey, *The Spirits and the Law,* 6–10.
16. Price-Mars, *Ainsi parla l'Oncle,* 44. Patrick Chamoiseau and Raphaël Confiant endorse the notion of imitation in early Caribbean literature in *Lettres créoles,* 37–39. Fischer observes regarding Cuba that the idea of imitation was "conventionally used in accounts of the cultural practices of people of color": *Modernity Disavowed,* 92.
17. Dash, "Afterword," 220. Dash reminds readers that, although Price-Mars's writings are founding texts for Haitian indigenism and negritude, they suffered from their association under the Duvalier dictatorship with black nationalism and authenticity and their use to attack mulattos.
18. Appendix C provides one of the submissions to the Académie française's 1823 poetry contest on the subject of abolition of the slave trade. (The submissions are in the Archives of the Académie française in Paris.) It purports to be written by "JC, an African," although non-European authorship is uncertain. The poem is not related directly to Haitian independence, but we have chosen to include it because it provides a useful point of reference for the existence of related Old and New World discourses on colonial oppression and black aspirations to freedom.
19. Janvier, *La République d'Haïti et ses visiteurs,* 520.
20. Those critics include Raphaël Berrou, Christophe Charles, Léon-François Hoffmann, and Duraciné Vaval.
21. Promoting national autonomy in Haiti was promoting independence and freedom from slavery which had been gained in the Haitian revolution. In contrast, in Cuba independence meant local autonomy which firmly supported the continued existence of slavery.
22. Vaval, *Histoire de la littérature haïtienne,* 246–47; Gragnon-Lacoste, ed., *L'Haïtiade,* 164; Morpeau, "Un Poème épique inconnu," 298. Isaac Louverture's notes similarly play an important role in "Mémoires et notes," which are appended to *Histoire de l'expédition des Français à Saint-Domingue,* ed. Antoine Marie Thérèse Métral (Paris: Fanjat aîné, 1825).

23. The prolific Edna Worthley Underwood (1873–1961) may be the first translator of Haitian poetry into English: see *Poets of Haiti,* 153.

24. Boyer presumably read the poem in manuscript form. See Bissainthe, *Dictionnaire de bibliographie haïtienne,* 177.

25. Jean-Fernand Brierre, introduction to Desquiron de Saint Agnan, *L'Haïtiade,* xiv. Brierre, a Haitian poet, dramatist, and statesman, wrote epic verse celebrating the heroes of Haitian independence.

26. Vaval, *Histoire de la littérature haïtienne,* 246–47.

27. Arnold D. Harvey, *Literature into History* (New York: St. Martin's, 1988), 131.

28. Haitians may also have learned to read in the aftermath of the Haitian Revolution by using colonists' books, which contained such references: see Hoffmann, *Littérature d'Haïti,* 76–77.

29. See Downs, "The Poetic Theories of Jacques Delille."

30. See Roman Jakobson, "Qu'est-ce que la poésie?" in his *Huit questions de poétique* (Paris: Seuil, 1977), 46.

31. See Griggs and Prator, *Henry Christophe and Thomas Clarkson,* 43.

32. Dessalines's proclamation of April 28, 1804: "Already at its approach, the irritated genius of Hayti, rising out of the bosom of the ocean, appears; his menacing aspect throws the waves into commotion, excites tempests, and with his mighty hand disperses ships, or dashes them to pieces": cited in Jenson, *Beyond the Slave Narrative,* 101.

33. Reinsel, "Poetry of Revolution," 48. Ironically, contrary to the opinion that Haitian writers at the time undoubtedly held, Hugo was not an abolitionist and even had racist tendencies for some period of his career. See Léon-François Hoffmann's scrupulous documentation of the issue of Hugo and race in *Haïti,* 80–95.

34. *L'Union,* May 4, 1837.

35. *Le Républicain,* August 15, 1836.

36. Edward W. Said, *Culture and Imperialism* (New York: Knopf, 1993), 51.

37. Ignace Nau and Coriolan's brother Beaubrun Ardouin, author of the eleven-volume *Études sur l'histoire d'Haïti* (1865), both held official administrative positions under Boyer. Beaubrun Ardouin renegotiated the 1825 settlement with France in 1838. Issues of both newspapers are available at http://gallica.bnf.fr.

38. Nau, *Histoire des Caciques,* 326.

39. Beaubrun Ardouin reports that Coriolan wrote one of his first essays about Coutillon Coutard, who died to save Pétion. See his "Notice Biographique," in Coriolan Ardouin, *Poésies,* xi.

40. See Jenson, *Beyond the Slave Narrative*, 106.

41. In 1822, Boyer unified the East (Santo Domingo, now the Dominican Republic) and West (Haiti) of the island of Hispaniola. The unification was a complex diplomatic enterprise involving renunciation of Spain, the help and then the dismissal of emissaries from the postcolonial complex of "Gran Colombia" in Latin America, and persuasion of Haitian and "Spanish" elites in the city of Santo Domingo that the unification was in their best interest. See Ramsey, *Spirits and the Law*, 57.

42. *L'Union*, January 31, 1839. The article from which this quotation is drawn is signed S. Faubert, le jeune, presumably a son or brother of Pierre.

43. Faubert's contemporary, the Cuban poet Gabriel de la Concepción Valdés, known as Plácido, also writes about other countries—in his case the struggles for independence in Poland and Greece. But unlike Faubert, who is writing four decades after slavery ended in Haiti, Plácido mentions these countries as a disguised way of calling attention to the lack of freedom in Cuba. See Fischer, *Modernity Disavowed*, 84, 98.

44. See Bongie, *Islands and Exiles*, chap. 6.

45. For the complete version of the poem that includes the second stanza, see Durand, *Rires et pleurs*.

What? Native race! Would you remain silent?

1. The term "indigène" or "indigenous" was used occasionally, but inconsistently, by both French and afro-diasporic members of the Armée de Saint-Domingue to differentiate soldiers of European from those of African heritage. In a separate genealogy of identities, the term "indigenous" also refers to the original inhabitants of "Hayti," the Taino Amerindian name for the island of Hispaniola. The slaves in Haiti were not indigenous, but they identified with the indigenous victims of the Spanish colonization of Hispaniola, and of the New World more generally, as evidenced in their use of the term Armée Inca (Inca Army) in some late-revolutionary correspondence. The poem begins with an outraged or sorrowful gesture to the muteness of indigenous peoples in the face of oppression. Nomenclature played a role in the evolving identity of the nation in the early years of its independence. This poem is set to the tune of the "Marseillaise," the French national anthem, whose first line appears beneath the title of the poem "Hymne haytienne" (originally rendered as "Hymne haytiène") as "Allons

enfants de la patrie." "Hymne haytienne" figures in a series of early Haitian government publications that the historian Julia Gaffield discovered in the British National Archives dossier of Edward Corbet, a British diplomat in Jamaica. A handwritten transcription identifies the document as dating from 1803—the period in which Napoleon's expedition to Saint-Domingue was defeated—but first published by the Haitian government of Jean-Jacques Dessalines on January, 21, 1804, "Dessalines being present."

2. The hero is Jean-Jacques Dessalines (assassinated October 17, 1806; date of birth not firmly established), a leader of the Haitian Revolution and the founding father of the Haitian nation. The spelling of his name as "Jacque," without a final "s," reflects the instability of orthography in some early Haitian texts.

3. In his proclamation of April 28, 1804, Dessalines would announce, "I have avenged America." In this poem, which appears to precede the proclamation, a hero avenges the indigenous people.

4. The sun is a resonant mythological topos in the early independence poems and can refer to Inca or other indigenous cults of the sun, which were occasionally featured in Haitian revolutionary rhetoric. This line refers most directly to the condemnation of captive Africans forced to labor under the baking sun in the fields. An alternate reading, in which the homicidal Frenchmen strike down the (indigenous) children of the sun, is also possible. We have chosen the second meaning for the translation.

5. The Haitian Declaration of Independence features the trope of the personified bones of the ancestors. Dessalines warns in the Declaration that the ancestors will reject their descendants from a shared tomb if those descendants fail to avenge them. Here watering the bones of the ancestors with the colonial tormentors' blood will make the bones speak the refrain of the poem. The poem as a whole is consistent with the early poetics of Dessalines's proclamations: unity with ancestry, warrior glory, avenging the tyranny of Europeans over the Amerindian inhabitants of Hayti and their African replacements.

6. Translator's note: I have chosen to translate the first- and second-person imperatives ("Vivons"/"Vivez") in the same way. The use of the second person in the third stanza of the original may be an error.

7. "Thunderbolt" (Tonnerre) probably alludes here to Dessalines's secretary Louis-Félix Boisrond Tonnerre.

8. The translation here emphasizes the Catholic valence of the word

"Patron" in the sense of Jacques as the patron saint, Saint James. Jacques could also be not a patron saint but a patron in the sense of "boss."

9. The poem ends with the letters CH, which may indicate authorship by Chanlatte, who, like Boisrond Tonnerre, was one of Dessalines's secretaries. In other works such as *L'Histoire de la catastrophe de Saint-Domingue,* Chanlatte uses the letters CH to indicate his name.

Let us now sing our glory!

1. The poem is designated "Couplets chantés et présentés à Sa Majesté Jacques Ier, Empereur d'Haïti par C. César Télémaque, contrôleur du département du Nord," although with respect to poetic form it is not composed of couplets. It was sung to the tune of "Vaude-ville du Devin du Village," from Jean-Jacques Rousseau's opera *Le Devin du village* (1752), which was adapted as a creole opera, *Jeannot et Thérèse.* This creole opera was one of the most famous and frequently performed works in Haiti, and so the notation of the Rousseau tune here can be seen as an allusion to it. The poem appeared in the *Gazette politique et commerciale d'Haïti,* November 15, 1804. César Télémaque had been a pro-French mayor prior to Haitian independence. This poem celebrating Dessalines as emperor indicates Télémaque's political evolution and can be considered an act of poetic diplomacy. The historian and critic Hénock Trouillot alleges that according to chronicles from the Pétion era, Télémaque was one of the rare former slaves who married a white woman: see his *Origines sociales de la littérature haïtienne,* 19.

2. This line suggests that it was conventional in 1804 to view Haiti as an islandwide rather than a regional (western) nation, although in January 1804 the French general Ferrand had established a French base in the eastern ("Spanish") region, which is now the Dominican Republic, and claimed that the eastern part was French.

3. The fourth line of the third stanza of the original French version is missing the word "ne" in the line "Il voit en nous que ses enfants." We have reproduced the poem as it appears in the original.

Nature, in wisdom infinite

1. The anonymous author's nom de plume may echo Dessalines's warning in an April 1804 proclamation that the Spanish, on the eastern side of the island, needed to swear fidelity to be recognized as "enfants d'Haïti" (children of Haiti). The poem was originally designated "Couplets chantés à la célébration de l'Anniversaire de

l'Indépendance d'Haïti" and published in the *Gazette politique et commerciale d'Haïti,* August 1, 1804.

2. Translator's note: I follow—though not slavishly—the original's unorthodox rhymes and repetitions; likewise its varying line lengths of eight and ten syllables, with a nine-syllable line recurring before the last line of the refrain. These vagaries were probably required by the melody to which these supposed couplets were meant to be sung.

3. Translator's Note, line 9: The original's rhyme of "mémoires" with "pères" and "frères" reflects the lingering eighteenth-century pronunciation.

4. The original reads "jette un regarde." We correct the poet's apparently inadvertent mistake.

You, O great Emperor!

1. Gautarel, as a "grenadier," represented a military elite. His simultaneous military and poetic vocation shows the continued connection between military culture and the use of poetry to celebrate the emperor, who had at the time of the Declaration of Independence chosen to be known as the "General in Chief" of Haiti. The identity of Gautarel is not further known from documents of this era, but in 1814 a "Gautarel" is listed as the music professor for the royal pages in the court of King Henry Christophe. The use of the familiar forms "toi" and "tu" in the French poem are significant. The poet evokes not just the notion of mastery over the colonial powers but the language of a soldier who feels a close bond with a leader identified, like the writer, with the tenacity of the warrior. Although the familiar form occurs throughout French poetry in the first half of the nineteenth century—for example, that of Victor Hugo—it generally is used in contexts that are personal or lyrical, not in addresses to leaders as in this poem.

2. A national celebration of Dessalines's feast day—July 25, coinciding with the Catholic feast day of Saint Jacques—was launched in the summer of 1805. See the Introduction.

What hustle-bustle, hurly-burly sound

1. The poem first appeared in "Couplets chantés à la célébration de l'Anniversaire de l'Indépendance d'Haïti," *Gazette politique et commerciale d'Haïti,* August 1, 1805 (the second year of independence). The celebration of the anniversary of the independence of Haiti, an occasion documented in the *Gazette,* has shifted chrono-

logically here to the summer, apparently in relation to Dessalines's July 25 feast-day celebration (see note 2 in "You, O great Emperor! above"). An unspoken rationale for the change is the nomination of Dessalines as emperor the previous summer, although that nomination had been backdated to earlier in 1804 for greater symbolic coherence with the early independence. This poem shows the intense importance ascribed to symbolic and communal representations of the proclamations of Dessalines's government. In documents from the time, fixed dates underlying this new cultural monumentalization were modified to create more chronological coherence.

2. Jean-Jacques Dessalines. See the notes to " What? Native race! Would you remain silent?" above.

3. For the sake of the rhyme scheme, the poet changes *emperor* to *king*.

4. We have supplied what appears to be a missing word, "notre," in the original ("offrez-lui notre hommage").

As his namesake sought to do

1. The 1814 *Relation des glorieux événements qui ont porté Leurs Majestés sur le trône d'Hayti,* by Julien Prévost, comte de Limonade, contains a number of literary texts, most of them anonymous. Prévost's role as an anthologist in this historiographical work raises the possibility that he himself may be associated with the authorship of anonymous Christophe-era poetic homages to the king. Prévost, a secretary, soldier, statesman, and contributor to the founding of the Haitian educational system, was a prolific writer whose publications included works co-authored with the important Haitian writer Pompée-Valentin de Vastey. In his notes on "As his namesake sought to do," Prévost comments that the inaugural song was followed by a hunting party in the style of Henri IV, "the good king whose virtues have been consecrated by history and who greatly resembles 'our Henry' [Christophe]." The inaugural song was also followed by a play, the *Siècle de Rhée,* and several other creative festivities. The current poem follows the "Chant inaugural" by Chanlatte (not included in this anthology).

2. This poem is based on an intricate analogy between the French king Henri IV and the Haitian king Henry Christophe. The analogy rests especially on Henry Christophe's presumed fulfillment of the ideals articulated by Henri IV, such as the notion of a "chicken in every pot," which here becomes a hen in the pot of every poor Haitian soldier. Henry Christophe (1767–1820) was one of the most prominent generals in the Haitian Revolution. He founded the

Republic of the North after the assassination in 1806 of Dessalines. On March 26, 1811, he was declared king of Haiti in the North. On October 8, 1820, ill and fearing a political coup, he committed suicide. The rise and fall of this would-be "creator" of the Haitian people—a national father figure long before the advent of "Papa Doc" Duvalier—is dramatized in Aimé Césaire's modern classic *La Tragédie du Roi Christophe* (The Tragedy of King Christophe; 1963).

3. The wife of Henry Christophe, Marie Louise. The syncretic fusion of her identity with that of the Virgin Mary is apparent here, in a structure that overlaps with the "Patron" Jacque metaphor in "Hymne haytienne" (see the notes to "What? Native race! Would you remain silent?," above) and in what we know about the feast days of Dessalines and his imperial spouse.

What sweet chants, these, that strike, entrance my ear?

1. For information on the text in which the poem appeared, Julien Prévost, comte de Limonade's *Relation des glorieux événements,* see the notes to "What his namesake sought to do," above. It was originally signed "Juste Chanlatte, comte de Rosier." This poem was sung on the occasion of the coronation of Henry Christophe on June 2, 1811. For more information about the poem, see the Introduction.

2. The chorus here served no doubt as a literal chorus as well as a classical motif. Collective singing roles were divided in the poem among the "general chorus," men, women, children, old men, soldiers, etc.

3. The first of several references to Mars, this mythological allusion connected the imagined classical realm to the Champ de Mars, a public square looking over the port in Cap-Henry (now Cap-Haïtien), where the poem was first performed. The daughter of Mars, god of war, may be interpreted here as either Nike, goddess of victory, or Harmonia, goddess of harmony.

4. Henry Christophe. See "What his namesake sought to do," above.

5. Clio, the muse of history, breathed new life into this verbal monument to Haiti's glory. Singing of Henry Christophe's "exploits" led to a new "engraving" of cultural memory.

6. The Hydra was an ancient multiheaded beast, guardian of the underworld, that was killed by Heracles.

7. Themis was the embodiment of divine order, law, and custom.

8. This stanza brings the guiding maritime inspiration of the poem into focus. The numerous classical water gods and spirits in the poem

allude to an unspoken local mythology: the Vodou underwater world, "anba dlò," presided over by the "loas," or spirit gods, Agwe and the Mermaid ("la Sirène").

9. The author refers to "la citadelle Henry" in the poem. Located on top of a large mountaintop in northern Haiti, the Citadel, also known as the Citadelle Laferrière or the Citadelle Henry Christophe, is one of the largest fortresses in the Americas, and is now a Unesco World Heritage site. The construction of this massive monument, along with that of Christophe's Sans Souci palace, is commemorated in such literary works as Alejo Carpentier's *El reino de este mundo* (Kingdom of This World) and Aimé Césaire's *La Tragédie du Roi Christophe* (The Tragedy of King Christophe).

10. This section, "La Marine" or "The Navy," alludes to the fact that the ceremony, performed overlooking the port, was in part the inauguration of Christophe's proud new naval force. Iwa Agwe and Lasirèn are typically represented in naval military splendor, sometimes in conjunction with Neptune or his Greek equivalent, Poseidon.

11. The Nereids, fifty beautiful young girls who formed Poseidon's cortege, were sometimes represented as sirens, half woman and half fish. Borne by seahorses, they carried tridents, victory crowns, or branches of coral. They were patrons of sailors and fishermen.

12. Jason, heroic leader of the Argonauts, obtained the golden fleece located in Colchis. He was thus entitled to be placed on the throne of Iolcos in Thessaly.

13. The Rutulian fields are the scene of battle in Virgil's *Aeneid*. It is there that Aeneas, Anchises' son, defeated the Rutuli, the local inhabitants of Latium, and became the founder of Rome.

14. The mythological name Sylvain, Sylvan, or Silvan refers to an association with the woods or to the forest itself. The term can refer to the person who resides in the woods or to a god or spirit of the wood. A dryad is a tree nymph, the female spirit of a tree. The dryads were friends of the goddess Artemis.

15. Orpheus was a legendary musician, poet, and prophet. He is known for the ability to charm all living things and even stones with his music; his unsuccessful attempt to retrieve his wife, Eurydice, from the underworld; and his death at the hands of Maenads, frenzied followers of Dionysus, either because he disrupted the god's worship or because he refused to love another woman after Eurydice.

16. The Christophe regime followed the lead of Dessalines in associat-

ing the "feast days" of the leaders with dates in the "Romish" calendar. "Marie," here, is no doubt a merger of queen Marie-Louise and the Virgin, just as "Henry" represents Henry Christophe and Henri IV.

17. The poem ends with an apostrophe to Minerva, the goddess of wisdom. Henry Christophe's commitment to and success in educating and uplifting the people of the North was noteworthy. Christophe can be read here as the Dawn, and the flowers can be read as the young people of Haiti.

Ascending to the heavens, I dreamt a dream

1. From *Le Télégraphe*, April 1815. Antoine Dupré died in 1816 in a duel. Neither his birth date nor biography has been documented. He fought in the resistance against Christophe and supported Alexandre Pétion, who had been in power in the southern Republic of Haiti since 1806. The historian and critic Hénock Trouillot calls him the national bard of Pétion's regime: see *Les Origines sociales de la littérature haïtienne,* 22. The Haitian lawyer Joseph Saint-Rémy wrote in the *Revue des colonies* that as a young man Dupré attempted a career as an actor in England. After he returned to Haiti, he wrote successful plays, including *La Jeune Fille* and *La Mort du général Lamare.*

2. The point of departure here, that in his dream the poet had attended a council of the gods, introduces the analogy between political councils and councils of the classical gods. This analogy leads to an allegorical encomium of the English Parliament's ban of the slave trade, contrasted with a scathing representation of political assemblies in France, where monarchy had been restored in 1814. Where abolitionist English parliamentarians plead universal rights for the peoples of Africa and the Americas, a god of fools has moved into France. The divinities of sacred rights flee France and take up permanent residence in Haiti.

3. William Wilberforce (1759–1833) was a British politician and abolitionist who helped pass the Slave Trade Act of 1807 and the Abolition Act of 1833. In his 1814 *Lettre à son Excellence Monseigneur le Prince de Talleyrand Périgord . . . au sujet de la traite des nègres,* he countered the arguments for the slave trade made by Pierre Victor Malouet, who is cited later in the poem. The other members of the Imperial Parliament in the House of Commons who are cited subsequently—Whitbread, Canning, Sidney Smith, and Protheroe— contributed to the 1814 arguments against the slave trade.

4. Author's footnote: "Frédéric Auguste, Régent d'Angleterre." This was the future George IV (1762–1830), who served as regent from 1811 to 1820 because of the mental illness of his father, George III.

5. George Canning (1770–1827) was a British statesman and politician who served as foreign secretary and, briefly, prime minister.

6. [William] Sidney Smith (1764–1840) was a British admiral who served in the French revolutionary war and who took up the slavery cause later in life.

7. Samuel Whitbread (1758–1815) was an English politician and abolitionist.

8. The poet misspells the name of Edward Protheroe (1798–1852), member of the British Parliament and outspoken proponent of the abolition of slavery.

9. Trouillot observes that the meaning of "liberté" in this poem implies opposition to the French and is closely linked to the notion of independence: see *Les Origines sociales de la littérature haïtienne*, 28.

10. Pierre Victor Malouet was the author of *Mémoire sur l'esclavage des nègres dans les possessions françaises* (1788), in which he articulated a proslavery position. More immediately for this poem, the Haitian writer Pompée-Valentin de Vastey had written a companion piece to his 1814 *Le Système colonial dévoilé*, titled *Notes à M. le Baron P. V. de Malouet,* in which he engaged polemically with Malouet's 1802 *Collection de mémoires sur les colonies, et particulièrement sur Saint-Domingue* as the ideological representation of the Restoration initiative to restore colonialism in Haiti.

11. Bellona was a Roman goddess of war. Her Greek counterpart was Enyo. She is typically depicted with a sword, helmet, spear, and torch.

O you, ancestral lord! O Sun

1. Dupré's poem was published by the politician and writer Hérard-Dumesle in *Voyage dans le Nord d'Haïti, ou révélations des lieux et des monuments historiques* (Voyages in the North of Haiti; or, Information About Historic Places and Monuments). The presumed date of the poem is 1815. Hérard-Dumesle contextualized the poem thus: "We include this hymn by Dupré solely to bequeath to the reader the pleasure of judging how much the feeling of freedom beautifies everything that it inspires" (340). Various anthologized versions of the poem have been published by Raphaël Berrou, Christophe Charles, Hénock Trouillot, and Duraciné Vaval. They vary in the placement of the second and third stanzas.

2. The sun, "god of my ancestors," is aligned in this poem with Enlightenment thought through the trope of "natural law." Yet this Enlightenment is tender, sensuous, and African. For more on the rhetoric of the sun, see "What? Native race! Would you remain silent?" above, note 4.

3. This feminine figure of liberty may seem at first to bear an association with the French icon of liberty, Marianne. But Marianne is not particularly identified with virginity. Dupré's virginal liberty evokes instead both the Virgin Mary and a secular liberty that has never been "consummated"—a virgin freedom. The eroticism of the subsequent imagery of flames, desire, feeling, and sighs suggests that liberty is then carnally embraced.

4. Just as the image of a feminine liberty evokes yet departs from the French figure of Marianne, the two final verses of the poem subtly evoke and yet transform the French national anthem, the "Marseillaise." In the "Marseillaise," the singers hope that the "impure blood" of the "horde d'esclaves"—the horde of slaves to monarchy—will water and nourish their fields. Here the poet imagines that if the colonial tyrants ever return, they will soon be put to flight, and the fleeing hordes will fertilize Haitian fields.

5. A final stanza of the poem is provided by Vaval: "Entends mes derniers adieux!/Si, quelques jours, sur tes rives,/Osent venir des tyrans,/Que leurs hordes fugitives/Servent d'engrais à nos champs!" (Yes, hear this last farewell of mine!/If ever on your island's shore/The tyrants dare their faces show,/Let their hordes' blood forevermore/Make our fields still more fertile grow!"). However, it does not appear in the Hérard-Dumesle version on which we base the provenance of the poem. Nor does it appear in the versions published by Berrou, Charles, and Trouillot.

Haitians all, come and rally round

1. Authorship of this poem is anonymously attributed to "A Haitian." It was published on October 1, 1817, in *L'Abeille haytienne,* a journal edited by Jules Solime Milscent that appeared from 1817 to 1820. The journal's motto ("Sword and Pen in the Service of the State"), discussed in the Introduction, reflects the sentiment expressed in this poem.

2. Alexandre Pétion, born in 1770 and educated in France, first entered the Haitian revolutionary arena as a member of the Napoleonic expedition of 1802, but soon transitioned to a role among his fellow Haitian military cohort. One of the founding fathers of Haiti,

he was elected president of the southern republic beginning in 1806 and ruled until his death in 1818. The concurrent Pétion and Christophe regimes reflect an era of North-South divided rule in Haiti. In this and many other poems found in *L'Abeille haytienne,* Pétion's cause was extolled. Pétion died on March 29, 1818.

3. In the French, the conclusion of each stanza with the refrain "Chantons tous vive PÉTION!/ Vive! vive notre PATRIE!" creates a visual alignment of "PÉTION" and "PATRIE." The two words have the same number of letters and begin with "P." Although the homophony is limited, the poem creates a visual analogy between head of state and the state itself.

4. Vincent Ogé (1755–91) and Jean-Baptiste Chavannes (1748–91) fought to gain representation for men of color ("de couleur," meaning of mixed race) in the French National Assembly. Their revolutionary cause became radicalized over time, and they were brutally executed after involvement in a local insurgency in 1791.

Join now our voices

1. Anonymous, from *L'Abeille haytienne,* September 1, 1817, sung to the tune of "La victoire en chantant nous ouvre la barrière." This poem appears to be connected to the celebrations of Pétion's birthday. The idea of celebrating the birthday of the head of state marks a departure from the earlier tradition of celebrating a leader's feast day. It is possible that the precise birthdates of Dessalines, his spouse, and Christophe were not known. However, Pétion, a "mulatto" from a well-to-do family, did have documentation of his birth. The Haitian lawyer Joseph St. Rémy gave April 2, 1770, as Pétion's birthday. If this is correct, the 1817 celebrations were not aligned with an actual birthdate. For more detail on Pétion, see "Haitians all, come and rally round," above.

To smite the tyrant's shackle-curse

1. Jules Solime Milscent published a number of his own poems in his newspaper *L'Abeille haytienne.* We have accessed this poem not from *L'Abeille haytienne,* however, but from the *Revue des races latines,* 644–45. Its thematic importance is noteworthy and prefigures later poems such as Pierre Faubert's "Frères, nous avons tous brisé le joug infâme" (Brothers all, we have now that foul yoke broken), reprinted below. The author seeks to rally support for a single republic of Haiti, but clearly it is the South that is called upon to yield to the North: "The North/Calls on the South ..."

Haiti watched as her children, rent asunder

1. The poem was first published in *L'Abeille haytienne* in 1818, and the author was identified there as Delile Laprée, Haitian. The header to the poem reads "Port-au-Prince, le 16 avril, 1818, an quinze de l'indépendance d'Haïti" (April 16, 1818, year 15 of Haiti's independence), which is notable because it places the inauguration of Haitian independence in 1803, not 1804. Delile Laprée was a secretary to Pétion and a mathematics professor in Pétion's educational showcase, the Lycée national de Port-au-Prince.
2. Alexandre Pétion, the "Hero." See "Haitians all, come and rally round," above.
3. Translator's note: the quote beginning in the first stanza is the voice of Haiti, and extends through the fourth stanza, within which the refrain is itself quoted. Stanzas 5–7 are either Haiti's or the poet's voice. The last stanza is again clearly in Haiti's voice.
4. Themis is the goddess of justice, law, and equity.
5. Pétion died at the age of forty-eight on March 29, 1818.
6. The emphasis on resting places in the seventh and ninth stanzas of the poem, indicated in the translation by the verb "rests," and in the original by the past participle "placée," calls to mind the unusual burial arrangements for Pétion, whose body was buried under the Port-au-Prince Tree of Liberty, while his entrails were buried in the Fort National, and his heart was given to his daughter.
7. Pétion's successor was Jean-Pierre Boyer, president of Haiti from 1820 to 1843.

Scarce does a new face shine forth from the old year's course

1. From *Le Télégraphe,* January 28, 1821. The poem is signed by General Juste Chanlatte. For information about the poem, see the Introduction.
2. The poem was undoubtedly composed for the constitutionally mandated "Fête de l'indépendance" (Independence Day), January 1. The description of weather and time of day suggests that the poem was performed publicly.
3. The reference in the original to the end of "civil horror" ("Des civiles horreurs les salpêtres éteints") alludes to the unification of the governments of the North and the South in Haiti following the suicide of Henry Christophe on October 8 the preceding fall, and the massacre of several of his court nobility, military officers, and heir later that month. The poet himself, Juste Chanlatte, a member of the Christophean nobility—the "Count of Rosiers—survived

by embracing the regime of Boyer. Chanlatte contextualizes the freedom of Boyer's unification in subdued terms, as the putting out of fires. The metaphor of saltpeter, an explosive used in warfare as an ingredient in gunpowder, alludes more generally to the explosive sparks of regional discord, now "extinguished."

4. Author's note: "President Jean-Pierre Boyer."

5. Freedom, Chanlatte suggests, is located not in the person of an individual leader but in God and the rule of law. The poem's sober, judicious tone reflects an attempt to calm dissent and represent Boyer not as a charismatic leader but as a bureaucrat or magistrate.

6. Pallas is an epithet for Athena, the Greek goddess of wisdom.

7. The founder of the Haitian independence was Jean-Jacques Dessalines. Here, Chanlatte merges symbolism of the current unification with that of an earlier independence, and implicitly suggests a unity of goals between Dessalines's "northern" and "black" identity and Boyer's "southern" and mixed-race identity. But it is the people, not the leader, who are the "living portrait" ("portrait vivant") of a God who transcends political regimes.

Why ply you your fickle ministry?

1. From *Le Télégraphe,* December 30, 1821. This was intended as a song, with music by one "Monsieur Cassian, Haitian." For more information about the poem, see the Introduction.

2. In Greek mythology Phoebe connotes the moon.

3. Like Chanlatte's "Scarce does a new face shine forth from the old year's course," this poem was created for a national independence celebration, the Fête de l'indépendance (January 1). Unlike that poem, which was published after the 1821 independence day event, this poem was published two days before the 1822 celebration. For its performance, see the Introduction. Chanlatte had created the generic contours of this performed poem with allegorical solos representing demographics of the involved community in his 1814 "What sweet chants, these, that strike, entrance my ear?"

4. Henry Christophe. See notes to "As his namesake sought to do," above. As noted in the Introduction, Chanlatte here condemns the leader whom he previously served. Chanlatte held positions in the nascent Haitian state under the consecutive governments of Dessalines, Christophe, and Boyer, each of which attacked the ethnic and political identities of the previous regime.

5. Alexandre Pétion. See notes to "Haitians all, come and rally round," above.

6. Jean-Pierre Boyer. See notes to "Scarce does a new face shine forth from the old year's course," above.

7. As noted in the Introduction, the column erected to Independence is a metonymic representation of the nation.

8. This poem is chronologically situated just prior to Boyer's unification of the Spanish part of the island of Hispaniola to the Haitian part in the west. Pétion's ghost proposes here that "one government," already unifying North and South within Haiti, will soon become the torch-bearer for the Americas. This larger hemispheric symbolism alludes to other independence movements including Venezuelan independence earlier in 1821. Pétion had been a close collaborator with Simón Bolívar, who had visited Haiti to gain inspiration and allies in 1812. Pétion arises from the dead in this stanza to hail the extension of the decolonization movements of which Haiti is the beacon or "phare."

9. For the allegorical figure of the spirit, see the notes to "What sweet chants, these, that strike, entrance my ear?" above.

10. In Attic drama, the Coryphaeus was the leader of the chorus.

11. Astraea was the goddess of nocturnal oracles and falling stars. She was the daughter of Phoebe.

12. In Greek mythology, the Titan Rhea is the Great Mother, a symbol of female fertility.

See that old planter

1. This poem was published in 1822 in *Le Propagateur haïtien, journal politique et littéraire, rédigé par plusieurs haïtiens*. As for who the "anonymous" author might be, it is worth noting that the newspaper involved a group effort, as noted in the title. Delile Laprée (see the notes to "Haiti watched as her children, rent asunder," above) was listed as the contact for subscriptions and submissions. Some contemporaneous sources claimed that General Joseph Balthazar Inginac ran the newspaper. Inginac served as a secretary, in what might best be described as a cabinet financial role, under Dessalines, Pétion, and Boyer. He was so powerful politically that some journalists saw him as the true mastermind of the Boyer government. However, other contemporaneous sources identified Noël Colombel, the son of a French colonist and a woman of mixed race in Saint-Domingue, as the founder of the paper. Colombel had also been involved in editing *L'Abeille haytienne*.

2. The "old planter" here can be read most directly as France but also as the allegorical figure of any former colonial power, includ-

ing Spain. For Spain in relation to Boyer's 1822 unification of East (Santo Domingo) and West (Haiti) on the island of Hispaniola, see the Introduction. This poem presents the colonists in general, not any internal group, as the true foes of the inhabitants of the island of Haiti.

3. "Us" represents the Haitian people.

4. The refrain "A genoux!" (Bend the knee!) articulates the sadistic privilege anachronistically wielded by France over its former slaves. It serves as the transition from the viewpoint of the Haitians—"See that old planter"—to the imperious denigrations in the voice of the planter himself.

5. The 1822 date of the poem is echoed in the planter's chronology: according to the planter, Haiti has had a delusion of independence now for "bientôt vingt ans" (two decades), which would situate the independence in late 1803.

6. The first Haitian Constitution was published under Dessalines in 1805.

7. The Code Noir was passed by Louis XIV in 1685. It imposed harsh controls over the conduct of slaves in the French colonial empire.

8. The torture of slaves called "quatre-piquets" consisted of attaching the slaves' hands and legs to four posts spread out on the ground.

9. The French general Jean-Baptiste Donatien de Vimeur, comte de Rochambeau used mastiffs, which attacked and even ate the flesh of rebelling blacks in the macabre final year of the Haitian revolution.

10. For Pétion, see the notes to "Haitians all, come and rally round"; for Boyer, see the notes to "Haiti watched as her children, rent asunder," above.

11. The colonist uses the symbolism of earthquake—all too familiar on the island of Hispaniola—to threaten a military conquest of the independent, unified island. Rhetorically, the poet stimulates Haitians to react against this threat.

From South and West

1. The poem is from a tragedy by Jean-Baptiste Romane (1807–58), *La Mort de Christophe,* which was performed in 1823. (For Christophe, see the notes to "As his namesake sought to do," above.) This excerpt was published in Paris in the short-lived satirical journal *Le Diable boiteux* in 1823, where the author was identified as a "jeune poète nègre" (young black poet). Boyer attended the play,

which refers directly and scornfully to him ("Hateful Boyer,/Who seized Pétion's reins"). In the journal excerpt it was noted that Boyer refrained from censoring these words, perhaps because the partisan viewpoint of the speakers—Christophe and his supporter Jean-Philippe—is clearly not endorsed by the poet. Christophe's death has been depicted in other Haitian works, including the dramatic poem "Au cœur de la citadel" by Jean Fernand Brierre (1909–92), the play *Le Roi Christophe* by Vergniaud Leconte (1868–1932), and the play *Monsieur de Vastey* by René Philoctète (1932–90).

2. For the politics of the South and the West, see the notes to "Why ply your fickle ministry?" above,

3. Saint-Marc is a coastal port city in western Haiti. It was at Saint-Marc, on October 2, 1820, that a mutiny sparked a revolt against Christophe.

4. For Boyer, see notes to "Scarce does a new face shine forth from the old year's course"; for Pétion, see the notes to "Haitians all, come and rally round," above.

5. Marcus Portius Cato the Younger (95–46 B.C.E.) was a Roman statesman known for his moral integrity. Marcus Junius Brutus (85–42 B.C.E.) was a Roman general who conspired to assassinate Julius Caesar. Both were prominent statesmen in Roman history who took actions involving figures of power, as did Christophe's generals.

About the lightning-flaring furrows

1. Hérard-Dumesle's 1824 narrative of his travels around the North of Haiti after the fall of the Christophe monarchy contains the earliest known transcription of the "Serment du Bois Caïman" (Oath of the Cayman Woods). See Appendix A, below.

2. Spartacus (109–71 B.C.E.) was a Thracian gladiator who led a major slave uprising against the Roman Empire. His struggle emblematizes slaves' fight for freedom. Guillaume-Thomas Raynal, in his 1774 history of the East and West Indies, queried, "Where is this great man . . . this new Spartacus"? Writers including Alphonse de Lamartine subsequently celebrated Toussaint Louverture as the "black Spartacus" (Spartacus noir). Hérard-Dumesle uses the figure of Spartacus to introduce a long series of analogies between classical and afro-diasporic revolutionary figures and motifs.

3. Aeolus is the Greek spirit of winds. The participants in the ceremony are the sons of the spirit of the winds, the thunder storm, which relates to Vodou practices as well as to tempestuous weather.

4. The symbol of the bamboo is one of numerous analogies between natural features in the classical mythological traditions and the Caribbean tropical environment.
5. The throne of nature.
6. Virgil (70–19 B.C.E.), a celebrated ancient Roman poet of the Augustan period. Ausonia, an ancient town in central Italy, was destroyed by the Romans in 314 B.C.E.
7. The clemency is nature's, that is, God's.
8. The poet refers here to different shades of brownness or, possibly, African practices of scarification, the etching, burning, or cutting of words or designs on the skin.
9. Geneva is an example of a great republic arising out of political ideals and philosophy, like Haiti. "Scaling hands" in the translation refers to the famous Escalade (the act of scaling defensive walls), which is celebrated annually in Geneva, Switzerland, in memory of the defeat of the troops sent by Charles Emmanuel I, duke of Savoy, in 1602.
10. Zephyr is the Greek god of the gentle west wind. Boreas is the Greek god of the north wind. The allegory of the winds in this poem may indirectly evoke the cardinal orientations with which Haitian leaders had been associated: Pétion in the South and the Southwest, Christophe in the North. Boyer, the leader at the time of the publication of the *Voyage,* united not only North and South, but also East (now the Dominican Republic) and West (Haiti).
11. The language of the forebears is here rendered in two forms: the first, as it appears in the oath quoted within the text of the poem, is an idealized, classical language of military oratory. The second, which appeared at the bottom of the page of the original publication is Creole. We reproduce it in Appendix A, below.
12. Allusion to lightning here again references the importance of Ogoun and thunderstorms as divine forces in Vodou.
13. Jason was a Greek hero and leader of the Argonauts in their quest for the Golden Fleece.
14. In the Islamic state, the caliphate, ruled by the caliph, is analogous to the Papal State, ruled by the pontiff. The poet appears to allude to the global multiplicity of systems of religious authority and spiritual protection.

Hail, distant climes!

1. Chopin appears to have been French. According to the *Revue encylopédique,* however, he collaborated with "un homme de

couleur" (a person of color) named Delanoue, and the poem was published thanks to the efforts of Chopin's students "of color." The poem's publication in the Haitian *Propagateur haïtien* indicates its integration into Haitian culture and politics. And although Chopin is identified as "un littérateur français" (a French writer) in a note to Pierre Faubert's *Ogé ou le préjugé de couleur,* performed in 1841 and published in 1856, his tribute to Faubert's mother quoted in the note attests to his close involvement with the Haitian community: "Her house was open to all Haitians: to see her, surrounded by so much respect and love, one would have taken her for the mother of this great family."

2. In the first line of the second stanza of the French poem the word *verdissent* has been substituted for *fleurissent,* which appears to be a misprint in the original or an error in our transcription of the poem.

3. "Royalty's eldest son" is Charles X. The poem appears to have been timed to celebrate his coronation as well as France's acknowledgment of Haiti's independence.

4. Leonidas was a king of ancient Sparta who led the Spartans against the Persians and died a hero in the Battle of Thermopylae. He was thought to be a descendant of Heracles and to have inherited his ancestor's strength and bravery.

5. In 1821, the Greeks revolted against the Ottoman Empire. Liberals implored European governments to help the Greeks, as Chopin implores Charles X to do in this poem.

6. The poet admonishes the Haitians to be good Catholics, which is in line with the abolitionist Henri Grégoire's efforts in Haiti at the time.

7. Chopin's French identity is corroborated by the expressions "our French arts" and "our depravity" in the final stanza.

What King, this, he whose weal outspread?

1. This poem appeared in *Le Télégraphe* on July 24, 1825. It was sung to the tune of "Soldats français, chantez Roland."

2. Haiti was the second republic in the hemisphere.

3. For Charles X, see the Introduction and notes to "Hail, distant climes."

4. As noted in the Introduction, allegiance to Haiti comes before that which is pledged to France.

5. Henri IV (1553–1610) was the much-venerated first Bourbon monarch.

6. The "Sons of Saint Louis" were French soldiers mobilized by Louis XVIII in 1823 to restore the Spanish Bourbon king Ferdinand VII to the throne.

The world has hailed your sons

1. Jean-Baptiste Romane first appeared in the literary record as the sixteen-year-old author of the play *La Mort de Christophe* in the *Propagateur haïtien* in 1824. The international press took note of this afro-diasporic prodigy, and the *Diable boiteux* in France added that the criticism of the Boyer government in the play was a sign that the Haitian government "has not yet recognized the advantages" of censorship. Indeed, Romane subsequently was integrated into the poetic vanguard of the Boyer regime, as the current poem demonstrates. The Haitian *Télégraphe* published this poem as part of a long account of the public figures and events connected with Haiti's celebration, which began on July 3, 1825, of France's recognition of the "full and entire independence" of its government. Amid these festivities, on July 11, Romane's "Hymn to Independence" was sung by the citizen Élie, a representative of the commune of Port-au-Prince, to an audience comprising the principal Haitian authorities as well as the baron de Mackau, the captain charged with delivering to Boyer the Royal Ordonnance signed by Charles X.

2. The palm represents the tropical vegetation of Haiti; the lily (fleur-de-lis) symbolizes France. Alexandre Pétion placed the palm tree in the center of the Haitian flag in 1806. For examples of the thematic centrality of the palm as a symbol of Haiti, see the first Haitian novel, Émeric Bergeaud's *Stella* (1859).

3. In wishing France and Haiti long life, the poet significantly places Haiti first. He also praises the Haitian forefathers in the second stanza before praising the French king in stanza 3. In the ordonnance of 1825, France's interests come first, with recognition of Haitian independence placed at the end.

4. The poet significantly emphasizes that Haitians were responsible for gaining their own independence.

5. The Artibonite River is the longest and most important river in Haiti as well as the longest on the island of Hispaniola. It forms part of the international border between Haiti and the Dominican Republic.

6. For Boyer, see the notes to "Scarce does a new face shine forth from the old year's course," above.

What looms there, shining afar before our startled eyes?

1. This poem first appeared in *Le Propagateur haïtien*, January 15, 1826.

2. As noted in the Introduction, the phrase "live free or die" evokes past battles for freedom.

3. For Charles X, see the Introduction and notes to "Hail, distant climes."

4. Lucius Quinctius Cincinnatus (519–430 B.C.E.) was regarded as a hero of early Rome. Having put down his plow to serve his country, he resigned when the enemy forces were defeated and returned to his field. The translation "plowshare-scepter" in stanza 5 reflects this legacy. Cincinnatus's willingness to resign absolute authority with the end of the crisis has made him a model of service to the greater good, lack of personal ambition, modesty, and virtue.

5. Ceres is the Roman goddess of agriculture and harvests.

6. See the notes to "Scarce does a new face shine forth from the old year's course," above.

One day, Lily to Palm says

1. This poem first appeared in *Le Propagateur haïtien,* January 15, 1826. Pierre Faubert (1806–68), from Aux Cayes and educated in France, was an adviser to President Boyer and director of the Lycée Pétion. He played a key diplomatic role in the Concordat between Haiti and the Papacy in 1860 under the rule of President Fabre Geffrard.

2. For the symbolic meaning of Lily and Palm, see "The world has hailed your sons," above.

3. Like other poets, including Chanlatte in the later years of his career, Faubert lavishes praise on Boyer and celebrates the accord he made with Charles X: see the Introduction.

4. King Henri IV (1553–1610) was prince of Béarn.

5. While *Liberté* remains the rallying cry in this poem, Faubert also makes the case that a new era of peace must replace one based on past animosities and hostility.

O Muse, now to new songs I tune my lyre

1. For a discussion of the *Haitiade,* see the Introduction.

2. The poem begins with a first-person narrator and then shifts to a different, omniscient voice.

3. The temporal focal point is 1802, twelve years after the onset of uprisings in 1790–91.

4. Toussaint Louverture (1743–1803) was the leader of the Haitian Revolution. Betrayed by Napoleon, he was captured and imprisoned

in Fort-de-Joux in France, where he died. Some historians are critical of what they consider his overly conciliatory relationship with France in the postrevolutionary period and his inclination to force freed blacks back to work under conditions resembling slavery. The poem's bias in his favor is reflected in the capitalization of his name throughout the poem.

5. Toussaint may have been involved in the planning of the Boukman rebellion of 1791. He joined the army officially shortly after the initial revolt.

6. A lambi is a large conch shell that was used as a trumpet to sound a rallying cry among slaves.

7. The rest of Canto 1 presents a reenactment that the major participants in the battle for Haitian independence and their troops are summoned to attend. Some, notably Pétion and Boyer, are eulogized. Others—in particular Christophe and Dessalines— are criticized for their ambition, cruelty, and tyrannical acts. Of diverse racial backgrounds and both sexes, the cadre of respected, committed Haitians is reunited as they were in battle. A note in the second edition states: "In grouping together the principal characters, and assigning to each the place he deserved, the poet tried, perhaps unwittingly, to fight against color prejudice, so regrettably embedded in the conduct of former slave countries" (Gragnon-Lacoste, L'Haïtiade, 165).

8. The "merveilleux chrétien" (divine intervention) was considered appropriate in the higher genres of poetry and especially in the genre of the epic, to which L'Haïtiade belongs.

9. Toussaint is typically depicted with his hat decorated with three white plumes and a grenadier's plume.

10. For Christophe, see the notes to "As his namesake sought to do," above. In the introduction to the third edition, Michel Desquiron refers to the statements about Christophe and Dessalines as errors of judgment (xvii).

11. For Dessalines, see the notes to "What? Native race! Would you remain silent?" above.

12. This stanza praises several generals in the Haitian revolutionary army including Philippe Clervaux and Gédéon.

13. The Chevalier de Bayard was known throughout medieval (and later) lore as "le chevalier sans peur et sans reproche" (the fearless, irreproachable chevalier). He was an icon of the courtly tradition.

14. Toussaint considered his nephew Moïse to be a traitor and had

him executed. The poet chooses, tellingly, not to dwell on this part of Toussaint's story.

15. The following stanzas continue the praise of generals in the Haitian revolutionary army: Télémaque, Beauvais, Inginac, Marion, and Bonnet.

16. Mole-Saint-Nicolas is a city in Haiti.

17. For Ogé, see the notes to "Haitians all, come and rally round," above.

18. André Rigaud (1761–1811) was a leading Haitian military and political leader who ruled the South and West.

19. For Pétion, see the notes to "Haitians all, come and rally round," above.

20. For Boyer, see notes to "Scarce does a new face shine forth from the old year's course," above.

21. Antilochus and Nestor in the *Iliad*, along with Telemachus and Mentor in the *Odyssey*, are seen as models from antiquity of sons and older men bravely fighting together.

22. The poet continues to name and eulogize key figures of Haitian history including Juste Chanlatte: see the Introduction.

23. Jean-Christophe Imbert (1779–1855), was acting president of Haiti in 1811.

24. For Cato, see the notes to "From South and West," above.

25. Noël Colombel, secretary to both Pétion and Boyer, was the editor of *L'Abeille haytienne*. Gragnon-Lacoste notes an anachronism in the poem: Colombel was a schoolboy in France at the time of the Haitian revolution.

26. Efforts were undertaken to recognize Haiti's independence, almost certainly at the price of the restoration of slavery, under Louis XVIII.

27. This is the first part of the poem that adopts Toussaint Louverture's voice: see the Introduction.

28. A return to the first person, as at the beginning of the poem, begins here. At the end of the poem, in Canto 8, a repetition of this same refrain occurs: see the summary of the *Haïtiade* in Appendix B.

29. History shows that emancipation was gained by the slaves, not granted by the French, as this poem suggests.

The Bechouans

1. *The Bechouans* consists of five poems ("The Dance," "Song of Minora," "The Bath," "The Bushmen," and "The Departure of the

Slave Ship"). The title page contains two quotations: the first from Judges 21, "Quand vous verrez que les filles de Silo sortiront pour danser avec des flûtes, alors vous vous élancerez des vignes, et vous enlèverez pour chacun sa femme, et vous vous en irez au pays de Benjamin" (And see, and, behold, if the daughters of Shiloh come out to dance in dances, then come ye out of the vineyards, and catch ye every man his wife of the daughters of Shiloh, and go to the land of Benjamin); and the second by Ignace Nau, "Un négrier sur l'Atlantique/Courait sans lumière et sans bruit" (A slave ship—darkly, noiselessly—was crossing the Atlantic sea). *The Bechouans* was originally published in Haitian newspapers in the 1830s and later republished by the poet's brother Beaubrun Ardouin in *Poésies de Coriolan Ardouin*(1881). "The Dance," the first of the five poems, was published in *L'Union* on November 29, 1838. It appears as "Fragment de poésie de feu Coriolan Ardouin (a poetic fragment by the late Coriolan Ardouin) and is titled "La Danse des Betjouanes: extrait d'un petit poème sur l'Afrique" (The Dance of the Bechouans: Excerpt of a Little Poem About Africa"). The precocious productivity of Coriolan Ardouin (1812–35), who died in his early twenties, recalls that of Arthur Rimbaud. But Coriolan, the brother of the historian-statesmen Beaubrun Ardouin (1796–1865) and Céligni Ardouin (1806–49), united African themes with a typically Romantic melancholy. The Ardouin and Nau brothers were an essential network for the dynamic moment referred to as the "Cénacle de 1836" or the "Cénacle romantique" in Haiti. The poetry of Coriolan Ardouin is in Nau, *Reliquiae d'un poète haïtien*.

2. The Amirantes belong to the Outer Islands of the Seychelles, which are located in the western Indian Ocean.

3. The Bechouans are alleged to be indigenous people of Bechuanaland, which now forms part of South Africa. However, references to other locations can also be found, undoubtedly because visiting Westerners in the nineteenth century used the same name for diverse regions.

4. Drums appear here and elsewhere in *The Bechouans* as a warning of impending danger and call attention to the musicality of Haitian cultural practices.

5. The assotor, called a *sotor* in the poem, is a large drum from Haiti. Its low, heavy sound can travel for several kilometers in the mountains. It is a traditional instrument in Vodou ceremonies. During the Haitian Revolution, when French troops sought to regain control of newly liberated regions, Toussaint Louverture reportedly made use of the assotor to send coded messages between the mountains and valleys.

6. "Song of Minora" appeared in *L'Union* on December 13, 1838.

7. Consistent with romantic poetry in France and Haiti at the time, "Song of Minora" uses local color to evoke non-European settings. See the Introduction.

8. The Kuruman (Koûramma) is a river in the northern Cape region of South Africa. The geographical references in this and other poems include a range of locations in south central and eastern Africa.

9. This poem contains an intimation that Minora's lover has been captured while away in battle.

10. The petals of this sensitive plant, a kind of mimosa, close up at night.

11. We have omitted a full line of ellipsis points that appear following this line in the original poem. Here and below, omissions of a line or more of ellipsis points are indicated in the poem by ellipsis points in brackets.

12. Although the term *bechouan* is imprecise, Amy Reinsel alleges in "Poetry of Revolution" that it can be identified with Bantu languages: *be-* is a prefix in Bantu for the human plural; *tjouan* is like *tswan* in *Botswana*. *Betjouanes* is feminine here to refer to women of the Botswana area, 79.

13. The Bushmen (Boschismens) of south central and eastern Africa were feared by other blacks for their bloodthirsty ways. Émile Nau states that they terrorized their neighbors, the Bechouans, invading their villages to obtain prisoners to sell: see his *Histoire des Caciques* (Paris: Guérin, 1894), 328. The term comes from the Dutch, meaning bandit or outlaw, which may be the sense in which Ardouin uses it. For the Bushmen's involvement with the slave trade see Reinsel, "Poetry of Revolution," 78–79.

14. The simoom is a violent hot wind that blows across the deserts of Africa.

15. A *Tonnelle* is a tent used for Vodou worship. It consists of posts erected to support a roof covered with palm or banana leaves. It is significant that Ardouin chooses here to call attention to Haitian practices of Vodou and their African roots.

16. This poem adopts a double perspective: that of the slave victim and that of an omniscient narrator. The first four lines of the poem reflect the slave girl's point of view.

17. *Halcyon* is the Greek word for kingfisher. The ancients believed that it laid its eggs on the surface of the sea, hatching them during the calm just before the winter solstice. The bird was also believed to bring fair weather, thus giving rise to the term "halcyon days."

18. The adoption of the slaves' perspective during the Atlantic crossing in this poem is unique in our collection.
19. Ardouin personifies the ship. He evokes the white sailors as being as blind to their destiny as the slaves they are transporting.
20. Émile Nau praises Ardouin's *Betjouanes* poems as a whole, but he finds the ending of this one to be too vague and lacking in a precise dramatic conclusion: see *Reliquiae d'un poète haïtien,* 17.

When the sky donned the setting sun's fine golds

1. From *Poésies de Coriolan Ardouin*. The version published in *Le Républicain* (January 1, 1837) does not contain stanzas 3 and 5.
2. Ardouin's romantic use of nature and local color are apparent in his evocation of the old soldiers.
3. The reference here is to Pétion, although his name appears only in the title. For Pétion, see the notes to "Haitians all, come and rally round," above.
4. Unlike *The Bechouans,* in which the impending doom evoked is capture and enslavement in Africa, in this poem the setting is Haiti and the threat is internal and political.
5. The use of "our" situates the poet within the crisis of his nation's destiny.
6. On November 8, 1838, *L'Union* published a poem titled "Célie au lit de mort de Pétion" (Célie at Pétion's deathbed). Represented as the younger daughter of "La Patrie" ("The Nation"), she deplores Pétion's death, which has left the country lost and near ruin. Pétion's daughter was given her father's heart at the time of his burial.

Oh! I recall that day

1. From *Poésies de Coriolan Ardouin*.
2. This poem calls attention to Haitian oral tradition. Mila's story is passed down to the first-person narrator, speaking here, from his father. The poem presents the romance of the "bossale" or African-born slave Mila, "the beautiful Angolan," once "the pride of Angola," with the Creole Osala. Mila works in the fields, singing of her love for Osala. The colonial master, Elbreuil, hears her Creole song and thinks that the Angolan is the most beautiful woman on the plantation, but she remains mistress of herself—unyielding. Osala in the meantime approaches, singing of his own love for Africa, accompanied by the music of the mandolin. The desire that the colonist, Elbreuil, feels for Mila leads to a tragic, unstated

moment in which Osala, chained far away, is unable to come to her aid, and she dies, presumably in the context of sexual assault by her master.

3. The quotations suggest a flashback in time and a shift to the voice and point of view of Mila, a slave.

4. Frangipane and sugarcane are among the distinctive Haitian products found in the poem. "Frangipane" refers to any variety of tropical American deciduous shrubs.

5. Translator's note: I took the liberty of changing the "hoe" in the original to a "scythe."

6. Similar analogies between birds and the plight of slaves occur in the poetry of the French romantic poet Marceline Desbordes-Valmore in the 1820s.

7. Ardouin emphasizes Haitian traditions of music and storytelling among slaves, as well as their love and nostalgia for the African homeland.

8. The variant of "Sahara" in French, "Sarah," is close to the Arabic word for the desert, "al-Sarah."

9. The lines in quotations depict Mila's jealousy in Osala's absence of an imagined rival, Marie.

10. The last part of the poem evokes cruelty toward slaves in terms of silencing their voices: the name that Osala cannot hear, the song that Mila cannot finish singing, the sounds that the mourners cannot utter.

There did he fall

1. From *Poésies de Coriolan Ardouin.*

2. The reference to the emperor and the title, "The Pont-Rouge," make it clear that the poem is about Dessalines, although he is not named until the last part. (For Dessalines, see the notes to" What? Native race! Would you remain silent?" above) The conspiracy to overthrow Dessalines allegedly included both Christophe and Pétion. Dessalines was assassinated en route to battle the rebels, north of Port-au-Prince at Pont Larnage, which is now known as Pont-Rouge. The date, which is not given in the poem, was October 17, 1806. After he was killed, a woman called Défilée (Dédée Bazile) took Dessalines's mutilated body to give him a proper burial. Hénock Trouillot, a Haitian historian and dramatist, is the author of a play about the incident, *Dessalines ou le sang du Pont-rouge* (1967); Jean Métellus also wrote a play, *Le Pont rouge,* in 1991 commemorating the event.

3. Although mention here of Dessalines's bloody deeds may seem to undercut his status as the founder of the nation, his courage and glory are celebrated in the rest of the poem.

4. In her doctoral dissertation, Amy Reinsel observes that the poem contains two temporalities: the time when Dessalines was assassinated in 1806 and his defeat of the French in 1804: see "Poetry of Revolution," 86.

5. Ardouin adopts the arrogant voice and viewpoint of colonists who thought they could prevail after capturing Toussaint Louverture. (For Toussaint Louverture, see the notes to " O Muse, now to new songs I tune my lyre," above) The mocking of white colonists here recalls the taunts found in "See that old planter."

6. The poem suggests that the violence against whites was justified and that it was needed to turn passive slaves into warriors.

7. The poem ends on a note that calls to mind the notion of "mains sales" (dirty hands) in Jean-Paul Sartre's political play *Les Mains sales:* there is no purity in politics.

Dessalines!... At that name, doff hats, my friends!

1. The poem was composed on December 31, 1838, and appeared in *L'Union* on January 3, 1839. It follows an article about the two treaties signed between Haiti and France in 1838 that reduced Haiti's exorbitant debt to France: see the Introduction. In 1838 the debt was reduced from 150 million to 60 million francs. In this poem, Boyer, who negotiated the 1825 treaty, is not mentioned. Thomas Madiou published an excerpt of the poem in *Histoire d'Haïti, 1827–1843,* vol. 7 (Port-au-Prince: Éditions Henri Deschamps, 1988), 266, noting that it was composed to honor the Haitian celebration of independence in 1839. For Dessalines, see the notes to "What? Native race! Would you remain silent?" above. He was identified as African-born in a variety of contemporaneous or early-nineteenth-century accounts.

2. Although Haitians who could or would have read this poem were limited to the educated elite, the address to the people ("my friends") is an indication of a national identity that extends beyond that elite. Similarly, the first stanza uses an inclusive "we" and proclaims all Haitians, heirs of the fight for independence, to be heroes.

3. The poem suggests that Independence Day in 1839 marks a new beginning. In 1838, Hérard-Dumesle, the leader of opposition to Boyer, was expelled from the legislature and imprisoned.

4. Through Dessalines, the poem celebrates the African and slave origins of Haiti. It suggests the critical attitude toward Boyer and the reigning mulatto elite. Numerous articles in *L'Union* focused on the history and legacy of slavery including the events of Ogé's death. *L'Union* published abolitionist writings by Agenor Gasparin and Thomas Clarkson.

5. Although this is not a direct quote from Dessalines's proclamations, it can be read as a paraphrase of them—for example, see the line in the Declaration of Independence, "Quand nous lasserons-nous de respirer le même air qu'eux?" (When will we weary of breathing the same air they breathe?)

6. The scene of Dessalines's composition of the act of independence is not historically accurate. It is an imagined re-creation in which the leader responds directly to the will of the people.

7. The phrase "tomorrow's sun shall rise" no doubt connects the audience to the first day of the New Year of 1839, while the lyrical celebration of nature at the end of the poem affirms an unwavering commitment to the Haitians' control of their homeland.

Oh, the delight of your days freedom-spent!

1. "To the Spirit of the Fatherland" appeared in *L'Union* on April 14, 1839, following an article rendering homage to the English abolitionist Thomas Clarkson. Various Haitian anthologies report that it was unfinished at the time of Nau's death and present truncated versions of it. The version we present here, which is drawn from its publication in *L'Union* in 1839, appears to be complete.

2. The "Spirit," the "Génie de la Patrie," perhaps derives from Dessalines's figuration of the "irritated genius" of Haiti: see the notes to "What sweet chants, these, that strike, entrance my ear?," above.

3. For Nau, whose loss of his beloved wife Marie is evoked in the poem, women are linked to nature and inspiration. In contrast, the Spirit is associated with Haiti's male heroic tradition. Because that tradition is masculine, Nau depicts male nourishment of the country. Although undoubtedly allegorical, male lactation is physically possible and was of interest in the eighteenth and nineteenth centuries to Alexander von Humboldt and Charles Darwin.

4. Nau argues throughout the poem that unity, equality, and peace are necessary for the country to move toward progress.

5. Pétion is presented here with the original blue-and-red flag created by Dessalines. It was maintained during Pétion's regime.

Father dear, how I love to cast my glance over these hills and fields

1. The poem first appeared in *L'Union* on March 24, 1839. Anonymous poems presented as a dialogue between an old man and a son can be found in several other issues of *L'Union* as well.
2. The association of nature with homeland and independence is a recurrent motif in poetry of the 1830s.
3. For the reasons for a renewed sense of hope in 1839, see the notes to "Dessalines!... At that name, doff hats, my friends!" above.
4. It is not clear who the "one man" is, but it seems unlikely that it was Boyer (see the notes to "Haiti watched as her children, rent asunder," above), who was criticized by the editors of *L'Union*. It is more likely that it is the founder of the republic, the much beloved Pétion (see the notes to "Haitians all, come and rally round," above).
5. For Ogé, see the notes to "Haitians all, come and rally round," above.
6. Author's note: "The Spanish."
7. Author's note: "Don Gracia."
8. This poem is in keeping with others in *L'Union* which glorify the heroism of Haitian leaders and consider the violence that occurred under Dessalines to have been justified.

Harried, we stand upon this shore

1. "Harried, we stand upon this shore" is from *Ogé ou le Préjugé de couleur,* which was performed on February 9, 1841. It was published in 1856. The three-act play, described as a *drame historique* (historical drama), is in prose and is followed, in its published version in 1856, by a series of poems titled *Poésies fugitives* (Fleeting Poems). "Harried, we stand upon this shore" is a rebel song that is heard in act 1, scene 5, when military forces appear. *Ogé ou le préjugé de couleur* was composed by Faubert as director of the Lycée national de Port-au-Prince for performance by his students at the annual prize ceremony in 1841. Subsequently, as Faubert notes in the introduction to his 1856 edition of the text, it was cited extensively by the French abolitionist Victor Schoelcher as an example of what he saw as the ideology of the *faction jaune* (yellow faction) in Haiti. Faubert summarized Schoelcher's interpretation that it was "carried out by order of [the Boyer] government, and that it was a work written under the influence of color prejudice" (13). Although Faubert notes that he was closely associated with the

Boyer government, he states that the play was completely independent of government influence (15). Faubert's work represents a view of Haiti's independence as deeply rooted in a lineage from Ogé through Pétion.

2. The motto "la liberté ou la mort" (freedom or death) recurs in works reclaiming political liberation.

All praise his power, the God of the oppressed!

1. This selection is taken from *Ogé ou le Préjugé de couleur,* act 2, scene 1.
2. For Ogé, see the notes to "Haitians all, come and rally round." Ogé is depicted "un drapeau à la main" (holding a flag).
3. Faubert chooses to depict Ogé as a champion of slaves in particular, not simply as a defender of the rights of persons of color in general.

Proudly I say, "I love you," negress mine

1. This is one of the "Fleeting Poems" included in Faubert's *Ogé ou le Préjugé de couleur.* See the notes to "Harried, we stand upon this shore," above.
2. We interpret this poem as celebrating black women's beauty, devotion, and capacity for true love, pace Hénock Trouillot, who contends in his anthology that the "negress" is only depicted as a sensual being and is portrayed as inferior to the white woman, Elina, who rejects the narrator of the poem. Moreover, Trouillot anachronistically sees the poem as emblematizing a lack of respect for blacks under the regime of Fabre Geffrard, who became president in 1859, seventeen years after Faubert's poem was written. See Trouillot, *Les Origines sociales de la littérature haïtienne,* 155–56. That the poem describes her beauty as "le doux reflet de l'âme" (a soul sincere) indicates that the black woman's sensual qualities are not her only or even most important attributes.
3. Translator's note: I've understood the French "épargnez-le" to mean "spare it" (i.e., love).
4. The narrator identifies himself as white. Although Trouillot affirms that Faubert was white (*Les Origines sociales de la littérature,* 156), the exact nature of his ethnic background is unclear and, we believe, ultimately unimportant. As other poems in this volume have shown, authors who may have been white were, like Faubert, firmly implanted in Haitian culture and politics, and had formed a Haitian identity.

Brothers all, we have now that foul yoke broken

1. This is one of the "Fleeting Poems" included in Faubert's *Ogé ou le Préjugé de couleur*. See the notes to "Harried, we stand upon this shore," above.
2. Here and elsewhere Faubert refers to the United States.
3. Jonathas Granville (1785–1841) was a Haitian soldier, diplomat, and civil servant who worked to encourage free blacks in the United States to immigrate to Haiti. William Wilberforce (1759–1833) was a British politician and abolitionist. His campaigns helped pass the Slave Trade Act of 1807 and the Slavery Abolition Act of 1833. The abbé Henri Grégoire (1750–1831) was the leading French abolitionist throughout the revolutionary period and the early decades of the nineteenth century. He was closely involved in Haiti in the years following independence in 1804.
4. "Pactole" in the French version refers to a source of riches such as gold mines. It refers to the Greek river which, according to legend, contained flecks of gold.
5. U.S. ambitions to annex Cuba were well known at the time.
6. In the 1830s, Hungary was rife with internal conflict. Habsburg monarchs tried to preclude the industrialization of the country, and nobles insisted on retaining their privileges. Reformers saw the urgent need for modernization and addressing the conditions of the peasantry. Faubert makes an ardent plea here for an end to civil conflicts within Haiti.

Appendix C. Once the Eternal

1. The poem is attributed to "JC, né en Afrique" (JC, born in Africa). It was submitted to the poetry contest on the abolition of slavery sponsored by the Académie française in 1823, the only one of fifty-four submissions to claim nonwhite authorship. As noted in the Introduction, its eulogizing of European civilization would have been in keeping with other poetry written by whites and nonwhites in the years surrounding France's recognition of Haitian independence but undoubtedly not to the extent found in this poem.
2. Author's note: "One will perhaps be surprised to see us apply to others than the Romans the title of 'masters of the world'; but we read in the eighty-first of Montesquieu's *Lettres persanes:* 'Of all the nations of the earth, there is not one that surpassed that of the Tartars in glory and in the vastness of its conquests.'"
3. Author's note: "We speak here of the centuries of feudalism and of the even unhappier ages that preceded it."

4. Author's note: "Blacks, like all primitive peoples, honor a God of goodness, just and benevolent, and fear a God of evil. One can, indeed, read in the accounts of travelers that the Africans picture the spirit of evil in the images that we present here."

5. Charles X, who recognized Haiti's independence in 1825.

6. Ausonia, an ancient town in central Italy, was destroyed by the Romans in 314 B.C.E.

7. Bartolomé de Las Casas was a sixteenth-century Spanish friar whose writings chronicled the first decades of colonization of the Caribbean and the atrocities committed by the colonizers against the indigenous peoples.

8. Fou[l]lepointe, located in Madagascar, seems out of place in this evocation of Africa. A reference to it in Bernardin de Saint-Pierre's *Paul et Virginie* (1787) suggests a literary rather than strictly geographical source.

9. The author acknowledges the ambivalent tone of the poem, which at times adopts a Haitian perspective and at other times seems to be written by a French author.

10. Anacharsis, a sixth-century B.C.E. Scythian philosopher, traveled to Athens, where he was known as an outsider to Greek culture and an outspoken "barbarian."

Appendix D. When our ancestors

1. Oswald Durand (1840–1906) is the author of *Rires et pleurs* (Laughter and tears), published in 1896 but including poems dating back to the 1860s. Noteworthy selections in this collection are the "National Song," which became popular as a presidential hymn, and "Choucoune," recognized as the first Haitian poem published in Creole. "National Song" was written in the 1880s. ("Choucoune" is the nickname of a Haitian woman.)

2. These lines are drawn from Durand's poem "Aux Cubains" (To the Cubans) included in *Rires et pleurs*. Durand saw Haiti's legacy of freedom as extending to all persons of African diasporic descent.

3. Durand envisions the poet's mission as promoting national identity, unity, and legitimacy.

4. In 1802, Brigadier Commander Lamartinière fought under Dessalines at Crète-à-Pierrot, a fortress on a hill near the village of Petite Rivière.

5. The vicomte de Rochambeau (1750–1813) was appointed to lead an expeditionary force against Saint-Domingue after the death of General Leclerc. He was known as a cruel slaveholder and brutal military leader.

6. Vertières in the north of Haiti was the site of a decisive battle fought under François Capois during the Haitian Revolution.

7. For Ogé and Chavannes, see the notes to "Haitians all, come and rally round," above; for Toussaint, see the notes to "O Muse, now to new songs I tune my lyre," above.

8. Durand makes a plea for the unity of Haitian and European culture and for persons of all racial backgrounds.

Bibliography

Newspapers and Periodicals

L'Abeille haytienne: journal politique et littéraire
Gazette politique et commerciale d'Haïti
Le Propagateur haïtien
Le Républicain: recueil scientifique et littéraire
Le Télégraphe
L'Union: recueil commercial et littéraire

Other Sources

Ardouin, Coriolan. *Poésies de Coriolan Ardouin.* Port-au-Prince: Ethéart, 1881.

Berrou, F. Raphaël, and Pradel Pompilus. *Histoire de la littérature haïtienne.* Port-au-Prince: Caraïbes, 1975.

Bissainthe, Max. *Dictionnaire de bibliographie haïtienne.* Washington, D.C.: Scarecrow, 1951.

Bongie, Chris. *Islands and Exiles: The Creole Identities of Post/Colonial Literature.* Stanford: Stanford University Press, 1998.

Bonneau, Alexandre. "Les Noirs, les jaunes et la littérature française." *La Revue contemporaine* 29 (December 1856): 107–55.

Castera, Justin Emmanuel. *Bref Coup d'œil sur les origines de la presse haïtienne.* Port-au-Prince: Henri Deschamps, 1986.

Chamoiseau, Patrick, and Raphaël Confiant. *Lettres créoles: tracées antillaises et continentales de la littérature, 1655–1975.* Paris: Hatier, 1991.

Charles, Christophe Ph. *Les Pionniers de la littérature haïtienne: textes choisis.* Port-au-Prince: Éditions Choucoune, 1999.

Dash, Michael. "Afterword: Neither France nor Senegal: Bovarysme and Haiti's Hemispheric Identity." In *Haiti and the Americas,* ed. Carla Calargé, Raphael Dalleo, Luis Duno-Gottberg, and Clevis Headley, 219–30. Jackson: University Press of Mississippi, 2013.

———. *The Other America: Caribbean Literature in a New World Context.* Charlottesville: University Press of Virginia, 1998.

Dayan, Colin (Joan). *Haiti, History, and the Gods.* Berkeley: University of California Press, 1995.

Desmangles, Leslie G. *The Faces of the Gods: Vodou and Roman Catholicism in Haiti.* Chapel Hill: University of North Carolina Press, 1992.

Desquiron de Saint Agnan, Antoine Toussaint, ed. *L'Haïtiade, poème épique en huit chants.* 3rd ed. Port-au-Prince: Imprimerie de l'État, 1945.

Devimeux, E. Z. "De la nationalité—de la communauté des peuples." *Le Républicain: Recueil scientifique et littéraire,* August 1836.

Doin, Sophie. *La Famille noire suivie de trois nouvelles blanches et noires.* Ed. Doris Y. Kadish. Paris: Harmattan, 2002.

Downs, John A. "The Poetic Theories of Jacques Delille." *Studies in Philology* 37 (1940): 524–34.

Durand, Oswald. *Rires et pleurs.* Nendeln, Liechtenstein: Kraus, 1970.

Faubert, Pierre. *Ogé ou le préjugé de couleur.* Paris: Maillet-Schmitz, 1856.

Fischer, Sibylle. "Bolívar in Haiti: Republicanism in the Revolutionary Atlantic." In *Haiti and the Americas,* ed. Carla Calargé, Raphael Dalleo, Luis Duno-Gottberg, and Clevis Headley, 25–53. Jackson: University Press of Mississippi, 2013.

———. *Modernity Disavowed: Haiti and the Cultures of Slavery in the Age of Revolution.* Durham: Duke University Press, 2004.

Francingues, H. "La Presse en Haïti." *Revue des races latines* 18 (1860): 642–46.

Gragnon-Lacoste, Prosper, ed. *L'Haïtiade, poème épique en huit chants.* 2nd ed. Paris: Durand et Pedone-Lauriel, 1878.

Griggs, Earl Leslie, and Clifford H. Prator, eds. *Henry Christophe and Thomas Clarkson; A Correspondence.* New York: Greenwood, 1968.

Hérard-Dumesle. *Voyage dans le nord d'Haïti.* Aux Cayes: Imprimerie de l'État, 1824.

Hoffmann, Léon-François. *Haïti: Regards.* Paris: Harmattan, 2010.

———. *Littérature d'Haïti.* Vanves, France: EDICEF, 1995.

Janvier, Louis Joseph. *La République d'Haïti et ses visiteurs (1840–1882).* Paris: Marpon and Flammarion, 1883.

Jenson, Deborah. *Beyond the Slave Narrative: Politics, Sex, and Manuscripts in the Haitian Revolution.* Liverpool: Liverpool University Press, 2011.

Jenson, Deborah, ed. "The Haiti Issue: 1804 and Nineteenth-Century French Studies." *Yale French Studies* 107 (2005).

Lespinasse, D. "L'Utilité d'un journal." *Le Républicain,* August 15, 1836.

Louverture, Isaac. "Mémoires et notes." In *Histoire de l'expédition des Français à Saint-Domingue,* ed. Antoine Marie Thérèse Métral. Paris: Fanjat aîné, 1825.

Morpeau, Louis. *Anthologie de la poésie haïtienne*. Paris: Bossard, 1925.

———. "Un Poème épique inconnu: *L'Haïtiade*." *La Revue mondiale* 150 (1922): 291–98.

Munroe, Martin. *Different Drummers: Rhythm and Race in the Americas*. Berkeley: University of California Press, 2010.

Nau, Émile. "De la poésie native en général et incidemment de la poésie des naturels d'Haïti." *Le Républicain*, March 1, 1837.

———. *Histoire des Caciques*. 2nd ed. Paris: Guérin, 1894.

———. *Poésies complètes*. Port-au-Prince: Éditions Choucoune, 2000.

Nau, Émile, ed. *Reliquiae d'un poète haïtien*. Port-au-Prince: Bouchereau, 1837.

Nicholls, David. *From Dessalines to Duvalier: Race, Colour, and National Independence in Haiti*. London: Macmillan Caribbean, 1996.

Prévost, Julien, comte de Limonade. *Relation des glorieux événements qui ont porté Leurs Majestés sur le trône d'Hayti*. N.p.: n.p., 1814.

Price-Mars, Jean. *Ainsi parla l'Oncle*. Montreal: Leméac, 1973.

Ramsey, Kate. *The Spirits and the Law: Vodou and Power in Haiti*. Chicago: University of Chicago Press, 2011.

Reinsel, Amy. "Poetry of Revolution: Romanticism and National Projects in Nineteenth-Century Haiti." Ph.D. diss. University of Pittsburgh, 2008.

Revue des races latines: française, algérienne, espagnole, italienne, portugaise, belge, autrichienne, roumaine, brésilienne et hispano-américaine 18 (1860).

Tessonneau, A.-L. "Dupré et la littérature jaune en Haïti sous Henri Christophe." In *Haïti 1804, lumières et ténèbres,* ed. Léon-François Hoffmann, 183–99. Madrid: Iberoamericana, 2008.

Trouillot, Hénock. *Les Origines sociales de la littérature haïtienne*. Port-au-Prince: Théodore, 1962.

Underwood, Edna Worthley. *The Poets of Haiti, 1782–1934*. Portland, Maine: Mosher, 1934.

Vaval, Duraciné. *Histoire de la littérature haïtienne ou l'âme noire*. Port-au-Prince: Fardin, 1986.

Index